DISCARD
RETIRÉ

THREE VOICES

Joan Hind-Smith

THREE VOICES

THE LIVES OF

Margaret Laurence
Gabrielle Roy
Frederick Philip Grove

CLARKE, IRWIN & COMPANY LIMITED / TORONTO, VANCOUVER

© 1975 by Clarke, Irwin & Company Limited
ISBN 0-7720-0732-2

Published simultaneously in the United States
by Books Canada Inc., 33 East Tupper Street,
Buffalo, New York 14203, and in the United
Kingdom by Books Canada Limited, 17
Cockspur Street, Suite 600, London SW1Y 5BP.
1 2 3 4 JD 78 77 76 75
Printed in Canada

For my parents, who were both born on the Canadian Prairie

PREFACE

Sometimes, when I was writing this book, I mentioned to friends the names of "my three"—the writers whose stories make it. When I did, the three names spoken together brought a far-away look as the listener tried to decide why I had joined Margaret Laurence, Gabrielle Roy and Frederick Philip Grove. "They are western writers—prairie writers—they all have connections with Manitoba," was usually the first conclusion. Or else an alert historian would point out that they suggest our diverse racial heritage: Margaret Laurence is of Scots-Irish ancestry, Gabrielle Roy is French Canadian and Frederick Philip Grove was German.

It is of course true that Margaret Laurence and Gabrielle Roy were both born in Manitoba and that Grove lived there for the significant first seventeen years of his life in Canada. He has a reputation as a prairie writer, even though only seven of his thirteen books have prairie settings. Gabrielle Roy acknowledges her indebtedness to Manitoba when she speaks of its wide skies and says, "It is they which have marked us." Her first novel, however, was set in Montreal, and her urban and northern books are as important as those placed in Manitoba. Margaret Laurence has given us the unmistakable flavour of the small prairie town in her Manawaka books, but her first reputation was as a writer about Africa and even her Manitoba works transcend parochial interests by exploring universal themes. It would be difficult to identify any of them as solely prairie writers even though that part of the land has undoubtedly cast its spell over each. Several people have pointed out that a high proportion of our best writers came from the Prairies and perhaps the choices were an unconscious tribute to that particularly fertile literary soil.

It is truer to say that they are joined by their racial differences. Each one speaks with a unique voice; there is no melting pot at work here. Margaret Laurence's fine ear has heard the peculiar nuances and mannerisms of the hard-working, God-fearing Protestants who pioneered Neepawa. Gabrielle Roy writes in French, and except for a book of Eskimo stories, her central characters are French Canadians. Her portrayal of her mother in particular is recognizably and abundantly French. Grove rendered us in tones caught from the harsh melancholy of the philosopher poets of east Germany where we now think he was born. His books are disturbing to many people who have never heard quite that minor key, that dissonance before—or since.

Nor was it, in fact, their distinctive backgrounds which caused me to write about these three. I chose them because each, individually, possesses the power of illumination—a mysterious, intangible quality which lifts their work above ordinary life and casts flashes of understanding upon ourselves and our lives. This book is my search for the magical quality. While I found many unexpected rewards along the way, I don't suppose that I ever discovered the elusive source of their insight, and indeed, I don't think that anybody could. I don't believe that psychological analysis can explain the root of artistic expression; nor do I think that the writers themselves know where it comes from. Margaret Laurence has said, "Writing is like a sleight of hand. The writer becomes a magician. . . . I don't know where my characters come from."

I did find a quality which they share, a quality which is possessed by every writer who has ever held us spellbound: the capacity for wonder. Each has a childlike sense of awe as he observes the phenomenon of human life on earth. Even the despairing Grove never lost his fascination for the spectacle of man's strivings.

I don't think, however, that any of these writers would claim to have found the answer to human existence. Margaret Laurence's characters struggle for fulfillment, and in the end, they seize the courage to divest themselves of pride and to extend love to those around them. They find freedom when they do this but they do not untangle the ravelled events of their lives, nor do they grasp the degree of love which they require for themselves.

Gabrielle Roy is a writer of paradoxes. Every human being needs opposites at the same moment, she says. We need the warmth of companionship and family—what she calls "solidarity"—but when we have it, we are forced by our individuality to try our wings alone, for it is only in "solitude" that we can discover in ourselves what we have to give others. We are constantly torn between the need for solidarity and the need for solitude and, in the nature of things, opposites do not come simultaneously. There is no satisfying the human spirit. Painful solitude is most often our fate, and her single flute note is essentially a cry of loneliness—her greatest paradox, for it joins us in mutual recognition of isolation.

Grove urged that man free himself from the need for worldly satisfactions and seek his "godhead" in the realm of imagination, art and knowledge for its own sake. However, his characters are trapped in dreams created by their imaginations—even dreams impose slavery. Grove's view is as enigmatic as those of the other two.

Besides the quality of wonder, the three share something else which I discovered in the course of writing. They all have a strong sense of the pioneers who made this country. We are young as a nation and so our origins are still close to us and close to the imaginations of our writers. Margaret Laurence said of *The Stone Angel,* "I was trying to explore my ancestors." In her bones she is acutely aware of the people who came before her and who founded Neepawa. Gabrielle Roy's parents were both of pioneer stock. They had come from Quebec, but her father pioneered in Manitoba and then worked as a colonizing agent for the federal government helping others establish themselves; her mother went west as a little girl with her parents by train to Winnipeg, and then in a covered wagon to the Pembina Mountains. Grove arrived in 1912 when pioneers were still breaking land and he set himself the task of becoming "the spokesman for a race," those who had come from far away to find new lives. In all this there is a great sense of youth, of beginnings, let us say of freshness, which can only come from writers who are speaking for people who believe they are creating a country. In the last story in her collection *Street of Riches,* Gabrielle Roy captures the spirit of anticipation when she speaks of her heroine's first job as a teacher in a little prairie school. The story ends, beautifully, this way:

"But we—all of us together—were warm and happy. The two little ones recited their lessons. Right next to us the gale, like a misunderstood child, wept and stamped its feet outside the door. And I did not fully realize it yet—often our joys are slow in coming home to us—but I was living through one of the rarest happinesses of my life. Was not all the world a child? Were we not at the day's morning? . . ."

This paragraph has always seemed to me to express something much richer than Christine's feelings at that moment. It is the voice of a writer who finds herself in the moment of beginnings. While it is true that we are troubled within (not as cosy as the children in the school) and the world weeps and stamps outside the door, it may be that we are living through a rare moment. I keep the hope that with these three voices—the compassion of Margaret Laurence, the artistry of Gabrielle Roy and the stubborn originality of Frederick Philip Grove—we have proof that we have begun. We are at the day's morning.

JOAN HIND-SMITH

TORONTO
SEPTEMBER, 1974

THANKS & ACKNOWLEDGMENTS

I owe a considerable debt to Margaret Laurence, Gabrielle Roy and Mr. and Mrs. Leonard Grove, son and daughter-in-law of Frederick Philip Grove, for interviews generously granted, for patient replies to innumerable letters and telephone calls and for correction of factual error in the respective manuscripts.

Three previous biographers have provided scholarly research which has been indispensable. They are Marc Gagné, who wrote a serious and thoughtful study of Gabrielle Roy in his book *Visages de Gabrielle Roy,* Margaret Stobie who did pioneer work on Frederick Philip Grove in Canada for her book *Frederick Philip Grove,* and Douglas O. Spettigue whose inquiries into the possible European identity of Frederick Philip Grove are reported in his two books *Frederick Philip Grove* and *F.P.G., The European Years.*

Generous assistance was given to me by Joyce Marshall, Gabrielle Roy's translator, who helped me with translation of Gabrielle Roy's works in French and who provided editorial judgement; by Robert Weaver of the Canadian Broadcasting Corporation whose knowledge of Canadian literature was always enlightening and who provided CBC material on Frederick Philip Grove; by Mrs. C. Morden Carter, Margaret Laurence's aunt, who contributed her knowledge of family background; by the librarians of the Willowdale Library, who were ingenious in their search for information and who allowed me access to the Library's Canadiana Collection; by the librarians of the Literature Section of the Toronto Central Library; by Miss Elizabeth Hall, librarian of the *Winnipeg Tribune*; by the librarians of the Mills Memorial Library, McMaster University, who allowed me to study the Margaret Laurence Papers in the Library's possession; by Miss Margaret MacKenzie, librarian at the Elizabeth Dafoe Library, University of Manitoba, who provided material from the Grove Papers owned by the University; by the librarians of the Bibliothèque Nationale, Montreal, who searched out early articles by Gabrielle Roy.

Photographs used in this book were kindly lent by Margaret Laurence, Gabrielle Roy, and Leonard Grove.

I should also like to thank the Canada Council for the Canadian Horizons Program grant which assisted me during the writing of this book.

CONTENTS

THREE VOICES

3.

1. Peggy Wemyss, as Margaret Laurence was called in 1943, age seventeen. The house, her grandfather Simpson's brick dwelling, became a formidable symbol in *A Bird in the House.*
2. Laurence at her retreat on the Otonabee River near Peterborough, 1971. She has named this property "Manawaka" after the fictitious town in her books.
3. Jocelyn, two; Margaret and Jack Laurence, 1954, Victoria, B.C., on leave from the Gold Coast.

Margaret Laurence

THE LITTLE TOWN OF MANAWAKA lies enfolded in rolling hills about a hundred miles north of Winnipeg. Below the hills the Prairie stretches far and wide. If you take a bus out of Manawaka at night, as Rachel Cameron and her mother did once, all you can see are the lights from the farm kitchens and the stars. A tough Irish Protestant from Ontario, named Connor, set up a blacksmith's shop there back in the 1880's. He prospered, so he sold the shop and bought a hardware store, and with his profits he built a big, gloomy brick house like a fortress. Then, as others grew affluent, they too put up solid dwellings. Soon it was known that the most respected people in Manawaka lived on the streets where the elms sheltered stalwart brick houses.

Jason Currie lived there. He was the richest merchant in town. When his wife died giving birth to their daughter, Hagar, he had a stone angel put up over her grave in the cemetery on the hill. Years later, after Jason died, his grandson John Shipley pushed the angel over while he was drunk.

Downtown, besides Jason's store, there is Simlow's Dry Goods where the ladies try on dresses; the Regal Café, run by a Chinese gentleman, Lee Toy; and several churches and a tabernacle. Some grain elevators and the CPR station stand prim and upright in the midst of the town slum.

There is a school where Stacey Cameron and Vanessa MacLeod once saw some boys beat up a little kid named Vernon Winkler because he had a sissy name and because he was small. When Vernon grew up and moved to Vancouver, he changed his name to Thor and wore lifts on his shoes so that no one would ever bully him again.

The town dump, distastefully called the Nuisance Grounds, is near the cemetery. There you can see Christie Logan, the garbage collector, roaming around the junk, claiming in a loud voice that he knows all about the town's people just from their garbage.

The Wachakwa River flows sluggishly through the town, the fields, and off into the farmlands.

Manawaka does not exist on any map. It exists in the mind of the Canadian writer Margaret Laurence. She made up the Indian-sounding word when she was a teenager writing stories and needed a name for the town where her characters lived. As a mature writer, she continued to use Manawaka in five of her books. It is a portable place which she carries with her wherever she goes, in her head.

And yet it bears some resemblance to the real place where Margaret Laurence was born on July 18, 1926 — Neepawa, Manitoba. The cemetery on the hill is there and so are the brick houses and the fields beyond, where the children play and the lovers walk. The Wachakwa River is not there, but the less romantically named Whitemud is. Margaret and her friends skated there on frozen winter nights.

She was born Jean Margaret Wemyss, and she grew up within a large, closely encircling family whose roots were plunged into the beginnings of the town and the province. Her great-grandparents, Dr. and Mrs. David Harrison, came to Manitoba from Ontario by Red River cart. Dr. Harrison entered politics and became Manitoba's Minister of Agriculture in 1886 and even Premier for a few weeks in 1887-1888 when his predecessor resigned.[1]

The Scottish side of her family came to Manitoba in the 1870's. Her Great-Grandfather Wemyss left a comfortable life in Helensborough, Scotland, not altogether from choice: while he and his wife were on a Canadian visit his business partner absconded with all the assets of their import-export business, leaving the Wemysses little alternative but to homestead on a farm near Portage la Prairie. Their son John, who was to be Margaret's grandfather, joined them after receiving his M.A. at the University of Edinburgh. He articled as a lawyer in Winnipeg and then headed north for the settlement of Neepawa. It was he who incorporated the town in 1883.[2] Several years later he had done well enough to build a fine, ivy-covered brick house with elegant green- and ruby-coloured leaded windows in the front hall, and he was able to resume the comfortable life he had known as a child in Scotland. Margaret Wemyss, his wife, set about re-creating the old civilization in the new town, filling their house with brittle Limoges china and hand-embroidered Irish linens. They had three children. The two boys, John and Robert, fought in France during the First World War and, luckily, both returned. Robert was to become Margaret's father.

Margaret's maternal grandfather, John Simpson, was an Irish Protestant from Ontario. He arrived in Winnipeg in the early 1880's by sternwheeler and then, with characteristic determination, walked fifty miles to Portage La Prairie. The travelling was even slower after that since he had to earn his way picking up jobs as a cabinet-maker, for that was his trade. Finally he reached Neepawa, decided that this was to be his home, and set up business. He combined the career of cabinetmaker with that of town undertaker, as always happened in the early days, for who else was to make the coffins?

He often told the tale of his dauntless travels to the restless young Margaret, making sure that she appreciated his hardships. She never failed to respond with an enthusiastic "Gee!" while privately thinking that it was one of the dreariest tales ever dinned into her unwilling ears. Later, she was to remember the story of her grandfather with pride.

"I come from a race of survivors," she has remarked. It is true that most of her people were self-reliant, hard-working, and purposeful. But Neepawa was a good place to be when the West was opening, and her family not only survived, it thrived. By 1883 the town was fully settled. It was on the CPR-CNR line to Edmonton and its seven grain elevators boasted that it was a major grain outlet. Merchants grew affluent servicing one of the oldest and richest agricultural regions of the province. There was a lively trade in dairy products and wood, and a salt deposit was discovered which brought added revenue. For many people, a small western town sounds like the end of the earth; for the inhabitants of Neepawa, the name of their town, after the Cree word meaning "abundance," had been truly chosen.

Grandfather Simpson also used his profits to build a brick house. However, there were to be no fripperies like coloured windows for him; his pride was his only self-indulgence, and his house was as plain and upright as he. Frugality, hard work, and obedience to a Puritan God governed his life. He was a stern man of commanding appearance who stalked through the streets of Neepawa in an ancient and foul-smelling bearskin coat. Many people depended on his strength. He and his wife brought up seven children and he also supported two of his own ne'er-do-well brothers. His character was admired, but he was a hard man to love. As though to soften the sharp edge of his personality, he married a lady of such sweetness and gentleness that everyone loved *her*.

One of their four daughters was Verna, a shy, reserved girl who was a gifted musician and gave piano concerts in Winnipeg. It was she who became Margaret's mother. She married Robert Wemyss, a boy she had known all her life, after he returned from war and articled as a lawyer with the same Winnipeg firm that had trained his father. When Jean Margaret was born in the summer of 1926 in the Neepawa hospital, her father was a partner in his own father's law firm, and she was the child of well-known and respected people.

She was also the object of pride and affection among a large group of aunts, uncles, and grandparents . . . a bright, dark-eyed, dark-haired little girl who was known as Peggy. Verna Wemyss, under her shy exterior, was a gay and affectionate mother. A little dreamy, she played happily with her baby, sometimes forgetting that it was time to put dinner on. In the summertime, the families spent holidays about a hundred miles north of Neepawa at Riding Mountain, vigorously renamed Galloping Mountain in Margaret Laurence's books, on the border of Clear Lake, which she renamed Diamond Lake.

The safe circle was broken when Margaret was four. Verna Wemyss died of a kidney infection long before the days when antibiotics might have saved her. Margaret Laurence has only one memory of her mother: she recalls lugging a new tricycle up the stairs of her grandfather's house, where her mother lay ill in bed, to show it to her. Verna Wemyss died shortly after.

With the death of Verna, the two families closed ranks to look after the bereaved child and her father. Margaret Simpson, Verna's sister, who was teaching primary school in Calgary, left her job and came home to Neepawa to keep house for Robert Wemyss and to look after his child. They lived in the old Wemyss house with Margarget's Grandmother Wemyss; her grandfather, John Wemyss, had died when she was one. Grandmother Wemyss was too old to look after the household and the young child, and furthermore, she had been used to servants who had disappeared once the Depression set in. It was therefore up to Margaret Simpson, for whom the child had been named, to take over.

Margaret Simpson was an alive and outgoing woman. In Margaret Laurence's affectionate words, "She was a magnificent lady, with a great sense of home and responsibility, and she was devoted to English literature."[3] Her knowledge of books was respected in the community; when Neepawa established a public library, Margaret's aunt was the spontaneous choice as the town's first librarian.

To little Peggy she was as loving as if the child had been her own; perhaps her experience teaching young children helped. A strong and affectionate bond grew between them and it lasted until she died, long after Peggy had grown up. It was inevitable that Robert Wemyss should marry her, and a year after Verna's death she became Peggy's stepmother.

Shortly after her mother died the child invented a set of imaginary companions, one of whom was called Blue Sky. Blue Sky appears as Blue Sky Mother in Margaret Laurence's 1974 novel, *The Diviners*, invented there by a child whose parents die. It is noticeable that Margaret Laurence's creative drive increases whenever she suffers serious loss and, sadly for her, there were to be several such losses in her life. It was also about the time of her mother's death that she began to make up stories, even before she was old enough to write them down. By the time she was in Grade 3 she *was* writing them down and in Grade 5 she had scribblers filled with poems and stories.[4]

Margaret Wemyss, her stepmother, took this writing seriously. Young Peggy was a rather lonely, solitary child, and her stepmother encouraged her writing in an attempt to help her express herself and overcome the loss of her mother. Moreover, she had a real understanding of creativity in children and a knowledge of writing. Peggy showed all her poems and stories to her. They were discussed, always tactfully, and best of all, Margaret Wemyss never laughed. "It must have been hard for her to restrain herself," Margaret Laurence said later with a wry smile, "especially over some of the poems." Mrs. Wemyss did, however, suggest from time to time that Peggy might better write of things she knew than of lords and ladies engaged in dire love affairs in ancient castles.

The atmosphere of the house was in many ways centred around literature. Because Margaret Wemyss was the Neepawa librarian, one of her duties was to guide the selection of new books for the library. The Library Board gathered on a Sunday night once a year to decide how to spend their money — the immense sum of about fifty dollars. Mrs. Wemyss made her choices with the zest of a millionaire buying first editions. Before the great day, the Wemyss house was filled with book pages from the New York and Winnipeg papers, while Mrs. Wemyss pored over them, trying to decide which books were worthy of the Neepawa library.

There were plenty of books in the house for Peggy to read — not children's stories like the Oz tales because depression budgets did not allow for that kind of expenditure — but the works of Rudyard Kipling, Robert Louis Stevenson, and Arthur Conan Doyle whose *White Company* was read and reread.

Her father was a good-natured, amiable man with the straight dark hair and brown eyes of all the Wemysses. He sported a military moustache and spats. Both were rather dashing decorations for depression Neepawa, but perhaps they were token remembrances of his more adventurous youth as a soldier in France. Peggy sometimes lingered in his library where he kept a collection of *National Geographic*'s, travel books, and the adventures of such men as Lawrence of Arabia. She wondered about the private dreams of her father, a respected lawyer struggling like everyone else with the Depression, but who had once glimpsed the world and now kept a library full of books about faraway places.

The Depression itself rolled over the children as something that had always been. While in hot dusty summers the adults shook their heads over burnt-out crops, the children roamed the fields among the wild flowers and launched flat-bottomed scows on the skimpy waters of the parched Whitemud River. In winter there were pirated rides on the horse-drawn milk wagon and skating at night under starlit skies which sometimes flared with the eerie life of the northern lights.

The predictable rhythm of Peggy's life was broken again by two events, when she was ten. Her father and stepmother adopted a little boy whom they named Robert. He was a beautiful child with rosy cheeks, and his appearance in a red snowsuit set all the ladies a-twitter. Margaret was torn between delight and jealousy. More seriously, a flu epidemic struck; her father fell ill, developed pneumonia and died in 1936 at the age of forty.

Margaret Wemyss was left to care for the two children. It was obvious that some changes had to be made in their way of life. The big old Wemyss house had to be sold. It had been a heavy burden in depression days anyway, and Grandmother Wemyss had left several years before to live with her married daughter, Norma.

There was now only one place for Peggy, little Bob, and Margaret Wemyss to go — Grandfather Simpson's. It was one thing to visit him every Sunday for dinner, or to watch him stride through the streets of Neepawa in his bearskin coat; it was another to live with him under the same roof. The only person to escape his lashing tongue was his wife, whom he adored without ever expressing his affection. Mrs. Simpson, with her patience and gentleness, was the buffer between her husband and the rest of the world, and Peggy loved her grandmother as much as she hated her grandfather.

The grief in the family was great when, only a year after the death of Peggy's father, the loving Mrs. Simpson died too. Once, when Margaret Laurence was asked what affected her writing most, she replied, "I think it was the number of deaths in my family." Her books are full of symbols of death such as funeral homes and cemeteries. "Most kids don't know they are going to die. I certainly knew."[5]

Peggy flung herself into her writing with greater energy than ever. "I was always a writer," she says. She wrote after school, or under the bedclothes at night, with a flashlight. When she was only twelve her first published story appeared: "The Case of the Blonde Butcher," a mystery, printed in the Young Writers' Page of *The Winnipeg Free Press.*

About the time she was thirteen she launched into an even more ambitious work — an epic novel about a pioneer family, called *Pillars of a Nation.* She had already filled two scribblers with this story when she showed it to her stepmother. Mrs. Wemyss commented with interest that it was about people like Grandfather Simpson, who had himself been a pioneer. Peggy glared in disbelief; she was not interested in writing a story about someone like *him.* *Pillars of a Nation* was abandoned.

In her early teens, she wrote her one and only drama. She had a reputation as a writer by this time, and one day the local Sunday-School teacher asked her to write a play for the kindergarten class, the Sunbeams, as they were called. She wrote the play and, with characteristic consideration, provided a part for every last Sunbeam.[6]

Margaret Laurence remembers herself as a lonely girl during this period of growing up in Neepawa. She says she was often depressed, subject to periods of "black, Celtic gloom." However, as far as anyone else could see, she was an ebullient, bright, popular girl who was refreshingly normal; she prayed that God would make a certain boy like her better than her best friend and also that she would make the baseball team. (She didn't.) When she became a student at Neepawa Collegiate Institute, she played violin in the school orchestra, acted in school plays, was on the debating team, curled, and played baseball. At sixteen she was editor of the school paper, *Annals of the Black and Gold*. Reticent about including her own poems and stories in the paper, she let herself go in the editorials. They were usually impassioned defences of freedom, in strong support of her collegiate's war effort.

Freedom concerned her a great deal, partly because the Second World War was going on, and perhaps also partly because the household dominated by her grandfather was so noticeably unfree. She wrote a poem called "Song of Spring," which did manage to creep into the school paper. With spring as a symbol for freedom, the poem was a plea for children to be able to run, touch and experience nature, and, in reference to the war, "To glance up, unafraid, at peaceful skies."

When she was seventeen she published another poem, this time in the more august pages of *The Winnipeg Free Press*, although the editors did not see fit to send her the customary one-dollar fee, perhaps calculating that a schoolgirl would be satisfied with seeing her poem and her name in print.

At the collegiate's graduation exercises in 1943, Peggy Wemyss was awarded the Governor-General's Medal. The citation that went with the medal praised her academic work, her participation in athletics and extracurricular activities, and took note of her leadership and initiative. She had received an average of 81 per cent in Grades 10 and 11.[7]

With a successful high-school career behind her, Peggy was growing restless, anxious to shake off the dust of Neepawa and, especially, to escape the iron hand of her grandfather. His personality had not mellowed with the years. He had retired from the funeral business and inactivity did not agree with John Simpson; he had become even more irritable. Mrs. Wemyss suffered her father's moods patiently, and often pointed out to the rebellious Peggy that he never turned his back on family responsibilities, even though he made it quite clear to all of them that they were an unwelcome burden. Peggy could see that his strong character was admirable, but she had inherited a good deal of his determination, and this did not ease the tension between them.

There was one final explosive battle between Peggy and her grandfather, which formed the decisive factor in her decision to leave home. During the war, when she was just seventeen, the little town of Neepawa had a sudden injection of life. An Air Force training station was established nearby, and there were dances, and dancing partners who were not boys she had known from the runny-nose stage. Peggy fell in love with an Englishman in the RAF.

The couple spent every spare moment together. They wandered the fields around Neepawa, talking of the future, the war, and life. Whenever the airman had a weekend pass he spent it at the brick house, sleeping in one of her aunt's old rooms. Peggy wanted to marry him.

Grandfather Simpson performed true to form during this courtship. He raged and sputtered, but the romance persisted. One night after dinner, while Peggy and her airman were sitting together in the living-room talking, Grandfather Simpson appeared, winding his watch with a flourish. Abruptly, he ordered Peggy to bed. She objected — it was not late. The man with the iron will did not tolerate opposition. An impasse had been reached; two strong-minded personalities faced each other. Then her grandfather took his revenge.

Margaret Laurence has told the story of her love affair with the airman in her book of short stories based on her childhood, *A Bird in the House*. Some of the details have been changed, but the confrontation with her grandfather is described exactly as it took place. After a second of silent anger, he broke the tension with the coldest and cruelest remark he could have made: "I'll bet a nickel to a doughnut hole he's married. That's the sort of fellow you've picked up, . . ."[8] This vitriolic remark was not based on any fact that he could have known; it was calculated to injure and it was insulting to both Peggy and the airman. She flared up, shocked and outraged, and fled to her room.

Her defence had been vigorous, but when the airman was sent back to England shortly after, he stopped writing to her. Looking back on the experience, Margaret Laurence relives the pains of youth: "When I was seventeen, the line was 'puppy love.' I have never subscribed to that. When you fall in love, it's real. People who insult the idea don't know what they're talking about."[9] Ten years later she learned by accident that her grandfather had been right — the airman had been married. However, she did not know that at the time, and nor did her grandfather. She blamed him bitterly for destroying a love affair which meant a great deal to her.

Life in the Simpson household was plainly intolerable. Searching around for a means of escape, she applied to the women's Air Force, but was turned down because they said they had enough recruits. What about secretarial school? Her real longing was to go to university, but her grandfather wouldn't help her at all, and the means to finance this posed real problems. Then, because of her outstanding marks in high school, she was awarded a Manitoba Scholarship. Life suddenly opened up. In the fall of 1943 she would go to United College in Winnipeg.

She had absorbed Neepawa into her bones. Later, she said, "Because that settlement and that land were my first and for many years my only real knowledge of this planet, in some profound way, they remain my world, my way of viewing. My eyes were formed there."[10] It was not only the place, it was the people and the experiences. Nothing had been brushed off lightly. Her love affair was not puppy love; it was real. Her grandfather was not a cantankerous old eccentric to be dismissed; he was a puzzle to be solved. The early deaths of her parents and her grandmother meant irreparable loss, but the closely encircling family proved that there were still people to whom she belonged; there would always be roots. At seventeen, however, roots are not of great interest; it is the future which is compelling. The unknown, and freedom, awaited Peggy in Winnipeg.

PEGGY WEMYSS CARRIED the certainty that she was to be a writer with her to college and she set about finding how to be one. She studied English literature and found that three writers were of particular interest to her: T. S. Eliot, Graham Greene, and Joyce Cary. Tracing their influence on her work is interesting, although her writing seems to be more closely linked to Canadian authors of an earlier generation. T. S. Eliot's depiction of modern life as a waste land has been so thoroughly absorbed that it no longer appears to operate as a conscious influence on most writers, although he may have had some effect on the frightening, contemporary environments created in Margaret Laurence's two latest novels, *The Fire-Dwellers* and *The Diviners*. Temperamentally, however, Margaret Laurence, with her rich, earthy sense of birth, sex, death, and family attachment, is at opposite poles to Eliot's abstractions. His details of domestic trivia reduce life to banality, while hers are suffused with a sense of fertility. Graham Greene is a topical writer, highly sensitive to climates of opinion. This is also true of Margaret Laurence, especially in her African stories, and in *The Diviners,* in which she expresses anxiety about the devastation of the environment. Probably it is Joyce Cary, one of her favourite writers to this day, who had the greatest influence on her writing. The characters in his books are bursting with life and they oppose conventional society for its hypocritical propriety. Margaret Laurence's early characters are often paralyzed by propriety, but when we read her books there seems to be an unspoken plea from her to her characters to loosen up and be more like Cary's bawdy old lady, Sara Monday, or Gulley Jimson, the rebellious painter. In her last book, *The Diviners*, the break is made. The writer, Morag Gunn, attempts to fit into middle-class life, and then casts it off as irrelevant and suppressive.

Canadian literature was not taught at United College, nor anywhere else in Canada at that time. Peggy was lucky to make friends with two of her teachers who not only knew Canadian writing but encouraged her own. The first was the late Professor Robert Hallstead who often invited students to his home to talk about Canadian literature. Long into the night Peggy and her friends discussed such writers as Morley Callaghan, Sinclair Ross, W. O. Mitchell and Ethel Wilson — to all of whom she now feels indebted. The other good friend was Dr. Malcolm Ross, who became a strong influence on Canadian writing as editor of *Queen's Quarterly* and as general editor of the McClelland and Stewart paperback series, The New Canadian Library. Dr. Ross, she says, "gave me much encouragement in the years immediately after I graduated, and in fact he was editor of *Queen's Quarterly* at the time when my first story was published in Canada, and gave me very sound editorial advice."[11] Both men encouraged her to publish in the college magazine, *Vox*.

Peggy created a certain amount of stir on the campus when she published a critical piece on the American poet Robinson Jeffers, commenting on his disgust for the modern world and his feeling that "the source of infection of society is its increasing introspection — mankind turning in on itself."[12] Her later work is a powerful plea for people to reach out and communicate with their fellows. She also published a good deal of original work in the same magazine, including a poem, "Bread Hath He," which won a college award in 1947. In the same year, her final one, she became assistant editor of *Vox*.

The sureness of Peggy's ambitions seems to have given her a notable sense of direction. The woman who was her roommate for two years said, ". . . she seemed freer and more independent of mind than the rest of us. Peggy had already found her personality; we were still surrounded by all the walls that are built around teenagers and that they build around themselves."[13] Her graduation photograph shows a girl with a candid, unselfconscious smile, unlike the usual carefully posed pictures of that kind. She was engagingly uninhibited. Stories are told of her declaiming poetry on a fire escape one foggy night until the boys in an adjoining residence threw a pail of water over her, and of how she used to tramp around the common room singing loudly and off key.[14]

Her sentiments were on the side of the anti-establishment. The students gathered at a restaurant called Tony's, where they ate spaghetti and argued. Here she defended her belief that Louis Riel and Norman Bethune were two of the greatest Canadians. Riel, she said, was an extremely brave man. He fought hard to maintain the rights of his people, the Métis, by defending their land, language, and religion — he was hanged for his efforts. Bethune was a gifted doctor who might have been expected to take up a lucrative practice in Montreal, but instead went to Spain and saved many lives on the battlefields of the Spanish Civil War. Independent fighters struck a responsive chord in Peggy.

When she graduated from United College in 1947, someone wrote a prophecy about her for *Vox*. Considering the amount of effort and success which had marked her college writing career it does not seem to have been taken very seriously.

> When Peggy was a little girl her mother inadvertently dropped her onto a volume of Robinson Jeffers on the floor. She has been writing poetry ever since. Seriously, she plans a career in journalism; after which, successful or otherwise, she will settle down, marry a man with at least a million dollars and raise an average Canadian family.[15]

Obviously, no sensible Canadian girl would continue to write poetry, but journalism was acceptable. *Vox* was right about a couple of things, however.

Peggy did marry, although not a millionaire. Staying at her boarding house was a civil-engineering student, several years older than herself, who was attending the nearby University of Manitoba in Fort Garry. Jack Laurence was a restless, wiry, handsome, rather quiet Albertan, who had joined the RAF during the war, transfering shortly after to the RCAF. "It was more or less love at first sight." Jack had spent several years in India during his service and had also seen something of the rest of the world. The far corners of the earth held his future, not a stationary job in Canada. He was a man, not a boy, and he possessed an attractive degree of sophistication. Even writers were a known quantity to him. His mother, Elsie Fry Laurence, had published her first novel anonymously when she was nineteen, and since then had been publishing regularly in small magazines and writing scripts for the Canadian Broadcasting Corporation.

Jack and Margaret were married in 1947 soon after she graduated. They honeymooned at Clear Lake where her family had spent the summers, and where the loons that haunt many of her stories make their home. Jack still had two years of university to complete.

Vox proved right on another count; Margaret became a journalist. In Winnipeg, a band of newspaper people had left their jobs on the two established papers, *The Winnipeg Tribune* and *The Winnipeg Free Press*, and formed the first cooperatively owned newspaper in

Canada, *The Winnipeg Citizen*. This adventurous enterprise appealed to Margaret, who was always attracted by rebels. She joined the staff at one hundred dollars a month to write a daily radio column, review books, and cover the labour beat (about which she says she knew nothing).

Newspaper reporting seemed to be an ideal job for a budding writer, but as Margaret worked at it, she found that there was a conflict between fiction, which she never ceased to write, and the kind of writing required by newspapers. The incisiveness of journalism was not what she was trying to achieve. Besides, after a day of hard work she had little energy left to write at home.

The dilemma was solved for her, though sadly, when *The Winnipeg Citizen* folded after only a year. Like the rest of the staff, Margaret found herself looking for a new job. She became registrar for the Winnipeg YMCA; there she was able to observe a variety of people passing before her desk, and the two kinds of writing were no longer at war within her.

Another year passed, and Jack graduated. For him, the years at university had been a necessary delay before returning overseas. Margaret was just as eager to travel as he, and taking chances on future jobs, they booked passage for England.

LONDON. A BED-SITTER on Finchley Road. Long line-ups with the other lodgers for the nightly bath. Adele Wiseman, the Canadian writer who was to publish her novel *The Sacrifice* in 1968, was in England and available to talk about writing. Margaret had a job with an employment agency down the street, and Jack had an engineering job, but they were broke anyway.

One day there was an advertisement in a London newspaper. It said that the British Colonial Service required a civil engineer in the Somaliland Protectorate to direct the building of thirty dams over an area of 6500 miles. Jack and Margaret caught their breath. Somaliland sounded a lot less confining than Finchley Road and it had the lure of faraway places, of the strange countries described in the *National Geographic*s Margaret had read in her father's library. They had no idea where Somaliland was, and rushed to a map to find out. There it was — on the east coast of Africa, bordered on one side by the Gulf of Aden and on the other by Ethiopia. Jack applied for the job and got it. There was, however, an initial complication. The Colonial Office regretted that they had no accommodation for married couples in Somaliland. Perhaps Mrs. Laurence would be able to join her husband in six or eight months. "This arrangement did not suit us at all," Margaret wrote later. Jack tackled the Colonial Office, explaining that his wife was a typical Canadian girl, used to living in tents and handy with an axe. Margaret had never lived in a tent, nor had she ever used an axe, but the Colonial Office was convinced. They were off for the Somaliland Protectorate.[16]

MOHAMED, THE YOUNG Somali houseboy, stood uncertainly in the doorway, balancing an elaborate tea tray. The sahib and the memsahib had announced again that they did not like tea in the morning. This was not comprehensible. *All* sahibs and memsahibs liked tea in the morning. He, Mohamed, had been trained to provide just such morning tea. What was he to do?

Mohamed's attachment to the household of Sahib Laurence was giving him plenty of trouble. Soon after their arrival, the memsahib had decided to walk from her proper place among the cluster of European bungalows to the Somali town of Hargeisa, some distance away. He had accompanied her, shambling along behind and highly embarrassed. When they reached the village she had wandered unconcernedly around the market. Why did she do this, causing him great worry, and making it necessary for two policemen to tail her discreetly through Hargeisa? It was not done: no western woman ever went to the village by herself, and no European ever walked. She had caused a great scandal.

Nor did the sahib and the memsahib spend their evenings drinking gin at the Hargeisa Club with the British administrators and their wives. Instead, the memsahib tried to learn the Somali language, bothering the death out of Hersi, the household interpreter.

Worst of all, one day when her husband was away in the desert, two elders of the local Somali tribe had appeared at the bungalow, asking to see Sahib Laurence. Memsahib Laurence actually invited them in for tea, and not only that, explained her husband's work to them. Mohamed had never beheld such behaviour in a woman. As soon as the visitors had gone, he explained in a frenzy that she must never do such a thing again. Somali women never entertained men alone, even if the men were eighty years old. As for the discussion of her husband's work, no Somali man ever talked about serious matters with a woman.

Margaret did not wish to offend the Somalis and she did her best to conform to their customs. One day, having learned enough of their language to catch the gist of a conversation, she overheard two Somali women commenting on her appearance when she was wearing slacks in the garden. They were both amused and shocked, and wondered what sort of being she might be — male or female? After that, Margaret never wore slacks in Somaliland again, even when the mosquitoes were most ferocious.

There was one thing, however, she was determined not to do, and that was to become a memsahib. She attended a few morning tea parties given by the English ladies, and found their conversation to be mainly complaints about the servants. She saw that they were making pitiful efforts to establish a kind of society in the desert that was vanishing even in England. The Somalis were dismissed as barbarians who presented ultimate proof of their stupidity by speaking English incorrectly. Margaret listened to this kind of talk with a cold heart. She had come from a country also considered a colony by these British, and she had observed the remittance men from England who turned up in Canada to sneer at the hard-working pioneers who had made the country, disdaining to do the same kind of work themselves. Margaret identified with the Somalis, not the English.

In spite of the fact that the Colonial Office in London claimed to have no accommodation for married couples, Jack and Margaret had been given a bungalow near Hargeisa on their arrival. Shortly after, when Jack began work, they were based at Sheikh and another bungalow was put at their disposal. It was a small, dark green house on a ridge away from the main settlement. Their possessions were placed there, and so, it became their first home.

Like a good housewife, Margaret set to work arranging furniture, putting up pictures, and embroidering pillows. Mohamed provided the Somali reaction to all this busyness; he simply did not understand it. Margaret looked out at the uncaring land and decided with relief to enter its calm. It was a moment of assessment for her, a judgment which was to remain: "Then I realized how much I needed Sheikh, how I had been moving towards it through the years of pavements, of doom-shrieking newspapers and jittery voices of radios."

Jack was thoroughly engrossed in his work. The thirty dams, or *ballehs*, were intended to catch the water which poured down in the rainy season, but which soon flowed away to the sea, leaving the land parched and the people in a state of terrible deprivation. When the dams were built they would each hold ten million gallons of water, and greatly decrease the peoples' hardships. Jack had his problems. He had to teach unskilled men how to handle bulldozers and trucks. Often machinery was damaged because it was not understood, and then he had to wait months for parts replacements from England. Little by little, though, the men learned, and soon some skilled mechanics developed. Jack also found himself conducting an informal tribunal for family and tribal quarrels. The Somalis engaged in long, involved conversations which were often difficult to follow and which seemed to have ritual rather than logical purposes. Jack was a logical man and found these conversations exasperating, to say the least. The elders, whom Margaret had mistakenly entertained, returned again to speak to Sahib Laurence. They expressed grave doubts about the *balleh* project. Perhaps the English — the *Ingrese* — intended to poison the water so that the Somali people would die. Or, again, they had heard that the *Ingrese* were going to build large towns around the *ballehs* so that the Somali people would not be able to use the water. They could not see, they said, what benefit these *ballehs* would be to Somaliland. Jack responded to all these comments as calmly as he could with countering questions: Why on earth would the English want to poison the water? Why would they build large towns for no reason?

The *ballehs* themselves were a hundred miles away from Sheikh, along the Ethiopian border, and there Jack set up camp. Margaret decided to go with him, forsaking the peace of Sheikh. It was in the desert camp that she discovered the Somali people.

It was the dry season, the *jilal*; no rain had fallen for a year. As they travelled over the desert in their Land-Rover, they saw the people struggling from well to well with their emaciated camels, trying to find grazing grounds. Carcasses of camels who had died of thirst lay on the ground, while vultures circled overhead. Graves of people were marked only with heaps of sticks, and relatives barely had time to mourn their dead as they moved on to the next well. Jack stopped to give water when they had it, but sometimes they had none.

Margaret was strongly moved by the Somali people. They awed her and made her think that she knew little of life. She wondered how they endured, not only the hardships, but the monotony. She noticed that despite terrifying difficulties the people were alert and energetic. "There are no bored Somalis," she was to observe later, perhaps thinking of the memsahibs or the malaise of contemporary suburbia. They were sustained, she thought, first of all by the demanding ritual of family and tribal life. A man or woman's role was clearly defined, and those who broke the taboos were punished. And then there was their firm adherence to the Muslim religion. It was a faith which focused on the after-life and carried a strong element of fatalism. "If Allah wishes the people to reach the well, they will reach it; if He does not, they will die," was a common remark. Her own religion, learned in Neepawa, placed much more emphasis on the idea that God helps those who help themselves; but she realized that her people had never been in a position of utter powerlessness.

She did the little she could to help fate with a first-aid kit stored in a tin box under her camp bed. Before long, a regular stream of Somalis appeared at her tent, with gashed fingers, thorns embedded in their flesh, and eyes sore from blowing dust. She bathed and bandaged, but sometimes the injuries were serious and, with a sick heart, she had to turn away the really ill people.

She discovered another reason for the Somalis' strength of spirit. At night a huge fire was built within the camp, and the people gathered around to sing songs and listen to their poets and storytellers. The storytelling was intensely dramatic; the narrators waved their arms, rolled on the ground, and grasped their listeners in the fervour of the moment. The stories could also be funny or cynical, often describing man's ineffectual struggle against the will of Allah. She discovered that many of the stories were very old, had never been written down and had passed to the present by being told and retold.

The poets were honoured members of Somali society. As well as being gifted, they had to be learned, possessing knowledge of Muslim theology and religious history, geography, plant life, medicine, and animal husbandry. Young poets attempted only the *belwo*, short lyric love poems. As they matured and became wise they graduated to writing the *gabei*, serious poems that were also about love, but which included other topics, particularly war.

Sitting under the desert stars, listening with some understanding of the language to poems and stories, Margaret became aware that this was a nation of poets. The harsh reality of their lives had not dulled their imaginations; on the contrary, their poetry and stories soared into realms of sensuous delight, full of silken clothes and beautiful women, rendered in terms at once sensitive and earthy. Unexpectedly, the scene under the stars stirred Margaret's memories of long winter nights in Neepawa, when everyone had gathered around a piano and sung lustily until three in the morning. There was a link between the peoples — the link of survivors. Both battled the land for a livelihood; both kept their spirits alive in communal entertainment. An idea began to form in her mind.

She knew a well-known Somali poet, Musa Galaal, who sometimes joined them in the evening and regaled them with Somali jokes and stories. Margaret ventured her first tentative suggestion, "Could some of the Somali poems be put into English?"

"Absolutely not! Impossible!" cried Musa. As far as he was concerned, the language of the cold English could never do justice to his beloved Somali poetry.

Margaret did not argue, but she was not deterred. There was a wealth of humour, beauty, and insight in the poetry and stories, she said to Jack, and none of them had ever been written down. Certainly they had not been translated into any other language, and few English even guessed at the richness of the Somali culture. Who could help her?

"Take it easy," Jack said. "It may not work out."

"Oh, I know that," she responded agreeably, and kept her own thoughts. Years later she would write, "But I did not know. What I really knew was that it would work out."

She set herself to learn the Somali language, a difficult task and one not encouraged by the Somalis. With persistence and tact, she finally persuaded Hersi, their household interpreter, to give her lessons. Hersi was a gifted storyteller, as she well knew, having seen him at night before a spellbound audience, waving his arms, his voice rising and sinking in hoarse dramatization. But when she asked him about the stories one day, his face grew withdrawn and blank. He pretended that there were no such things as Somali stories. "We are not having such things presently times," he murmured. His distrust of the *Ingrese* was intense.

Nevertheless, the poetry translations took a sudden leap forward. Musa Galaal had finally succumbed to the project. Forgetting the inhibitions he usually felt in the presence of an *Ingrese* and a woman, he gave Margaret literal translations which she then worked into poetic form.

With the poetry in hand, she decided to approach Hersi again. She mentioned casually to him that she had heard from Musa a famous story about a man named Igaal Bowkahh, a rascal who prospered, and wondered if he had heard it too. When Hersi found not only that she knew the story, but that the much-respected poet Musa had told it to her, he was silent for a moment. Then he cried out, "Why are you never telling me you wishing to hear such things? . . . Who is knowing more of the consideration than I? I know ten thousand!" After that, Hersi not only told her stories, but appointed himself chief story-researcher, and tirelessly sought out tales from the elders and the people living in desert camps.

In 1952, Margaret found to her joy that she was going to have a baby. After a near miscarriage though, she decided that the rigours of camp life were too risky and returned to their original bungalow at Hargeisa, where Jack could visit on weekends. It was tiresome alone; the Somali translations were nearly done and time lay heavily on her hands. She was rescued, however, when the Administrator of the Somali Protectorate offered her a job as his secretary. She decided to take it. Although restrained and formal with the Somalis, the Administrator was not one of the pompous sahibs. One day she showed him the completed translations, and with great excitement he declared that the book should be published. He would try to get an allotment from the British Government to do so. "It would be worthwhile for this one passage in your introduction," he said, pointing to her description of the people's plight during the *jilal*, "even if there was nothing else in the book."

Margaret decided to call the book *A Tree for Poverty*, from two lines in the *gabei* poetry:

On the plain Ban-Aul there is a tree
For poverty to shelter under.

The heritage of poetry and stories was like a sheltering tree, she thought, for people who had little else as a buffer against hardship.

One day, two years later in 1954, when Jack and Margaret were living in the Gold Coast, Margaret received a package in the mail. It was *A Tree for Poverty*, published in Nigeria. "It took us a while, but we have managed at last," said a note from the Somaliland Administrator.

A Tree for Poverty was a landmark twice over: it was the first collection of Somali poetry and stories ever to be written down and translated; and, for Margaret, it was her first published book. It served to stimulate further interest in Somali literature, and to familiarize members of the American Peace Corps in Somaliland with the surrounding culture. Printed in a small edition, it was difficult to find until 1970 when the University of McMaster Press republished it. At the time of the second edition, it was reviewed by a Kenyan student at the University of New Brunswick, who had a rather cynical view of westerners in Africa and was therefore all the more surprised by Margaret's perception. Micene Mugo wrote: "What Laurence does here is remarkable, especially when we place it in the context of the 50's. The book is an attempt to show just how much Somalia has to offer the world of literature. . . . She is one of the very few who tried to learn and understand."[17]

While she was working on the translations in Somaliland, Margaret's efforts to write her own stories had not ceased. In fact, it was at this time, she said, that she began seriously to write. The results were discouraging; publishers returned manuscript after manuscript, until finally in 1951, Whit Burnet bought a story for inclusion in his annual anthology, *Story*, published in the United States.

In 1952, after Margaret and Jack had been in Somaliland for two years, the time came for their regulation leave. The *ballehs* were not

yet finished, and although Jack longed to see their completion, the
first Somali engineering graduate had just returned from England —
properly, the job should go to him. Besides, the labourers were well
trained now; it was best to let the people do their own work. Re-
luctantly, they left Somaliland for good. In England, they would
await the birth of their baby.

The effect of Somaliland on Margaret the writer was to stretch her
natural capacity for understanding to its utmost. The people were
foreign to her in almost every way. In her later novels, even those
about Canada, she searches into characters who are difficult and
baffling. Superficial differences seem to challenge her, and her
method for achieving insight is to find the universal characteristics
which link us all. In the case of the Somalis she found the drive to
survive, the life force of the fighter, which she recognized as being
common to her own people. It is a trait which she continued to
explore.

ABOVE ACCRA, THE capital city of the Gold Coast, a plane circled,
ready to land. Jack and Margaret Laurence peered down at the city
which was to be their home for the next four years. Beside them,
their three-month-old daughter, Jocelyn, with dark-gold hair and
her mother's brown eyes, slept in her Karri-Kot.

It was late 1952, only a few months since they had left Somaliland, and here they were, back in Africa. Jack had been appointed
engineer in charge of building the port harbour of Tema in Accra.

It was Africa, but it was a different Africa from Somaliland. The
sparse, starved landscape of the east had changed to rich, steamy
jungle farther west. Accra, with its teeming life, provided the opportunity for a more informal contact between blacks and whites,
and Margaret could walk through the streets and markets without
causing a scandal. She became friends with an African who was a
university teacher — a kind of relationship which would have been
impossible in Somaliland where the people distanced themselves
thoroughly from the Europeans. But the greatest difference between
the two countries lay in their sense of national identity: in Somaliland, Margaret had had to go out and search for this; in the Gold
Coast, the people were loudly proclaiming their individuality in

their political drive toward independence. Just four years after Jack
and Margaret's arrival, the Gold Coast would emerge, confusedly
but triumphantly, as the new African state of Ghana, a nation which
would run its own affairs without the domination of the colonizers.
When Jack and Margaret arrived in the Gold Coast, excitement
hung in the air, beat out by the drums and the continual background
chant, "Free-Dom, Free-Dom." Here, Margaret could see that tensions, still suppressed in Somaliland, were coming to a peak. She
could also see that the changes ahead would cause anguish for both
Africans and Europeans. The Africans were already experiencing
a struggle between the old tribal ways and the new life with its education, industrial society, and modern politics. For the Europeans it
was the end of a period in history. Many of them loved Africa and
had built lives there, but soon there would be no place for them.
Even Jack's contribution to the emerging nation had a curious
double edge: he was wanted, and yet not wanted.

The dramatic situation clarified certain feelings which had been
lying dormant in Margaret for some time, perhaps since childhood.
As a writer, she grasped themes which were to engage her for many
years. She saw that the people of the Gold Coast were not only
about to throw off the dominance of the Europeans, but of their
own ancestors as well. The tribal fathers were trying to entice the
young people back into the jungle villages, but the new African did
not want that any more than he wanted to be controlled by the
colonizers. The reverberating question of ancestors provides a central tension in Margaret Laurence's work: our forefathers provide
roots and a sense of identity; they also enslave with a subtle
stranglehold which prevents the individual from finding his own
identity.

Margaret began to work. Her first act was cathartic — she threw
out everything she had written, all the stories done in Somaliland,
more that she had done in the Gold Coast, and two novels she had
started. "I had begun to realize," she said, "that a writer must develop for a long time; most of what he writes is not very good."[18]

Out of renewed effort appeared a story called "The Drummer of
All the World." It is set in the dynamic political and social milieu
of the changing Africa; in it, Margaret reveals the psychological
stresses in both Africans and English. She possesses an acute ear

for dialogue, and she uses the rhythms of Gold Coast English to convey the musicality and exuberance of African life. Added to this is a telling sense of detail. The story is a fine and touching one. "It was my first proper story," she said.[19]

When it was finished, she spent some time pacing the floor, a nervous habit which accompanies the completion of all her work. Finally, she sent it off to Canada to Dr. Malcolm Ross, editor of *Queen's Quarterly,* her old friend from university days. "When this story landed on my desk there was never any doubt that it had to be published," Dr. Ross said.[20] It appeared in 1956. The drummer in the title refers to a folk-religious figure, a gigantic drummer who beats on his own vast belly. The message he resounds to all the world is the message of the times: oppressed people will submit no longer.

THE BIRTH OF "The Drummer of All the World" coincided with the birth of Margaret's son. David was born in Accra in 1955. Margaret was amused to find that wary though she was of the power of ancestors, she herself was strongly protective and even matriarchal — "a tendency I have to watch."[21] It is, however, a sensible attitude in the tropics, where children are prone to malaria and other diseases incubated in the heat.

When David was only two months old, she began the first of her published novels, *This Side Jordan.* Set in a Gold Coast heading pell-mell towards rebirth as Ghana, it tells parallel stories of an African school teacher, Nathaniel Amegbe, and a British businessman, Johnny Kestoe. Nathaniel is struggling to help himself and his people towards the new ways; Johnny is swimming against the tide of events, contemptuous of the Africans, and part of a small enclave of British who are terrified that some day the Africans will take over their business. Nathaniel's fumbling efforts finally bring him recognition from the headmaster of the school where he teaches; he is asked to draw up a curriculum which will prepare the boy students for roles in the new nation. Johnny at last takes a hand in bringing Africans into his firm; when he does so his superiors from London give him a nod of approval, thus indicating that his future will not be so perilous as that of his stubborn colleagues. The book ends as the wives of both men have babies at the same time in the same hospital; a future for Africans and responsible British seems hopeful. Technically, the book is a matching interchange of action between the two men: first we observe Johnny, then Nathaniel, as though we were watching a cautious dance with blacks and whites as untouching partners. In fact, the novel begins with a dance in a night club, when Johnny, slightly drunk, dances with an African girl, to the embarrassment of his own party and to the anger of the girl's African escort.

Margaret did not throw this manuscript out — the fate of her two earlier novels — but set it aside for further thought. She continued to write short stories.

Jack and Margaret Laurence left Africa with the children just as Ghana achieved independence in 1957. Margaret's experiences on that continent aroused an affection which she has not lost, but she did not feel that she belonged there, nor did she think that she could truly understand Africans: "An outsider can never really get inside. There were hundreds of things I could never know." This comment is remarkably modest; most of her readers, including Africans, feel that she *did* get inside.

However, her conviction that she could not grasp subtleties about Africa led her to the conclusion that, as a writer, she would have to deal with her own background. Every person is created by, and forever linked to, his roots. That was why Africa belonged to the Africans and why the Europeans could not participate in its growth. It was also why her own affection for Africa was only "a seven years' love affair . . . not basically a lifetime commitment."[22] Paradoxically, Africa revealed the significance of Canada for her.

When Margaret Laurence left Ghana at the age of thirty-one, these ideas were forming. She was on the threshold of her professional career, a career which would receive a painful assessment two years later when she faced up to her novel *This Side Jordan* in the rain-hung air of a city half way around the globe — Vancouver.

OUTSIDE, A DOGWOOD TREE, its broad leaves weighted with rain, its blossoms faintly obscured by the persistent mist; inside, Margaret Laurence, seated at a desk. She gazed with gloom, first at the wet-soaked tree in her backyard and then at a manuscript and a letter which lay before her.

Margaret, Jack, and the children had been living for two years in a house on West Twenty-First Street in Vancouver where Jack was working. Margaret's life now included all the duties of the Canadian housewife, the cooking, the cleaning, the shopping — a somewhat different pattern from that in the Gold Coast. Jocelyn was seven and David four.

On this particular spring day in 1959, she had settled herself in her study for a few hours. She again turned her eyes from the tree outside to the papers on her desk. The manuscript was her novel *This Side Jordan* and the letter was from an editor of *The Atlantic Monthly*, the magazine to which she had sent it. "I was only reasonably nauseated by the lengthy interior monologues of the main character," wrote the gentleman editor.[23] He went on to say, however, that her portrayal of the central African character, Nathaniel Amegbe, was very fine, despite the monologues. The characterizations of the Europeans did not come off so well, he thought. Mrs. Laurence's obvious dislike of these people had served to leave them thin and unrealized. If she could see her way to reconsidering parts of the novel, they would be willing to look at it again.

Margaret thought despairingly that she had already rewritten half the novel since she had come to Vancouver. With the perspective of several thousand miles, she had seen at once that she had been unfair to the English. The rewriting had been an attempt to show that they were frightened, uncomprehending people, forced to leave Africa and find jobs and lives elsewhere. The changes had evidently not been sufficient.

So far her success as a published writer was small. True, the University of British Columbia magazine *Prism* had published another of her Gold Coast stories, and it had brought a letter from Ethel Wilson, who liked the story. This had been encouraging and so had the remarks from Malcolm Ross. As yet, however, she had never even met a publisher. The only writer whom she knew well was Adele Wiseman.

This Side Jordan had remained unobtrusively on a shelf, but insistently on her mind. The thought of rewriting did not enchant her. "A quick cup of hemlock would be easier," she wrote later. "However, as we were a little short on hemlock just then, I got the manuscript out instead. . . . I hadn't looked at it for months, and I saw to my consternation that the gent with the upset stomach was undeniably right in some ways. I managed to cut some of the more emotive prose. . . ." Time at her disposal was not plentiful, what with caring for small children; but by spending two nights a week, she rewrote it by half again. Then she sent it to McClelland and Stewart, the Toronto publishers. In 1960 *This Side Jordan*, her first novel, was published.

When the book appeared, there was great surprise that a white woman, and one from faraway Canada to boot, had grasped the African characters and the situation in Ghana so well. The Europeans were still uneasily drawn, as she is the first to admit. Nevertheless, *This Side Jordan* marked the emergence of an important new writer.

With it, Margaret moved into a period of confident creativity. She wrote more about Africa, and her stories began to appear regularly in a variety of publications, including *The Tamarack Review, The Saturday Evening Post* and *Prism*. The African stories continued to investigate encounters between the African and the European. The Africans always won, albeit a little bloodied, because their roots were in the land, and the Europeans' were not.

The list of published works was growing; a flurry of recognition followed. *This Side Jordan* was a Book Society Recommendation in England, and in 1961 at the Canadian Authors' Association meeting in Toronto, it won the Beta Sigma Phi Award as "The Best Novel of the Year." Her African stories "A Gourdful of Glory" and "The Tomorrow Tamer" were awarded The University of Western Ontario President's Medal of Excellence in 1961 and 1962 respectively.

All this, however, was preliminary to a book which was to make her not only an important writer, but a major one. Around 1960 she began to work on it. The main character had been in her mind for several years, and the story was almost completely formed in her thoughts. This novel was to be a total breakaway from anything she had written previously. It was about her own background, and therein lay a great source of nervousness. When she was writing about Africa, she was writing from the outside; but when she began to face her own roots, she touched on matters which lay very close to her. It took some time to summon the courage to write it down; when she did "It almost wrote itself. . . . I experienced the enormous pleasure of coming home in terms of idiom. With the African characters, I had to rely upon a not-too-bad ear for human speech, but in conceptual terms, where thoughts were concerned, I had no sense of knowing whether I'd come within a mile of them or not. With Hagar [the name of her heroine], I had an upsurge of certainty."[24]

The first draft of the book took a year to write; written, it caused as many tremors as it had unwritten. Instead of sending it to a publisher, she put it aside for a time, and turned to another kind of writing.

When she was in Somaliland she had kept a diary, and one day she began to glance through it. Amused though she was by remarks which she had made ten years earlier and which now seemed naïve, she decided to turn the diary into a book. It was published in 1963 with photographs which she and other people had taken. She called it *The Prophet's Camel Bell*, from James Elroy Flecker's poem "The Gates of Damascus":

> God be thy guide from camp to camp,
> God be thy shade from well to well.
> God grant beneath the desert stars
> Thou hearest the Prophet's camel bell.

The book was her attempt to hear "the Prophet's camel bell," or the ring of the inner Somali spirit.

MARGARET LAURENCE IS a sympathetic, unpretentious woman. She is also one possessed by her work. The characters "talk inside my head" — the matter of being a writer is something over which she feels she has no control. Jack Laurence is equally driven by his temperament and work; he is happiest rambling about the face of the earth, exploring unknown corners. In 1962, he accepted a job that would take him to East Pakistan. This decision forced him and Margaret to assess their marriage. It could not have been foreseen, but their paths were diverging. As Margaret said later, they were ". . . two people with totally different life styles, both legitimate, but different."[25] Unhappily, the solution seemed to be a legal separation. When the separation arrangements had been made, Jack left for the East. Margaret Laurence has never cared to speak much about her marriage or her personal life.

Now free to go where she liked, Margaret decided to move away from Vancouver. England attracted her: "Like many Canadian writers, I wanted to see what the great literary world of London was like."

As it turned out, Jack Laurence's work led him into the underdeveloped countries, with England as his base. He and Margaret saw a good deal of each other in the years to come, and he was able to visit his children. She packed up the children (and her unpublished Canadian novel) and set forth on a new beginning. She was thirty-six years old.

Arrived in London, it did not take long for her to be caught up in everything she had come to find. She met writers and the people in her English publishing house, Macmillan; she found a flat and schools for the children; then she began to work. First of all, she collected ten of her African stories for publication in one volume. It was called *The Tomorrow Tamer* and was published in England in 1963, the same year as *The Prophet's Camel Bell*.

In England, Margaret was enjoying a reputation as the writer with unusual insight into Africa; in fact, she had moved away from that continent as a setting for her fiction. She encountered a whole new imaginative region when she wrote the first draft of her Canadian-set novel in Vancouver; that manuscript was now waiting attention.

The novel gave the first public introduction to the fictional town of Manawaka. Manawaka in itself was not important; it simply provided an authentic background in which Margaret could confidently move. The splendour of the book lies in the creation of one of the most powerful characters in Canadian fiction — Hagar Shipley, a ninety-year-old woman about to die. Hagar is Margaret Laurence's attempt to penetrate the mysterious inner workings of someone like her Grandfather Simpson, stubborn, proud, and unable to reach out to those he loved. She has made Hagar comprehensible by applying infinite compassion; and yet she regards her with awe, as indeed do all the other characters in the book.

Hagar, whose whole life has been one mighty battle, engages in a last struggle to stave off death just long enough to assess her life before it ends. With her, in flashback, we follow her painful recollections of a life which has been thwarted and blackened by pride. When her son Marvin attempts to place her in Silverthreads Home for the aged, Hagar runs away on a bus to a forest park called Shadow Point, a place which reveals many of the shadows of her life. Her pride has been understandably come by. She was the favourite child of Jason Currie, Manawaka's richest merchant. Handsome, spirited, and brainy, she had the mistaken notion that she was invulnerable. It was not only her position in the town and in her family which provided her unrealistic hauteur, but also her father's legendary tales of her proud Scottish ancestors whose battle cry was "Gainsay who dare!" Frighteningly, this became Hagar's inner cry.

In rebellion against her father's possessiveness, Hagar marries, abruptly and without thought, a widower farmer, Bramwell Shipley, with a broken-down homestead. Her furious father cuts her off forever from his fortune and his presence. Having cast her future with Bram's, she manages to destroy all possibility of joy there too. He is, in an essential way, "her man," but he is rough and obscene in his speech, and an affront to her genteel upbringing. She nags ceaselessly in a futile attempt to refine him, and saddest of all, she never speaks to him of the real response and respect she feels for his masculinity, and which he never guesses. The pity and waste of human relationships which never truly touch is one of the poignant themes in this novel.

Bram and Hagar have two sons. Marvin, the eldest, who is still hovering anxiously over Hagar in her old age, was always the conscientious, hardest-working man on the farm. He waited around after filling his mother's wood box, hoping for a word of approval, but Hagar always shooed him away impatiently. Only once, when he went away to war at the age of seventeen, did she feel that she wanted to reach out to him, but propriety held her back: "I wanted all at once to hold him tightly, plead with him, against all reason and reality, not to go. But I did not want to embarrass both of us, nor have him think I'd taken leave of my senses."[26]

Her favourite son was John, born ten years after Marvin. John has inherited all her wild flair and rebellion and so perhaps he is more truly her son than the comparatively pallid Marvin. John, however, feels only cynical contempt for his mother's overweening family pride. As far as he is concerned, his family is the source of agonizing and guilty humiliation — they are poor, and his father's shambling appearances in Manawaka, begging for lemon extract and stale doughnuts, are unbearable to him. John's bitterness leads him to a life of drunken parties and disreputable companions, but Hagar, refusing to see him as he is, imagines that he will carry on the proud Currie family tradition. When John falls in love with a neighbour's daughter, Hagar plots to prevent the marriage by arranging with the girl's mother that she shall go away. The girl had been a lifeline to John, who in drunken despair over her impending departure, takes her in a truck across a railroad trestle, where they are struck by a train and both are killed. John's death is the most terrible of all Hagar's terrible memories, because she knows that the most beloved being in her life has been indirectly destroyed by her.

Near the end of the book, Hagar is found by Marvin in the forest and, seriously ill, is taken to hospital. In retrospect she has seen her whole life: "Every good joy I might have held, in my man or any child of mine or even the plain light of morning, of walking the earth, all were forced to a standstill by some brake of proper appearances — oh, proper to whom? When did I ever speak the heart's truth?" Now she mourns the "incommunicable years": "Pride was my wilderness, and the demon that led me there was fear. I was alone, never anything else, and never free, for I carried my chains within me, and they spread out from me and shackled all I touched."[27]

Transfigured by this self-revelation, Hagar realizes that there is one thing she can do to free herself. The woman who never allowed herself to express affection to anyone remembers Marvin, now old himself and still waiting for a word of recognition from his mother. He enters the hospital room and says in a low voice: "If I've been crabby with you, sometimes, these past years, I didn't mean it." He suddenly grasps her by the hand, and she gives him her blessing: "You've not been cranky, Marvin. You've been good to me, always. A better son than John."[28]

Like the biblical Jacob who, struggling with the angel, said, "I will not let thee go, except thou bless me," Marvin can now let

Hagar die. She dies as she lived, fighting, impatiently demanding a glass of water from her long suffering daughter-in-law, clutching independently and clumsily in her own hands this symbol of life. Margaret Laurence has also drawn on the Genesis story of Hagar, the bond-woman who bore Abraham a son and who, because of her pride, was cast into the wilderness. Hagar Shipley's ill-fated son, John, is like the biblical Hagar's son, Ishmael, described in Genesis: "And he will be a wild man; his hand will be turned against every man, and every man's hand against him."

At first it would seem that the message of this book is that pride must be forsaken for humility, but there is always ambivalence in Margaret Laurence's view. While we shudder at the effects of Hagar's blind pride, we observe her irrational life force with wonder and admiration. There is grandeur in her struggle. Although Hagar never achieves her potential or the rewards she longs for, Margaret Laurence makes it plain that life exists in the struggle, not in the achievement — and Hagar is never dulled or bowed by the hardships and sorrows that besiege her. The book is a celebration of life, not in spite of its tragic nature, but because of it.

In England, Margaret Laurence sat down to read over the manuscript she had produced in Vancouver. She felt that the book was nearer completion than she had formerly thought. She rewrote the death of John, made normal corrections, and her book was finished. Later on, she had some misgivings about the flashbacks and especially the chronological order in which they were arranged, but at the time she was satisfied. While writing the book, she had thought it was about freedom; looking at it again, it seemed to be more about survival. She called her novel "Hagar." Gathering her courage, she took it to Macmillan in London. The reaction there was highly favourable; the book would be published. She then sent it to McClelland and Stewart in Toronto. The book would appear in England and Canada in 1964.

At the same time, Alfred Knopf in New York had become interested in Margaret Laurence's work. He wanted to publish three of her books, all of which would be new to American readers. The three were the new novel "Hagar," *The Prophet's Camel Bell,* and the collection of short stories called *The Tomorrow Tamer.* He was not, however, pleased with her choice of titles. For American publication, he wanted to call the book on Somaliland *New Wind in a Dry Land,* and the title "Hagar," bothered him considerably. Margaret Laurence conceded the new title for the Somaliland book, but said, "At least let me name my own novel." She picked up the book and glanced over the first sentence: "Above the town, on the hill brow, the stone angel used to stand."[29] There, in the first sentence, was the title, *The Stone Angel.* It is the controlling image for the central character, for Hagar was like the stone angel: "Summer and winter she viewed the town with sightless eyes. She was doubly blind, not only stone but unendowed with even a pretense of sight."[30] Tragic Hagar never did see the qualities of the people she loved; nor until the end of her life did she see that her own life had been stunted by her stubborn pride.

The Stone Angel was published in three countries in 1964. In New York it appeared on the same day as *New Wind in a Dry Land* and *The Tomorrow Tamer,* and as a publishing event this was probably unique. Alfred Knopf said, "It certainly isn't common practice for a publisher to introduce a new writer by bringing out three books on the same day. Indeed, I have no reason to think this has ever happened before. I think Mrs. Laurence is one of the best writers Canada has produced in a long time."[31]

IN LONDON, MARGARET was caught up in the whirl of literary life. She no longer felt isolated from the writing world as she had in Vancouver, but she was also bored by the glitter of it all. An unassuming woman, she puts on no airs, is very warm with her friends, but a little reticent with strangers, particularly if their surface manners seem false. The hardships of the Somalis had meant a great deal to her; self-conscious literary cliques in London did not. Having met some people whom she really liked, she was prepared to enjoy them and her own privacy, outside London. She does not like cities anyway, and she thought that away from the bustle she could be herself, free from the role of celebrity. "I'm a private person, not a public one," she has said firmly. "I certainly know a number of celebrities, but I'm not interested in circles, not one bit. I don't think they work very well."[32] She began to think longingly of the lovely English countryside and the little villages.

Late in 1963, she heard of a house for rent in the town of Penn, Buckinghamshire, halfway between London and Oxford. When she went to look it over, she saw, first of all, a thicket of trees. Hidden behind the trees was a large grey house made of pebbledash. There was a garden stretching over two-thirds of an acre of lawn, trees, climbing roses, and rhododendron. It had six bedrooms, fragile plumbing, an eccentric heating system, and was, as she said, "a rambling old house designed by a lunatic that has been added to over the past two hundred years by more lunatics."[33] She loved it, rented it, and moved in. It was called Elm Cottage, and was to be her home for the next ten and a half years.

The study was a writer's dream. It had been the kitchen in the original house, and it had a red tile floor, a fireplace, and a large bay window where she placed her writing table, overlooking a forest of beech, rowan, and fir. She set to work filling the plentiful bookshelves with a large collection of Canadian books, a good American representation, and some English, including novels by her old favourites, Joyce Cary and Graham Greene.

Young Canadians came to stay in increasing numbers — novelists, poets, journalists, song writers. "In England, there are about half a dozen young writers that I care about desperately," she has said. "If they need meals and a place to stay, they're welcome. Writers know you can't pay it back to the people who gave you the help and encouragement, so you pass it on to the next generation — and they'll do the same thing. Whom can you rely on if not members of your own tribe?"[34] She began to refer to herself as the Low Commissioner of an unofficial Canada House. Jack Laurence, now an authority on irrigation for Britain's Ministry of Overseas Development, was also a frequent visitor — as he had been in London — while on leave from India, Africa, and all the other places which drew his professional attention.

In 1965, when she was happily settled into Elm Cottage, an unexpected honour came from the land of the *ballehs*. The British Protectorate of Somaliland had travelled a far route since Margaret's departure in 1952; it had combined with the southern region of Somaliland, previously under Italian administration, to form an independent nation, the Somali Republic. Margaret was invited to attend their independence celebrations. *A Tree for Poverty* had played a part in the people's development of national awareness and in their drive toward independence.

It was now time for Margaret to confront Manawaka-Neepawa again, and another novel began to take form. This particular novel, *A Jest of God,* had not been her first intention. She had begun another about a Vancouver housewife, but for some reason it was not working, and she found instead that *A Jest of God,* firmly placed in the familiar setting, was coming to life of its own accord. If her readers had concluded that her gift was for creating larger-than-life characters like Hagar, they were in for a surprise when they discovered Rachel of *A Jest of God.* She is the reverse of the overwhelming Hagar. While Hagar rushes blindly into life, the thirty-four-year-old teacher, Rachel, is psychologically paralyzed into immobility. She intensely desires both a husband and children, but unlike Hagar, her strength of will has been frozen. Here, Margaret Laurence's preoccupation with the influence of ancestors surfaces again; while Hagar's arrogant pride in her ancestors has hurtled her without fear into a chaotic life, Rachel's ancestors have applied the hand of death. Her father, Niall Cameron, had in fact been a funeral director, who quietly drank himself to death in his business establishment below the apartment in which they lived. But it is her mother, still living, who keeps Rachel in the bondage of semi-childhood. A hypochondriac who conveniently suffers a heart attack every time Rachel attempts to lead her own life, her mother has managed to stifle Rachel's developing womanhood. Rachel is tied like a child to her mother who is equally tied like a child to her.

Rachel not only needs to break the pattern of spineless obedience to her mother, she must come to terms with her dead father too. He was a shadowy figure to her, mostly because he spent all his time in the dusty recesses of his business place drinking.

One night, restless and sleepless, she wanders downstairs to the funeral parlour which is now run by a homey, cheerful man named Hector Jonas. Hector asks her in for a drink. He seems to have the worldly idea that funeral parlours are for the benefit of the living, not the dead, and to that end he has transformed the musty establishment of Rachel's father into a shiny, antiseptic place complete with a neon sign. He is therefore the very person to give Rachel a no-nonsense view of her father, which she is in fact seeking. The chapel, however, makes concessions to the spirit of the dead, and there in the subterranean blue light which Hector has proudly installed, Rachel finds out something about her father and about herself. Most of Margaret Laurence's work could be called realistic; but in all her fiction there is usually one scene or story which has a surreal quality, a spookiness which adds another dimension. In *A Jest of God* this comes in the scene between Rachel and Hector, when Rachel manages to blurt out the real question about her father: "Did he like them?"

"You mean — did he like the stiffs?" Hector asks.

"Yes. The stiffs."[35]

It is Hector's opinion that it was not exactly the dead whom Rachel's father liked, but an absence of the living. A comparison between Rachel and her father hangs in the air. Is she, too, afraid to touch life?

During the summer holiday, Rachel does reach out; she falls in love with a Ukrainian schoolteacher, Nick Kazlik, whose ability to freely express his feelings is a revelation to her. She falls in love with Nick in a limited, infantile way, expecting him to take over and solve all her problems and, of course, marry her. She is not woman enough for Nick, who simply sees her as a rather attractive girl, and at the end of the summer, he goes away. The experience is a painful one for Rachel; moreover, she believes that she is pregnant. She sums up the courage to visit the Manawaka family doctor and finds, ironically — in a jest of God — that she only has a benign tumour, which is removed. It seems to be Rachel's fate to be tantalized by the children she wants so badly: this one of Nick's who turns out to be no child at all, and those whom she teaches and sometimes loves, but who inevitably pass out of her class. Margaret Laurence has named her after the Rachel of the Old Testament, mourning for her children.

The experience with Nick has, however, given Rachel something. She has experienced love, even if of a limited kind. It was a reaching out into the sunlight (and the scenes of her love affair take place in the sun) beyond the blue shadowy light of the dead, and her mother's stuffy apartment. She has suffered both the bereavement of an unhappy love affair and the fear of having an illegitimate child, but the suffering has given her strength and a new perspective on herself. She realizes that for her, at least, Manawaka represents confining fear, and that she will never be able to seize life again until she escapes its shadows. She applies for a teaching job in Vancouver and gets it. Over the protests of her clinging mother, she makes preparations to move. Although she takes her mother with her, their relationship has subtly changed now that Rachel has taken the initiative for her own life. Her mother becomes even more like Rachel's child, but Rachel will never again be her mother's child.

The book ends as they leave Manawaka at night on a bus, with only the lights from the farm kitchens and the stars. Rachel's courage lies in her knowledge that she can expect no miracles in the future: "Where I'm going, anything may happen. Nothing may happen. Maybe I will marry a middle-aged widower, or a longshoreman, or a cattle-hoof-trimmer, or a barrister or a thief. And have my children in time. Or maybe not. Most of the chances are against it. But not, I think, quite all. What will happen? What will happen. It may be that my children will always be temporary, never to be held. But so are everyone's."[36]

A Jest of God received the Governor-General's Award in 1966 for the best Canadian novel. Many people felt that it should have gone to *The Stone Angel* the previous year, and that the award in 1966 was the committee's way of making up for its oversight. Rachel is a more subtle figure than Hagar; her struggle is inturned and personal, while Hagar's is on a monumental scale and ravishes the lives of others. For this reason most people think *The Stone Angel* a more impressive book. Margaret Laurence is, however, unconcerned by such comparisons: "Writing is an addiction with me. When the people and the story are there I have to put them down. Some of my books are probably better than others. But I don't care. . . . I'm not in competition with myself."[37]

About the time that *A Jest of God* was published, Margaret and her children suddenly found that they were in danger of losing their beloved home, Elm Cottage. The people from whom they rented wanted to sell, and the only way she could stay there was to buy it. "I couldn't even afford a down payment," she said, "and I was just leaving for Canada to publicize *A Jest of God,* but I said, 'Don't sell until I get back — maybe a miracle will happen.'"[38]

A miracle did happen. Far away in New York, a theatrical agent, who represented the actress Joanne Woodward, happened to be leafing through a copy of *Life* magazine. He found himself reading a review of *A Jest of God,* and it struck him that the part of Rachel might appeal to Joanne Woodward. The book had not yet reached the bookstores, and they had trouble finding a copy. Finally, they borrowed the galley proofs from the publisher. Joanne Woodward saw the possibilities in Rachel immediately. When Margaret Laurence returned to England, wondering what to do about her house, the telephone rang. It was *her* New York agent calling to say that Paul Newman, Joanne Woodward's husband, wanted to buy an option on the film rights for *A Jest of God.* Margaret Laurence agreed, but there were a few initial problems: "Nobody was interested in producing and directing it, and finally Paul Newman said okay, he'd do it and it was the first film he'd ever directed. He took up the option and bought the rights right away."[39]

The fee which Paul Newman paid for the film rights bought Elm Cottage, and so the Laurence's were safe in their home. *A Jest of God* was retitled *Rachel, Rachel* when it was made into a movie. When the author saw it she was relieved that it had fallen into good hands: "I thought I was luckier than most writers whose novels have been filmed, mainly because Paul Newman directed so expertly, and Joanne Woodward really got inside the character. Stewart Stern who did the film script managed to convey all the essentials. I didn't think I'd care how the film was done, as it was not my work, but I found I was concerned after all."[40]

Although Margaret took no part in the production, she did have dinner with Joanne Woodward one night in London to discuss the role of Rachel, and found her highly intelligent, with a genuine understanding of the character. Joanne Woodward's sensitive portrayal of Rachel brought her an Academy Award nomination, and Paul Newman won the New York Critics' Award as the best director of the year.

A few Canadians complained because the film was set in the United States instead of in Canada, but that did not worry Margaret: "The main point as far as I was concerned was to get inside Rachel, and they did that."[41]

Her children were impressed by their mother's foray into the movies. Jocelyn found a story about it in one of the English Sunday newspapers, all about the Newmans and mentioning their mother as the book's author. "Fame at last!" cried Jocelyn. Her mother's re-action to this enthusiasm was wry amusement: "So you see I could go on writing until I was ninety-five and cut no ice with them, but the movie connection was something else."[42]

Africa was now to preoccupy Margaret again. During the 1960's Nigeria was experiencing a literary boom similar to the one Canada was soon to go through. The writers were using the English lang-uage — there was more English written there than in any other African country because of the numerous English universities estab-lished when Nigeria was still a British colony. Also, Nigerian plays were being seen on the London stage and were causing great interest. Margaret sometimes had lunch in London with visiting Nigerian writers; in her talk with them and in her reading of their work, she found that they were reassessing their past, rediscovering their in-heritance, and interpreting themselves both to their own people and to the rest of the world. This national awareness was something with which any Canadian could sympathize, and the idea of writing a book on Nigerian literature was too interesting to resist.

She called her book *Long Drums and Cannons,* from a line in a poem by Christopher Okibo, one of the Nigerian writers whom she most admired. In it she commented that Nigerian writers, unlike black Americans, were not concerned with being Negro *per se.* They did examine the psychological damage done during the period of colonization, but in social, cultural, and religious terms, rather than racial ones. They saw themselves as "neither idyllic, as some nation-alists think, nor barbarian as missionaries and European administra-tors wished and needed to believe."[43]

The whole Nigerian renaissance came to an end shortly after *Long Drums and Cannons* was published in 1968, when a political and tribal holocaust broke. Some of the writers discussed in her book were either killed or imprisoned. The massacre of the Ibos presented tribalism in its most chilling aspects. Saddened as she was by these things, she never said that she was disillusioned by Africa: "What has happened, with Africa's upheavals, has been happening all over the world."[44]

DURING THE SUMMER of 1967, Margaret again attacked her novel about Stacey MacAindra, the Vancouver housewife. The first few chapters went well and then suddenly she was blocked once more. It was strange that the character of Stacey who had been in her mind for many years and whom she knew well should cause such difficulties. The novel, which eventually became *The Fire-Dwellers,* did in fact develop a point of view which was essentially different from that of *The Stone Angel* and *A Jest of God.* The difficulties for both Hagar and Rachel lay within themselves, and their conflicts were resolved to some degree when they achieved self-knowledge. Stacey's dilemma was created by a hostile, cold outer world; it may be that this reversal of attitude was difficult for Margaret to meet. She took to pacing around her lawn, trying to see her way to the next action. As she did so, she noticed that her grass was being dug up by moles. Every day she cleared the mounds of earth off her lawn, only to find it dug up again the following morning.

She began to think that there must be a regular city of moles living under her garden, and so her first children's book was born. *Jason's Quest* was a means for her to escape for the moment from her preoccupation with Canada. Her only book to be set wholly in Britain, it reflects a thought which bemuses many North Americans when they visit England — the old country appears to be a vast museum in which the people are paralyzed by their reverence for their own history. *Jason's Quest* was the perfect vehicle to express the nightmare side of Margaret's conception of ancestral power. The story is about a mole named Jason who lives in an ancient mole city, Molanium. This city is run by elderly moles; they base all their laws on the ways of their revered ancestors, who came to Britain with Caesar's forces. The city is dying of a mysterious illness; the moles are lethargic and careless; the city is falling in ruins. Jason decides that he will go out into the world to discover the cause of the illness, then return to save his people.

On the way to London, Jason and three companions — two cats and an owl, meet with hair-raising adventures, including an unpleasant encounter with a gang of street rats, whom they manage to disband. In a London night club for small animals, Jason meets a glamorous girl mole who is a singer named Perdita, somewhat reminiscent of the English singer, Petula Clark. Jason falls in love with her immediately. He explains his quest, telling her of the sickness which has overcome his tribe in Molanium.

Perdita, who is a very bright mole, recognizes immediately that the moles are dying of boredom. She believes that their reverence for their ancestors has sapped their interest in the present. She agrees to marry Jason and accompany him back to Molanium to stir things up a bit and cure the moles of their sickness.

Faced with unexpected terrors, the travellers had reached a working philosophy: "Reasonable care, . . . we must just take reasonable care — and then bash on, regardless."[45] This kind of advice would have been well understood by Rachel, for, like her, the moles of Molanium were sick because they were afraid to change, afraid to dare. The overall motto of the four adventurers is "I'll try." The most cheerful and triumphant note is struck by Calico, one of the cats, who tells Jason, "I think you've discovered that you can act more bravely than you feel"[46] — a message which Hagar, Rachel, and even Nathaniel Amegbe of *This Side Jordan* all find to be true.

This children's book, published in 1970, gave her a great deal of pleasure. It is charmingly illustrated by a Swedish artist, Steffan Torell, who has managed to capture the spirit of the English pubs and Covent Garden Market. "I'm just like a kid about this book," Margaret has said. "Just delighted by it, possibly because it was pure pleasure to write. I felt it was a small gift which arrived unexpectedly out of nowhere at a time when I needed it."[47]

Now, quite suddenly, the problems with *The Fire-Dwellers* resolved themselves. It was written, and finally published in 1969. Perhaps part of the trouble had been Margaret's doubts about the popular reading appeal of a thirty-nine-year-old housewife with a husband and four children. "Who on earth," she asked herself, "is going to be interested in reading about a middle-aged housewife, mother of four? Then I thought, the hell with it — some of my best friends are middle-aged housewives; I'm one myself, but I deplore labels so let's just call one another by our proper names. I was fed up with the current fictional portraits of women of my generation — middle-aged mums either being presented as glossy magazine types, perfect, everloving and incontestably contented, or else as sinister and spiritually cannibalistic monsters determined only to destroy their men and kids by hypnotic means. I guess there are some women like the latter, but I don't happen to know any of them. There are no women like the former; they don't exist. Stacey had been in my mind for a long time — longer than Rachel, as a matter of fact. She's not particularly valiant (maybe she's an anti-heroine), but she's got some guts and some humour. In various ways she's Hagar's spiritual grand-daughter. When I finally got going at the novel, I experienced the same feeling I had had with *The Stone Angel,* only perhaps more so, because this time it was a question of writing really in my own idiom, the ways of speech and memory of my generation, those who were born in the 20's, were children in the dusty 30's, grew up during the last war. Stacey isn't in any sense myself or any other person except herself, but we know one another awfully well. She is concerned with survival, like Hagar and like Rachel, but in her case it involves living in an external world which she perceives as increasingly violent and indeed lunatic. . . ."[48]

The title *The Fire-Dwellers* expresses the threatening environment. While Stacey can see quite plainly that it *is* violent, she is bewildered because nobody else seems to acknowledge it. Though her neighbours have appalling problems — potential suicide and insanity ultimately reveal themselves — no one would guess the tensions underlying the carefully contrived exteriors. Even her own children are reluctant to speak of their problems of growing up. They keep to themselves, in troubled solitude. Stacey's chief block in her efforts to break the rigidly imposed silence is her husband, Mac. Raised by his minister-father who taught him to control himself, Mac is the most uncommunicative of men. He plods day by day through an unrewarding job as salesman for a questionable company, but when Stacey attempts to speak to him about his work he snaps at her irritably.

It is not only the smothered anxieties of the fire-dwellers' world which trouble Stacey; she is also unsure of her own role. Nobody, it seems, wants the traditional womanly gifts of comfort and reassurance which she, unlike Hagar or Rachel, can give in abundance. What is her purpose anyway? Once she had been an attractive girl named Stacey Cameron who loved to dance at the Flamingo Dance Hall in Manawaka; now, suddenly, she is a useless, middle-aged housewife with spreading hips. How did she get here? In the early part of the book she tries to connect with the Stacey who once was — drinking gin, she dances to the records of her teenage daughter, but she dances alone.

As the book progresses, Stacey makes a number of attempts to capture the promises which youth had seemed to hold out, but dead-end love affairs and esoteric courses are only devices to evade the central problems of her life. It is through Mac that she comes to understand what it is to be a grownup, and it is a difficult lesson. Following a job crisis, Mac becomes the British Columbia manager for his firm. This outcome seems to be a triumph, but really it is not. Mac knows that the company is fraudulant, and that his job is just a job — no glory. But he intends to cut out the false promises made by his company and so a kind of honesty does enter. Seeing Mac ready to do a job only because of family responsibilities, Stacey faces up to the fact that she will never again be the Stacey Cameron who danced at the Flamingo Dance Hall. Significantly, she gives up dancing; but as Margaret Laurence said, "She did keep her sense of humour and that was her way of dancing"[49] — a more realistic way. Stacey reflects: "When we've got all four kids through university or launched somewhere, and Mac retires and is so thin you have to look twice to see him and I'm so portly I can hardly waddle, we can go to Acapulco and do the Mexican hat dance. I can't stand it. I cannot. I can't take it. Yeh, I can, though. By God, I can, if I set my mind to it."[50] Stacey's interior monologues are, in fact, very funny, although wryly despairing, as when she contemplates the future.

Stacey's role, as she now sees it, is to lend as much order as she can to her own small universe by providing love, even though it is hardly recognized. They make room in their already crowded house for Mac's father who is going blind and is unable to look after himself. Then Stacey receives news that her sister, Rachel, and her mother are coming to live in Vancouver. They too, though they will not live in the same house, must be seen to.

The last scene in the book is a replica of an early one, as Mac and Stacey get ready for bed: the same jumble of Stacey's castoff clothes, the same neat pile of Mac's, the same unread books on the bedside table, the same litter of make-up and children's photographs. Life is the same, but not quite, because Stacey has accepted her lot.

Stacey was met with startled recognition by thousands of women who saw their lives pinpointed in *The Fire-Dwellers*. "What I care about trying to do," Margaret Laurence has said, "is to express something that in fact everybody knows, but doesn't say."[51] Like Hagar, Stacey seems so real that some readers have said that they would not be surprised to see her walking down the street. Margaret Laurence is sometimes stopped by people who inquire anxiously, "How is Stacey MacAindra . . . how is she getting along?" Her unvarying answer is, "She'll survive."[52] It does not strike her as particularly funny that people find Stacey real — she says she would not be surprised to meet her herself someday.

Male reviewers of the book were inclined to think that Margaret Laurence was too preoccupied with the miseries of being a woman. She does focus on women a good deal of the time, but their problems are symptomatic of the whole society. Although *The Fire-Dwellers* is about Stacey, Mac too receives a good deal of sympathy, and his plight is made clear.

"I think universal themes can be approached only through the particular," she says, countering arguments that each of her novels is concerned only with one individual character and one sex. One of the universal themes in *The Fire-Dwellers* is the starvation of human relationships when there is no communication. Another theme, which emerges at the end of all her Canadian novels, is the necessity of coming to terms with oneself. Only in this way, are Hagar, Rachel, and Stacey released from bondage.

Even while Margaret was writing novels, she continued to produce a flow of short stories. These appeared in a variety of magazines: among others, *The Ladies Home Journal, Holiday, Chatelaine, Saturday Evening Post, Tamarack Review,* and the *Atlantic Advocate*. Some of these stories were also dramatized by the Canadian Broadcasting Corporation. There were about twenty altogether, and of these eight separated out as a group. Known as the Vanessa MacLeod stories, they are about Margaret Laurence's early years in Neepawa, or Manawaka, as the town continued to be called. Vanessa is the fictional name Margaret gave herself. The stories, "while based on my childhood, are a very fictional version in many of their details. The characters, I hope, are reasonably true to those of my family and perhaps even myself as a kid, but lots of details happened in life differently. Fiction and reality get intertwined, so sometimes I have to recall from my own life which is mine and which Vanessa's. I should say that although she is based on myself as a kid, she is me and not me, as has to happen in fiction, I think, even fairly autobiographical fiction."[53]

Grandfather Simpson appears, renamed Grandfather Connor, but he is easily recognizable, even though Margaret Laurence has turned him into a blacksmith and hardware merchant, in place of an under-taker-cabinetmaker. Her stepmother is simply Vanessa's mother; no mention is made of Margaret's own mother's death. Vanessa's father's death, however, occurs as Margaret's father's did, and the story reveals her sorrow that he died before she was old enough to know him — the sense that she had lost him before she had found him. Vanessa's gallant, wisecracking Aunt Edna, who kept house for her parents when she could not find work, was based on Margaret's real Aunt Velma; but Velma was a nurse who came home only periodically when she was unemployed, and she never kept house for the elderly Simpsons. In the stories, Vanessa's Uncle Roderick was killed in the First World War, but Margaret's real uncle, John Wemyss, returned and settled in Wilkie, Saskatchewan. One of the stories tells how Vanessa's uncle was shot in the eye with a BB bullet, by her father, when both were boys. Margaret's real uncle was injured in the same way, but she says, ". . . at this point I don't know whether it was my dad who fired the shot or not."[54]

The Vanessa MacLeod stories were gathered together into one volume and published in 1970 under the title *A Bird in the House*. Looming like a malevolent hawk over the entire book is the dominating figure of Grandfather Connor (Simpson). *A Bird in the House* is, among other things, Margaret's struggle to put him in his place, to clear herself of his domination. However, as late as 1974, she said, "Whatever I did he disapproved of." He is associated in this book with hawks and bears, creatures who haunt the nightmares of young children; he also has strong satanic associations. When he is enraged at his household he stomps off to his post near the furnace in the basement, where he keeps everybody nervously aware of his indignation with the loud squeaking of his rocking chair. Obviously his real place is in the nether regions close to infernal fires. His house stands as his most formidable symbol; the book begins and ends with descriptions of his gloomy bastion.

Grandfather Connor represents the harshly crushing forces of earth, and it is clear that one must be strong to survive them. The gentle, sensitive people have a difficult time. Vanessa's cousin Chris in the story "Horses of the Night," retreats from Grandfather Connor and the horrors of the Depression into unrealistic dreams of the future, and finally succumbs to a world of total unreality in an institution for the insane. The sapping presence of the Depression itself leaves Vanessa even more exposed to her grandfather. Her affectionate father, Dr. Ewen MacLeod, died as an indirect result of its hardships. Overworked during a flu epidemic, he developed the pneumonia which was too much for his exhausted body and spirit. It is the tough ones — Grandfather Connor and Vanessa — who survive. In this book one begins to understand Margaret Laurence's obsession with survival.

"Tough" is perhaps not the exact word for Vanessa, but the lesson she learns — and it is a running theme in this book — is self-reliance. The manner in which members of the family survive Grandfather Connor is of their own choosing. Even he is seen more as a disaster to himself than to anyone else. Our demons lie within. The proud, extremely Protestant conviction that we hold our fate in our own hands is central to Margaret Laurence's thinking: in *The Prophet's Camel Bell,* when speaking of a bitter employee who had to be fired, she wrote, ". . . his truest and most terrible battle, like all men's, was with himself."[55] This holds true for Hagar and Rachel and, to some degree, for Stacey. When she was pressed as to whether she really thinks that we can control our own lives, Margaret Laurence said, "Of course there are many things which happen to us that we can do nothing about, but it is within the power of the individual to survive with dignity."[56]

She had managed to survive with dignity herself by transforming her hatred for her grandfather into a compassionate understanding of the suffering which his personality caused him. After *A Bird in the House* was published she said, ". . . I think I honestly kept on disliking him until I'd got all the way through these stories . . . and when I finished the last story [the one about the old man's death] I realized that I didn't dislike him anymore, but that there were things about him that I greatly admired."[57] Her epitaph to him comes near the end of that particular story when Vanessa describes the way she felt at his funeral: "I was not sorry that he was dead. I was only surprised. Perhaps I had really imagined that he was immortal. Perhaps he was immortal, in ways which it would take me half a lifetime to comprehend."[58]

Margaret had long since passed the youthful stage of longing to cut loose from her roots; she had reclaimed them in all her Canadian books and, most directly, in the autobiographical Vanessa MacLeod stories. In 1967, her roots reclaimed her. United College, from which she had graduated twenty years earlier, made her an Honorary Fellow; she was the first woman and the youngest person ever to be so honoured.

While she was in Winnipeg for these ceremonies, she decided to go to Neepawa. That, too, was a ceremony, a solitary one. It was nearly forty-one years since she had been born there; twenty years since her grandfather had died. She wrote about this last visit in the final pages of *A Bird in the House:*

"I went alone. It would have no meaning for anyone else. I was not even sure it would have any meaning for me. But I went. I went to the cemetery and looked at the granite and the names. . . . I did not go to look at Grandfather Connor's grave. There was no need. It was not his monument.

"I parked the car beside the Brick House. The caragana hedge was unruly. No one had trimmed it properly that summer. The house had been lived in by strangers for a long time. I had not thought it would hurt me to see it in other hands, but it did. I wanted to tell them to trim their hedges, to repaint the window-frames, to pay heed to repairs. I had feared and fought the old man, yet he proclaimed himself in my veins. But it was their house now, whoever they were, not ours, not mine.

"I looked at it only for a moment, and then I drove away."[59]

Vanessa MacLeod's good-bye to Manawaka was Margaret Laurence's good-bye to Neepawa. The place Margaret Laurence had known was no longer there.

WITH THE FAREWELL in 1967 to Manawaka-Neepawa came a change of wind affecting many matters which had been linked to Margaret's childhood. As it turned out, she was never to be free of emanations from her roots, but, for the time being, she sensed a decided shift in her course. She felt, first of all, that her writing would change. In 1969 she wrote: "At the moment, I have the same feeling as I did when I knew I had finished writing about Africa. I've gone as far as I personally can go, in the area in which I've lived for the past three novels. A change of direction would appear to be indicated. I have a halfway hunch where I want to go, but I don't know how to get there or what will be there if I do. Maybe I'll strike it lucky and find the right compass, or maybe I won't."[60]

A new novel did begin to form a little later, but no one, not even her publisher Jack McClelland, knew what it was about. "I have one basic superstition about my writing," she remarks. "Don't talk about it. If you do it'll slip away or it'll change."[61]

Her marriage came to an end in 1969 when she and Jack Laurence decided to divorce after twenty-two years of marriage, including seven of separation. "If you reach a point where your goals are no longer the same and it's no good for either of you, then it's foolishness to continue. I know marriages that hang on together 'for the kids.' Well, I'm not sure that it isn't rotten for the kids. Anyway, there's no animosity in our situation. . . ."[62]

She began to sense further changes in her personal life. The children were growing up. In 1969, Jocelyn was seventeen and David fourteen. It would not be long before they would leave home and she was not about to become a clinging mother: "One really has to be very careful of oppressing what you yourself want on your children."[63] Given their future independence, she began to think about her own future, and where it might lie. Her thoughts often turned to her own country. Would Canada be the place to go?

Then an opportunity arose to live in Canada for a year. The University of Toronto invited her to be writer-in-residence during 1969-70, to live on the university campus and to be available to students. She accepted the job partly because she was interested in finding out whether or not she could live happily in Canada. In the past twenty years she had spent only five in her own country — the years in Vancouver. Perhaps Canada had changed; perhaps she would feel like an exile. A year would give her a chance to find out.

The children, who were at school, could not come with her, so she arranged for a Canadian writer and his wife to move into Elm

Cottage and keep an eye on them. Their father also visited them when he could.

In Toronto her readers were waiting. Her books have always sold better in Canada than anywhere else. "I'd starve if I depended on English sales,"[64] she has said, and adds that American sales help. She was conscientiously available to all: budding writers, students, the general public, and a stream of journalists. She appeared on television several times, and newspaper columns were full of interviews with Margaret Laurence. She set aside six hours a week to see writers, one at a time; she found that most of them were male poets. While discussing their work, she was especially gentle when it was bad. "I didn't make qualitative judgments on submissions. I'd never dream of saying, 'Look, kid, you'll never make a writer,' because who knows, he might."

The warmth of her personality stimulated a response among all the people she met. For instance, her meetings with students very often veered off the subject of writing into the subject of life itself. "Whoever said this generation is inarticulate? They never stop talking — but I enjoy it," she remarked, still looking a little stunned at the recollection. The young people expressed a sense of doom which she recognized as different from her own experience. "They are living in a very different world from the one I knew at that age. They have a permanent sense of helplessness. People didn't have that feeling even during the Depression or war. Now they feel that the machine has taken over. These kids are faced with the destruction of the planet. They're afraid their children won't live. My world was much safer; it was smaller. Even through war and Depression it was possible to agree with Job: 'The earth endureth forever.' "

"I have to believe that man will prevail and that he is going to live forever," she says, holding firmly to her own faith in the future. "I *have* to believe it. That is the thesis and text of my books. It is true that American writing carries a greater sense of doom than Canadian, but if the Americans really believed the game was up they would answer with silence. The game is not up; they are yelling. I am still prepared to do battle and save the planet. I put a lot of faith in the young and also in the ability of the people of my age to change. I believe in the human will. It is true that we quite often can't control the circumstances of life, but there are things we can do. The control of pollution, for instance, is up to us. Writing itself is more than an act of will; it is an act of hope and faith; it says life is worth living."

The anti-materialism of the students pleased her — "They don't want a colour TV in every bathroom, and I'm glad they feel that way"[65] — and struck a responsive chord: "I don't care if I pass on anything material to my children. Maybe one copy of each of my books for them to read if they want to. Enough education. Not things of a material sense. . . . Personally, I don't believe in security. If I tried to make things safe until the day I die, forget it. . . . I hate the word 'own'. . . . All I ask is enough money and a place to live for two years, to write another book — if God is good."[66]

At the University of Toronto she encountered the Women's Liberation Movement, who attempted to include her in their ranks. Perhaps they were thinking of Stacey, the trapped housewife, as an illustration of the need for the liberation of women. Margaret Laurence, however, is wary of organized groups:

"There are a great many things these people are after which I have long felt and believed in, but the reason why I don't take part is not because I disagree with the aims, but because my way of dealing with it is not protest or propaganda. It's a case of reform tactics versus revolution and my way is at the individual psychological level using fictional characters.

"Some of their tactics put men down," she went on to observe, "and I think this is one of the great problems. I'm not sure men need to be attacked. Men have a lot of problems. Life is a very anxious thing for a man who has a family to support, rent to pay, a job to keep. This is the kind of thing I was trying to express in the case of Mac. . . . So women must be concerned about doing a minimum of damage. The aim is not to stab to the heart."[67]

She felt more comfortable talking to small groups of students than addressing large crowds; but the adults who filled the libraries and auditoriums where she spoke were treated with the same courtesy as the students. She was never impatient with the endless questions as to whether she uses a ball-point pen or a typewriter; she does not expect everyone to be an expert in her trade. Some of her fictional interpretations have evidently struck nerve endings: at one public meeting she was asked whether she is prejudiced against well-adjusted people and why her characters are so gloomy. She replied that she does not think she is prejudiced — her characters come from her subconscious, she does not know how or why — and that while she thinks the world is gloomy she does not think her characters or people generally are: "There's faith in most people that will come out."

WHEN MARGARET'S JOB as writer-in-residence at the University of Toronto ended in the spring of 1970, she was close to accepting Canada as her real home. She had found that she was not an exile; she was inextricably locked into the rhythms of the country; she had never been far away in a psychic sense. All the books she had written in England, except the children's book, *Jason's Quest*, had been set in Canada. The physical distance had given her perspective on her own country, and the great literary world of London no longer seemed so captivating: "I found it was the same as anywhere else; some good writers and a lot of indifferent ones, and that, as in Canada, I wasn't really interested in writers' groups! I also discovered, through letters to friends in Canada, and through reading Canadian books and through visits back, that I was really more interested in what was going on in Canada than in England."[68] Even Elm Cottage had been a kind of Canadian environment — most of her guests had been Canadians.

That summer she took her first step towards her Canadian future. She bought a small cedar cottage on the Otonabee River near Peterborough and moved in for the summer. With the unconcern for house decoration which she had learned long ago in Somaliland, she furnished the house in jig time out of the catalogue: "It was a kind of childhood wish fulfillment. Looking at the catalogue and picking out what you'd order IF. . . ."[69]

Another sign that she was home — she planted one that read "Manawaka" at the gateway to her long narrow property. Manawaka now really exists — but not a hundred miles north of Winnipeg.

She spent a month there, working on a new novel and learning to live alone. The aloneness took some getting used to: "When I first came here I missed the children so much I thought I'd die, and then

I found that not only could I live without them, but more important, they could live without me. . . . I need privacy and aloneness quite a bit but I'm by no means a recluse. I have a great number of friends and I need to talk. The disadvantage here is that sometimes when I'm not working and I have a free evening, that's when the aloneness hits me. But if I'm willing to handle a fairly large telephone bill, I can call somebody and talk it out. Of course, the situation isn't wholly idyllic, but what is? I don't aim at perfection, even in furnishings. In terms of one's life, it's not humanly possible to have everything you want, so you have to arrange things as best as you humanly can."[70]

In spite of her efforts to overcome her feelings of aloneness, at the end of the month she was anxious to get home to the children. She packed up her infant novel and flew back to Elm Cottage.

But a physical link had been reestablished with Canada, and for the next two summers she returned to the cottage on the Otonabee. She seemed to feel that not only had she come home to her own small corner of Canada, but that she had returned to the land where her ancestors had lived. In the winter of 1972 she wrote: "The land still draws me more than other lands. I have lived in Africa and in England, but splendid as both can be they do not have the power to move me in the same way as, for example, that part of southern Ontario where I spent four months last summer in a cedar cabin beside a river. 'Scratch a Canadian and you find a phony pioneer,' I used to say to myself in warning. But all the same it is true, I think, that we are not yet totally alienated from physical earth, and let us only pray we do not become so. I once thought that my life-long fear and mistrust of cities made me a kind of old-fashioned freak; now I see it differently."[71]

She worked very hard during those country summers, writing a new long novel, longer than anything she had done previously. She worked at a broad oak table in front of the window overlooking the river, and wrote in a firm legible hand in a red school scribbler. Nearby stood a divining rod, used by the man who had found the well that supplies water for her cabin. The most noticeable decorations in the room were two large posters tacked firmly and commandingly to the wall: one of Louis Riel, the other of Norman Bethune.

IN MID-SEPTEMBER of 1972, Margaret Laurence flew back to Elm Cottage for the last time. The children were now grown young people. Jocelyn, twenty, had decided not to have the university education which had once meant so much to her mother, and had taken a job when she finished high school. On May 12, 1973, she married an English painter — "a good one," her mother says. David, a tow-headed, friendly boy, finished high school in July and then began to consider his future — whether to stay in England or go to Canada. "We'll see one another when we can; it's not a great problem among us,"[72] his mother remarked.

It had been a busy winter. The long novel, which she had been working on for three years, was finished. It was to be published in the spring of 1974 by McClelland and Stewart in Canada, Macmillan in England, and Alfred Knopf in the United States, where it was chosen as a Book-of-the-Month Club selection.

Margaret began to prepare for the final move to Canada, which would come in August 1973. As the time approached to leave Elm Cottage, an inevitable sadness came over her. The eccentric old place had been the scene of many jolly Canadian gatherings, and she had hoped, a little, that someone would take it over who would carry on the tradition of her unofficial Canada House, but this was not to be. Most of her major work had been written there — *A Jest of God*, *The Fire-Dwellers*, *Jason's Quest*, and many short stories including those in *A Bird in the House*. She had read proofs of *The Stone Angel* in the fine old study.

Another ending. Another beginning. Margaret Laurence stepped off the plane in Canada in late August 1973. She headed straight for her cottage on the Otonabee. It was a little dusty, a few mice had found winter shelter, and the river was still following its ancient course. There was peace and silence for a few days, then she began the search for a new house, a new home. The cottage would not do in winter, although she said, "I'll keep my shack — I love it, and I feel that I need a small place on the river to go to, in the summers, to get away from cities and towns entirely, and just to look at the river."[73]

Perhaps Peterborough would be her new home. "I *like* Peterborough," she said in a burst of enthusiasm. "It has two main streets." Two are plenty, but in the end she chose Lakefield, a little farther north, with one main street wandering between sturdy brick houses built by prosperous pioneers. She found an old yellow brick house and bought it for occupancy in March 1974.

So much accomplished, she set out for London, Ontario, where she was to be writer-in-residence at The University of Western Ontario until Christmas, and then, closer to home, for Trent University in Peterborough where she would hold the same position.

Her novel *The Diviners* appeared almost simultaneously with her move into her new house. She had come full circle in more ways than one. Lakefield and the yellow brick house were as familiar as childhood dreams. As for the novel, if she had thought that her internal compass was going to point away from Manawaka, she was wrong. It pointed directly there and, much more deeply, to the source of the Canadian pioneer experience, encompassing the Métis, and the shadow of Louis Riel. *The Diviners* draws on our short history in order to discern some rational basis for contemporary life, which, as Morag Gunn, the heroine, describes, is "an accomplished nightmare."

In this novel, Margaret Laurence not only encompasses the Canadian historic consciousness, she has also scooped up her own fictitious characters from earlier books, now seen from the viewpoint of Morag. We see Stacey MacAindra of *The Fire-Dwellers* when, still Stacey Cameron, she is accompanied by her terrible mother on a visit to Simlow's Dry Goods, where Morag is a clerk on Saturdays. Mrs. Cameron cannot resist making one of her patronizing remarks to Morag, to the intense embarrassment of Stacey. Both Stacey and Vanessa MacLeod are Morag's classmates; Vanessa receives the coveted soloist's part in the Sunday-School concert, to Morag's chagrin.

It is, however, the Métis family, the Tonnerres, who loom up large and painful as the most significant revival in this book. Among fleeting Tonnerre appearances in previous works, Piquette Tonnerre figures in *A Bird in the House* as a sullen Métis girl with bone cancer, cured by Vanessa's father and invited by him to stay with them one summer at their cottage at Diamond Lake. Later, Vanessa learns that Piquette has burned to death with her two small children in one of her father's shacks, while drunk on home brew after her Anglo-Saxon husband has abandoned her. This horrifying event is experienced first-hand by Morag Gunn of *The Diviners*, who is sent to report it for the *Manawaka Banner*. There, she finds old Lazarus, Piquette's father, standing alone in the snow beside the charred ruins; nearby, two of his young sons are huddled together. Morag vomits into the snow in revulsion at this evidence of the misery experienced by the indigenous people. Many recent Canadian writers are exploring the Indian-Métis factor in the Canadian consciousness, as though the shame which we conveniently bury must be faced before we can recognize ourselves.

It is significant that Morag should be the only one of Margaret Laurence's heroines to experience intimately the cast-out Métis. Unlike the privileged, establishment-family girls, Stacey, Vanessa, and Rachel, Morag is one of the dispossessed. Both her parents died of infantile paralysis when she was five; she was then adopted by the town garbage collector, Christie Logan, who lived in the poor district. One of Margaret Laurence's fighters, Morag is determined to overcome the shame of being poor and despised. By using a heroine who is uncertain of her position, Margaret Laurence probes a new area of Canadian consciousness. She presents the idea that all Canadians are dispossessed — those who came from Europe have been dispossessed of their ancient homes and traditions, while the Indians and Métis have been dispossessed by the Europeans who took away their land and dignity.

What, then, do we have in place of our ancient ties? We have our legends. For the Métis, these are the tales of Louis Riel and the hard-fought, lost Battle of Batoche. For those of Scots origin, like Morag and her foster father, Christie, they are memories of embattled ancestors, driven from Scotland by rapacious landlords. When Christie is in his cups, or when the mood is upon him, he thunders at Morag about her forebear, Colin Gunn, a Scottish piper who piped heart into his people when they fled from Scotland and landed in the almost unbearable hardships of Canada. The book is full of pipers, and Christie is one of them. By piping the legends of Morag's people Christie imbues his foster daughter with a sense of heritage. At his grave she insists, to the embarrassment of the funeral director Hector Jonas, whom we remember from *A Jest of God*, that a piper play the pibroch, the Scottish lament.

How much of the old stories are fact and how much are legend?

It is hard to say, and it is also hard to tell which is more important. The legends woven into our history give us "the strength of conviction" and it is doubtful whether we could do without them.

Morag's three lovers cast some light on the relative importance of fact and legend: the first one represents her attempt to renounce her roots; the other two, however, give her both a Métis and Scottish heritage. When she goes away to college in Winnipeg she meets a cultivated professor of English, Brooke Skelton, and at the end of her first year she marries him and moves to Toronto. Brooke is the antithesis of the cussing, rough-mannered Christie; he is the means by which Morag escapes the humiliation of poverty in Manawaka. Ashamed to tell her dazzling new husband about her humble life with Christie, Morag insists that she has no past. Brooke has had a painful childhood himself and is only too happy to pretend that both he and Morag are without history; he is also afraid of the future and refuses to allow Morag to have the child she longs for. The marriage fails because it denies the significance of both the past and the future, and Morag, developing as a woman and a writer, feels herself suffocating within the narrow confines of Brooke's conception of her as a perpetually innocent young girl. She releases herself by running away to live for a few weeks with Jules Tonnerre, a member of the Manawaka Métis family who has turned up in Toronto. Jules is brother to Piquette who died in the fire, and he was Morag's classmate in the Manawaka school. She bears Jules' child, a little girl whom she names Piquette, in memory, and so she links herself forever to the Métis.

Her third lover, a Scottish painter, Dan McRaith whom she meets in England, gives her unexpected insight into the meaning of her Scottish heritage. Dan comes from near Sutherland, the home of Morag's ancestor Colin Gunn. Morag visits Dan thinking that she will take the opportunity to see Sutherland itself. In the end she does not go, explaining to Dan, "The myths are my reality." She has at last come to understand that the real Scotland is not her source. "I always thought it was the land of my ancestors, but it is not," she tells Dan.

"What is, then?" he asks.

"Christie's real country. Where I was born."[74]

On top of this realization comes the news from Manawaka that

Christie is dying. "Pique, we're going home," she tells her child, and *home* is what she means. She cannot, however, settle in Manawaka, which represents too many destructive forces. Instead, she finds a piece of wilderness in Ontario, much like Margaret Laurence's property on the Otonabee, although this one is a farm on a river near a town with a suitably Scottish name, McConnell's Landing.

To some degree Morag has come to terms with the past, but there is still the future to be dealt with and that must be through her daughter, Piquette. Pique is eighteen when the book ends, the blue-jeaned, long-haired, guitar-strumming, hitch-hiking figure familiar in contemporary times. Like Morag before her, Pique is searching for her own path; for Margaret Laurence, all of us are pioneers trying to find a way in strange territory. Pique senses that she may find salvation if she seeks out her ancestors. She has learned her Scottish inheritance from her mother, and now she believes that she must find the people of her father, Jules Tonnerre. Jules, one of the pipers, has already provided her with some of her past in copies of the folk songs which he sings in night spots to drunken, uncaring white men. They are laments for his grandfather, Jules Tonnerre, who fought with Louis Riel at Batoche; for his father, Lazarus; and for his dead sister, Piquette. Pique leaves for Galloping Mountain, where Jules' brother Jacques lives with a large family of Métis children, his own and others'.

At the end, Morag is finishing a novel alone in her old farmhouse, but living nearby are a few friends. One of these, Royland, is a well diviner, a man who can find water using a forked willow branch. Royland suddenly loses his gift for well divining. He does not know how; indeed, he never understood how he possessed it in the first place. He does know, however, that somehow the gift has been passed on to a younger man. The diviners, like the pipers, are those who possess faith and grace — gifts, which in the optimistic ending of this book, flow from generation to generation. Writers are both diviners and pipers, and they too, may lose their power. The book's ending hints at personal finality, as though Morag's gift for divining novels were slipping away: "Morag returned to the house, to write down the remaining private and fictional words, and to set down her title."[75]

The whole novel, not only the ending, has the finality of a summation. It is so total a raid on Margaret Laurence's sources that it gathers up between its covers even her earlier works. When we find that she has resurrected past characters, we wonder whether she has done so in order to gaze on them one more time before saying good-bye. She has sorted out the ghosts, put them in their places, and said: "Rest in peace. Haunt me no more."

THE APPEARANCE OF *The Diviners* in May 1974, was hailed as the Canadian literary event of the season. It was widely and enthusiastically reviewed in Canada, the United States, and England. Flocks of journalists made their way to the hamlet of Lakefield to interview the author. There they found one of Canada's most successful and widely acclaimed writers, full of housewifely pride, buoyant and hearty, but quite plainly shy and nervous in the face of such attention. She announced adamantly that *The Diviners* would be her last novel. It would not necessarily be her last *book*; she would like to write another children's story, but never another novel which would force her to roam relentlessly among the shadows.

Perhaps. Although it seems unlikely that the divining power upon which she places such faith could suddenly desert her when she is in the full flower of her artistic and intellectual strength.

Does she really imagine that the restless spirits have no further claims?

1.

2.

3.

1. Gabrielle in 1940, shortly after her return from Europe, when she had decided to give up teaching and make her way as a writer in Montreal.
2. On holiday in Greece with her husband, 1961.
3. Roy family portrait, 1912. "La Petite Misère," Gabrielle, aged two, at bottom, centre. Top row: Bernadette, Clémence, Adèle, Anna, Rodolphe. Second row: Léon, Germain, Mélina. Only Joseph, of the eight living children, is missing.

Gabrielle
Roy

IN ST. BONIFACE, Manitoba, there still stands, at 375 Rue Deschambault, a rambling wooden house which has the air of being left over from an earlier time, a time when there was all the space in the world to build such generous houses and the wide, uninhabited Prairie stretched not far from its very doorstep. The capacious house, originally painted yellow and decorated with a pillared porch, was built in 1905 by a gentle, studious man named Léon Roy, as a home for himself and his wife, Mélina, and their large family of children. Now St. Boniface is a busy city, but when Léon built the house it was little more than a town, a French settlement across the Red River from the bustling city of Winnipeg.

Late on the night of March 22, 1909, the front door of the house flung open, and a young girl, hurriedly buttoning her coat around her, ran down the steps. Mélina had just given birth to her eleventh baby and, lying in bed with the newborn Gabrielle, had asked that someone hurry to the Cathedral and arrange for bells to be rung to announce the birth. The quick footsteps of the messenger echoed through the empty, snowy streets. She reached the heavy doors of the building only to find that not a soul was about and that it was too late to rouse the bell-ringer. No bells rang that night.

It did not really matter. Mélina Roy was a woman for whom imagined bells always sounded sweeter than real ones, and indeed, her triumphant demand for bells was proof that her imagination had once more overcome the obstacles of reality. When she had discovered, at the age of forty-two, that she was to have another baby, her feeling had been one of dismay, not joy. Léon had been even more anxious; he was sixty, and quite frankly felt too old to take on the responsibilities of parenthood once more.

It was true that some of the older children had already left home. Joseph, the eldest boy, had set out on his own at an early age, much to his father's despair since Léon had a great respect for books and learning and had wished Joseph to continue his education. Joseph, however, was to become a successful self-made man, first as a settler, then as a miner, and finally as a wheat buyer. The two eldest girls, Anna and Adèle, had also left to teach and had since married. There now remained Clémence, Bernadette, Rodolphe, Germain, Agnès, and the new baby, Gabrielle, with her blonde hair and clear blue-green eyes.

Two of Léon and Mélina's children had died. One had been named Agnès, for there were two Agnèses in the family. "The first one, whom I never knew, died of typhoid at fourteen," Gabrielle Roy remembers. "My father was inconsolable after the loss of this young girl who was, they say, sweetness itself, and of exquisite charm. So much did my father and mother grieve over the death of Agnès, that when another girl was born in our family, they gave her the same name."[1]

To support his brood of lively, handsome children, Léon worked as a colonizing agent, a job he loved. Under the French-Canadian Prime Minister Sir Wilfrid Laurier, a great flood of multinational immigrants, the poor and persecuted people of the world, poured into the Canadian West. Léon's job was to help them select farmland and settle in the new country. Like a patriarch, he led bands of Doukhobors, Mennonites, Galicians, and Slavs into the wilderness of Saskatchewan and Alberta. They trusted him as a wise and reliable leader who guided them through difficult times. Many French Canadians resented Sir Wilfrid Laurier's immigration policy as doom to their dreams of another Quebec in the West, but Léon did not share this feeling. He saw Sir Wilfrid Laurier as an admirable man who strove to unite Canadians. Léon had a vision of the great Canadian plains, settled by people who would make the land productive and enrich the country with their cultures. He had been a pioneer in the Prairie himself, the first of the Roys, followed soon after by two of his brothers, to leave Beaumont village in Quebec at the end of the nineteenth century. His wife, Mélina Landry, had also been of pioneer stock. She had come as a child with her parents, who were of Acadian origin, from St. Alphonse, Quebec, and they had settled at St. Léon, near Somerset in Manitoba. Now, both Léon's brothers and all Mélina's brothers and sisters were well established in farms and villages across the Prairie Provinces, and Léon hoped to do as well for the new arrivals under his care.

Léon's work took him away from his family for weeks at a time. One summer morning, when Gabrielle was a year old, he set forth once more on a journey, suitcase in hand. He crossed the wide front porch of his house, with its row of rocking chairs and its imposing pillars — a note of grandeur in the otherwise sensibly built house. His wife's fragrant stocks bloomed in the front yard. He walked along the wooden sidewalk of Rue Deschambault until he came to Rue Desmeurons, and there he caught a yellow trolley which took him over the Provencher Bridge across the Red River into Winnipeg where he boarded the train for Saskatchewan.

While he was away, there was a terrible accident. Gabrielle Roy recalls it, even now, with horror: "The other little Agnès died too, tragically, at the age of four, having set a little fire at the back of the house, which caught onto her starched dress, and in no time the child was all in a blaze. My father was away then amongst his immigrants. The news my mother sent him, telegram and all, never reached him. When he returned home several weeks later, he had no knowledge that the child was dead and buried. He called her name softly as he entered the house and before mother could rush to tell him the news. I was then a baby. Later, the tale of the second Agnès's death was told and retold to me many and many a time and I cried endlessly for the company of the little sister I had not known. For a long time in our family we hated calm Sunday afternoons in summer."[2]

Agnès's death had reverberating effects upon Gabrielle. She was now the only little one — her brother Germain, the next youngest, was eight, too old to be a playmate. "The last child in a family is alone," she has said, "and is in a sense an only child. I had no one to play with because my brothers and sisters were so much older. I was often very lonely."[3] Her mother, however, found comfort for the loss of Agnès in the new baby, and a strong bond grew between Gabrielle and her mother.

In 1911, when Gabrielle was two, a national political event took place that was to affect the Roy family. Wilfrid Laurier's Liberal Government was defeated by the Conservatives, led by Robert Borden. Laurier's defeat was partly brought about by his own people of French descent in Quebec, who interpreted his middle-of-the-road attitude towards British imperialism versus Canadian independence as too strongly pro-British. Even the immigration policy which provided Léon with his work was suspect, since it was administered by Clifford Sifton who was remembered for his anti-French sentiments in Manitoba. When the Government changed, many of Léon's Civil Service colleagues found it provident to change their political allegiances from Liberal to Conservative. But not Léon. He continued to hang a full-length portrait of Wilfrid Laurier in his study at home; and the only time this charming, gentle man ever exchanged angry words with his associates was in defence of Laurier. He found those who changed loyalties for political advantage contemptible, and he said so.

In 1913 the realities of political patronage came home to roost. Léon at this time was sixty-four, only six months away — after his long years of service — from his retirement and the pension on which he would then live. One day, returning from one of his settlements, he stopped in at his Winnipeg office and found a letter from the Government. It informed him that he was to be replaced by a younger man, someone with more up-to-date methods. As Gabrielle Roy wrote bitterly many years later, this excuse hid the real reason for his dismissal: "We must hand over your job to a man of the right political party. . . . What we need is not a servant of the country, but a servant of our own. . . ."[4]

Léon Roy was fired without even the security of his pension. Many people whom he had helped wrote letters to the Ministry in his defence. He himself went through the humiliation of pleading with the officials, but it was no use. The personal effect on the man was devastating. He lost his confidence and he was stunned by the betrayal; years of devoted service meant nothing because he had not bowed to political expediency. For the Roy household the result was instant hardship.

Gabrielle Roy speaks of her mother as heroic. Mélina Roy took roomers into their big house: "We found some of these people good company; others we forgot as soon as they left."[5] Her mother was an expert seamstress and made dresses and mended for the neighbours; somehow they survived. Gabrielle Roy has written a story called "By Day and by Night" about the tragic effect that this disaster had upon her father, but she finds it painful to speak of still. She was only four at the time, and does not remember the occasion; she only knows that as she grew up thrift was essential; there was a good deal of worry and few luxuries. "We were the genteel poor," she says. "We were not the sort of people to take in boarders. Poverty is perhaps hardest for middle-class people who fight through it to keep up a certain 'rank'."[6]

Determined as Mélina Roy was to see her family survive, she was equally determined that poverty should not reduce their life to the ugly and ordinary. Gabrielle remembers one day when her mother took her out to buy a new hat. They went to the place that represented all that was splendid in the outside world — Eaton's department store in Winnipeg. On entering the front door they passed one of Winnipeg's landmarks — the massive statue of Timothy Eaton — and then proceeded to the hat department. Gabrielle's mother went immediately to the less expensive models. Gabrielle listlessly tried on a few, but her eye strayed constantly to another table where stood an elegant brown velour sailor hat with ribbons down the back. She wandered towards it and tried it on. It was wonderfully becoming, but her mother tried not to notice. Gabrielle tried on a few more of the ordinary sort, and then in a burst of extravagance her mother announced, "Let's be foolish just this one time and buy the beautiful hat. We will make up for it by being very thrifty in other things."

They sailed out of Eaton's with the hat on Gabrielle's head. Then remorse overtook her mother. They walked home to St. Boniface in order to save carfare, and all the way her mother kept saying, "We shouldn't have bought it. Don't tell your father what it cost. I don't know how I will account for the big hole in my allowance." Gabrielle herself was torn between joy and guilt — admiring herself in the store windows as they passed, yet conscious that she had no right to the hat. "I have always remembered that beautiful hat. Thus I acquired a taste for the exquisite in the midst of poverty and thank my mother for it."[7]

Mélina Roy's feeling for elegance never died. It was part of her indomitable spirit. She made beautiful clothes for all the children, from the finest materials bought on sale at Eaton's after careful hunting.

She had another quality which made her children forget their poverty. She was able to bring a kind of magic into the house with her gift for story-telling. She had a dramatic flair and imitated the voices of the people in her stories. While Gabrielle sat on the kitchen floor stroking her kitten, and one of her sisters embroidered nearby, Mélina, at the stove, would launch into stories about her childhood in Quebec or into some account of her misadventures at Eaton's, where her uncertain English often brought her difficulties. "My mother was quite capable of exaggerating, but we did not mind.

I was fascinated by her tales."[8] Mélina Roy often spoke of the little village of St. Alphonse in Quebec where she was born and which had been blessed by sheltering hills which seemed particularly appealing when she looked out onto the flat plains of Manitoba. This village, according to her mother, was the most beautiful in the world, with charming trees all around and hills leading from one grand view to another. Gabrielle went to St. Alphonse later and found a few craggy stones and some wispy trees — not at all as her mother had described. Mélina also told her children about her voyage west as a child in a covered wagon, a trip she described to Gabrielle as a spendid journey of discovery.

Mélina was also musical and piano lessons were provided for all the young ladies in the Roy family, come inhumane governments or everlasting macaroni dinners. A young girl with long hair tied back in a ribbon could usually be seen seated in the parlour playing Mozart or Rachmaninoff.

It was just as well that Gabrielle's mother retained her spirit in the midst of difficulties, for Léon Roy, the man who had once been so convivial, turned silent and morose in misfortune. The child Gabrielle, too young to understand or remember him in good times, thought this meant that her father did not like her. In an effort to reestablish himself when Gabrielle was fifteen, he used some small savings to buy a store in St. Boniface. He was seventy-five at the time and besides, unsuited to business. The venture soon petered out in disaster and his situation was as dispiriting as ever. Sometimes at night Léon's old joy returned, and he told stories about the days before *the* letter came. Léon was a good story-teller, but of a different order than Mélina. He was a studious man with a reverence for fact, and he was sometimes impatient with the impossible embellishments which his wife added to her stories. He often told Gabrielle not to expect too much from life. But it is inconceivable that her father disliked her. He was an intensely sensitive man who was greatly worried by the vulnerability of children, especially since three of his had died. He felt too old to be a proper father to his youngest, and he was also stung by his inadequacy to provide for his family. Gabrielle was a tiny child and to him she seemed pitiful. Once, when she was about eight, she became ill with jaundice and had to go to hospital. On her return home, she lay weak and pale for several weeks on the front porch. One afternoon, as her father turned into the walk of his home, he found her crying and struggling with an old board which had been left by workmen who were tearing up the wooden sidewalk on Rue Deschambault in order to replace it with cement. The other children in the neighbourhood had snatched up the rest of the planks and had run off to make playhouses. Léon Roy, at the sight of his weak and pitiful Gabrielle, immediately nicknamed her "Petite Misère" — Little Miserable One. She was crying because only one board had been left for her, and to make up for this he made her a playhouse himself, in the backyard. Nevertheless, the nickname "Petite Misère" stuck, and it secretly angered her. She did not intend to be miserable — like him.[9]

There was a good deal of fight in the child who had to struggle hard for attention in a house where all the brothers and sisters were engaged in the important comings and goings of growing up. As the baby, she was adored — sometimes. Other times she was pushed impatiently out of the way and warned not to snoop or to ask so many questions. Gabrielle felt particularly left out by the stir created when her older sister, Bernadette, made the decision to become a nun. Bernadette was a pretty girl, affectionately called Dédette, and Léon and Mélina were both sad and proud on the day she left for good to become a cloistered nun. Her dedication affected them profoundly and Gabrielle was left with a strong feeling that Dédette had done something impressive, although she was not quite sure what it was. What must *she* do that could be spendid enough to affect her parents so strongly?

Her eldest sister, Anna, was interviewed by *The Winnipeg Tribune* about Gabrielle many years later when her youngest sister had become famous. "What she wanted she went after," Anna said. "She was a proud child and restless — she always seemed to be reaching beyond herself in search of accomplishment."[10] Anna felt that some of Gabrielle's pride was knocked out of her as a result of being one in a large family. Far from being the result of pride, Gabrielle's drive to achieve was a fight to become worthy of attention and to match all those superior, grown-up brothers and sisters.

Gabrielle exuded buoyancy. Yet, she could be full of joy one moment, and then at the least hint that she was not liked, not loved, droop like a crushed bird. "Petite Misère" suited her sometimes.

When these moods came upon her, she crept away to the attic to be alone; on the third floor of the yellow house there was a low-ceilinged room with a window where she could watch, as a detached observer, the world below which had rebuffed her. The room was a storehouse for all the old books belonging to her brothers and sisters, and the times spent in the attic were not always unhappy. Sometimes she went there simply to be quiet — to read, to dream, to invent.

In spite of her father's troubles, Gabrielle's life was secure and peaceful in the French town of St. Boniface, firmly grounded as it was in the rules and rituals of the church, the town, and the family. The end of her street, Rue Deschambault, drifted off into the Prairie and, only a short distance away, there were fields where the children played. Since there was no industry to speak of in St. Boniface, the men worked in Winnipeg; thus during the week the streets were almost deserted. What traffic there was was gentle: "It seemed to me that every day in the streets of our town we could see children passing two by two with a nun, whose beads we could hear clicking." The harshest sound she heard was the ringing of church bells and, on Sunday, the people appeared: "I can still see the streets filled with people all walking in the same direction; I remember a whole town flowing towards the door of the Cathedral."[11]

Gabrielle herself soon joined the line of children walking under the surveillance of the nun. Her parents sent her to St. Joseph's Academy as a day pupil where she was taught by the Sisters of the Holy Names of Jesus and Mary. She was a quick and hard-working student who stood at the top of her class. Mélina was not content to let Gabrielle's education stop there. She sent her off to play with neighbouring Irish children to learn English. "There is no one from whom you cannot learn something,"[12] she said firmly.

By the time she was ten, Gabrielle had become a writer and one with an audience too. She wrote a play which contained a villain, a hero, and a murder. "I had three or four neighbourhood children at my disposal, and for several summers we put on this play, using a nearby tree as the main prop. This tree was sometimes a castle, or a forest — and sometimes, a tree." The audience was called upon to be the chorus, as in a Greek drama. Her favourite line was uttered by a little boy called Louis, who cried out: "There lies the rotting carcass!" Louis' mother did not care for this language and, hearing him rehearse, forbade him to use it. Gabrielle had great trouble with Louis for some time, until she discovered that his mother had interfered with her best line. With great firmness, she demanded of Louis: "Who is the author of this play, your mother or me?" Louis conceded in a small voice that it was she, Gabrielle, and from then on proclaimed the line with satisfactory gusto. Gabrielle had defended the inviolable rights of the author at an early age.[13]

Her second literary work was a novel written when she was about eleven years old. It extended to only two chapters, although the title page bore the proud announcement: "A Novel in Twelve Chapters by Gabrielle Roy." She hid away in the attic to write it. The novel was about her uncles, those who lived on farms scattered around the countryside and whom she often visited on holidays. She had a great fondness for these uncles, who cast a special spell because of their grand drooping moustaches which made her think of Russian muzhiks, although she also often referred to them as "my uncles, the Archdukes of Russia." When she had finished two chapters she showed it to her mother. Mélina was horrified at the imaginative rendition of her brothers, and flung the manuscript into the fire.

"I didn't write anything else for a long time; I was afraid." But it was not her mother she feared; it was rather the fear of taking a big step, of finding herself challenged and alone. It took her a long time to make the irrevocable decision to be a writer; when she finally did, she was twenty-nine. In her teens and early twenties she sometimes mentioned the idea to her mother, but Mélina begged her to talk sense. For her mother, writing meant being poor in a garret, loneliness, and suffering. "I was very good at composition at school," Gabrielle would argue, but then she was good at everything, and Mélina was not going to see her carried away by a foolish, impractical, and dreamy notion.

Mélina was unalterably opposed to her youngest daughter becoming a writer; and yet, if ever a woman was born to be the mother of a writer, Mélina Roy was that woman. Inspired with imagination, her stories could change small events into moments of significance, and protect her children from falling into the despair of poverty. She preferred a good story to colourless truth, and Gabrielle Roy has always said that it was her mother who taught her to prefer fiction to fact. "What would I be without the memory of my mother?" she wrote years later. "If she had not been as she was, would I have been capable of transcending facts? I doubt it."[14]

Mélina's stories planted a strong desire to see the world. Gabrielle's own longing for the unknown crystallized one brilliant summer morning when she was sixteen, staying on holiday at her Uncle Excide's farm near Somerset. She awoke snug and happy in the farmhouse, with the smell of toast and coffee drifting up from the kitchen. She could hear the trees rustling outside her window and the birds singing. She ran downstairs to breakfast — and then outside to the edge of her uncle's far-stretching wheat field. The house itself was cradled in a grove of poplars, but the wheat field was open to the wide Manitoba sky. The day was so beautiful that as she looked away to the horizon she felt that the future would be splendid. How, she did not know, but she felt certain that destiny held great promise. Then she ran back to the farmhouse. "They are immense, the skies of Manitoba," she wrote later. "They have made us different than we would have been otherwise. The immense sky invites us to know, and to go and see, always, that which is at the end of the horizon. It is because of it, no doubt, that we have left Manitoba, but it is that which has marked us."[15] The memory of these two images caught in her youth — the cradled farmhouse and the open plain — provide the central tension within Gabrielle Roy's writing. On the one hand she longs for the safe, enclosed shelter of family and friends, and on the other she is driven towards the loneliness of achievement.

When Gabrielle had just turned eighteen and had nearly finished high school, her mother pointed out that it would be necessary for her to earn a living. This came as something of a shock to the romantic Gabrielle. "Must life be earned?" she wrote later. "Was it not better to make a gift of it once for all, in some beautiful impulse?"[16]

Once again, to the exasperation of her mother, Gabrielle mentioned her desire to write. It was quite obvious to Mélina what career Gabrielle should follow. Her daughter had been a brilliant student, winning gold medals, bursaries, and scholarships. Naturally, she should be a teacher, and Mélina was prepared to pay for the training from the last of her husband's savings. In the end,

Gabrielle was given a scholarship by the French-Canadian Teachers' Association of Manitoba, and in the fall of 1927 she entered the Winnipeg Normal School.

In 1927, while Gabrielle was at school, Léon Roy died. After his death, Gabrielle learned to her bewilderment that the crushed, silent man she had known had once been charming company. She began to comprehend the blow he had endured when he was dismissed from his job. Although the influence of Gabrielle's quick-witted, fanciful, and courageous mother on her character and writing is easily perceived, Léon Roy's darker presence left an equally strong impression. He lived a tragedy that could not be overcome by flights of the imagination. In her later writing she described immutable sadness, yet as a balance to this reality there was the saving grace of imagination. One result of her imaginative power was her ability to laugh at the machinations of officialdom, deflating the power of inhumane institutions by refusing to take them seriously. Some of her funniest writing is about the strange gyrations of bureaucracies, institutions, and committees. One of her most amusing stories is about the installation of a telephone in an Eskimo tent; but, as she has said herself, "It is not really funny. At least, not as it lingers in the mind."[17] However, she was not always able to reduce cruelty with humour; as in the case of her father, there are some tragedies which cannot be reduced. He left her the image of a gentle man caught by harsh circumstances. She has said, "I write mostly of the gentle people. I do not wish to write about violence. I know only too well that it exists, but what would another book about violence achieve? The world is already full of them."[18] Nevertheless, the violence done within a man she well understood, and wrote about.

With Léon's death, it was more necessary than ever for Gabrielle to stand by her mother. The challenge of the horizon was set aside. Upon graduation from the Normal School, she accepted a teaching job for one summer month in the poverty-stricken village of Marchand. Her experience there gave her a singular view of human misery. On the first morning in class, she called the roll. One child did not answer. After a silence, the other children, whom she had found listless and unresponsive, told her that the child had died the night before of tuberculosis, a common cause of death among the young there. In an attempt to reach these children, who were largely

Métis, ragged, and undernourished, and who had had a rapid succession of bored teachers, she suggested that they all go to see the dead child. After school they did so, and found her alone in a pitiful cabin. The parents were not there; Gabrielle guessed that they were away making funeral arrangements. She encouraged the children to place flowers around their dead companion. The experience came back to her over forty years later when she included the story of the dead child in a collection of stories about summer.[19]

In spite of the fact that her ultimate hopes lay elsewhere, they were not yet fully realized and she was far from unhappy as a teacher. The affection of the children warmed her, and looking back later she said that the first year teaching was "the happiest time of my life." Intimacy with other people is something she misses painfully when she is writing.

Her desire to write, however, was not entirely forgotten. When she was twenty she wrote two murder stories, one in English and one in French. The English story was sent to *The Winnipeg Free Press* and the French one to *Le Samedi* in Montreal. Daily she watched the mail for the publishers' replies, while her mother remarked scornfully, "They will never pay you for such a thing, Gabrielle."[20] Both papers did pay, however, and they published the stories. The fee from *Le Samedi* was two dollars, such a small amount that Gabrielle pretended to her mother that this was only an advance on a larger sum. Both stories embarrass her now.

In the fall she taught for a year at Cardinal, near Somerset, a place she knew well from summer visits to her uncles. She has written a story about this year called "To Earn My Living. . . ." It expresses her happiness at being in the warm, snug little school, safe with the children while a winter storm raged outside.

The following year she was able to teach in St. Boniface and live with her mother. She was appointed teacher of a class of six- and seven-year-old boys at the Institut Collegial Provencher, a bilingual school, but one which attracted students from a wide variety of national backgrounds. She taught at the Provencher Institute from 1930 until 1937. A photograph taken of one of her classes shows four rows of extremely sturdy-looking little boys lined up on the steps of the institute. The teacher, standing behind them, is pretty and slender, and wears a checked shirtwaist dress and tie. She appears to be very much in command of the situation. From this photograph one would guess that Mademoiselle Roy ran an orderly class.

During her years of teaching, Gabrielle was able to use another of her talents. A very good actress, she joined Le Cercle Molière, the St. Boniface theatrical group run by Monsieur and Madame Arthur Boutal who were important figures in the cultural life of the French Canadians in western Canada. Gabrielle travelled to Ottawa twice with Le Cercle Molière to take part in the Dominion Drama Festival. On both occasions the group won the Bessborough Trophy, first award for French-language productions. She also acted in English plays in Winnipeg, and became well known as a local actress. At school she produced plays with the children.

Acting was great fun. Gabrielle loved the excitement of production and the lively companionship backstage. Her flair and humour found expression in the plays and they were qualities which both her fellow actors and the audience appreciated.

As far as anyone could see, Gabrielle's life was all it should have been. She was a good teacher, she genuinely enjoyed her job, and she was earning her living in a respected profession. She and her mother were close companions. It was something of a mystery to Gabrielle's friends why she did not marry; she was an unusually beautiful girl; but she had her mother to look after, so it appeared understandable.

No one seems to have guessed that beneath the surface Gabrielle possessed a fierce longing to see the world and to find possibilities beyond St. Boniface. In 1937, when she was twenty-eight, she dropped a bombshell. She announced that she was going to Europe to study theatre. She did not say that she was going to write; in fact, she did not even admit this to herself — the old fear still held her. No, she would go to Paris and London and find out whether she could make her way as an actress. The reaction to this announcement among her friends and family was one of disbelief. Young girls at that time did not suddenly just pack up and go to Europe — certainly not to study drama, of all things. During the Depression anyone with a job was lucky just to be drawing a salary, and here was Gabrielle, trying to outreach herself as usual.

All this adverse reaction made Gabrielle very unhappy. She was not as sure of herself as she appeared to be and she was worried about leaving her mother alone. Some of her later writing about this period reveals that she never overcame her anxiety about her mother. Nevertheless, there was something else at stake and she stuck to her guns. The objections continued: she did not have enough money; everyone would worry. By some miracle, however, Gabrielle had managed to save eight hundred dollars — the idea of going away had obviously been on her mind for a long time. On a starting salary of one hundred dollars a month, which dropped to ninety dollars during the Depression, she had helped her mother and had also patiently and regularly saved towards . . . something. She borrowed a little more and reassured the protesters, "It will only be for a year."

Mélina Roy, now an aging lady of seventy, was not to be comforted. Although at first she had refused to take Gabrielle's plan seriously, when Gabrielle continued to speak of it her unhappiness grew. Finally, they stopped speaking of her departure at all.

Her plan was to sail in September, and in June she left the Provencher Institute. She had two months to put in and she was anxious to earn a little more money for her travels. She had heard that there were summer schools in the North, often in need of teachers, and she decided to apply for such a job. The result was an experience of a kind of life she had never known before, of people living on a remote island — untouched, simple, and innocent. Much later the experience resulted in a book, *Where Nests the Water Hen*.

Finding the place was in itself an experience: "At the Board of Education, they didn't even know how to get there, it was such an out-of-the-way place. But the postmaster at St. Boniface had become inspector of the post offices in the north of Manitoba, a very charming man, Mr. Vermandeer, of Flemish descent. I rang him up, and I said, How does one get to the Water Hen district? That is a joke, he said, because I am going there myself day after tomorrow, and if you can be on the train from Dauphin, well, I'll be renting a car; I'm going to Meadow Portage to visit the last post office in that region . . . so I got on the train and we met at Rorketon and took this rented car and a guide, and we travelled to Meadow Portage, that little village of nothing at all . . . which I thought was my post. But it turned out that this was not my post: this was the *village*, this was a *big* place; my appointment was to the island, eighteen miles farther away. Well, I was a city girl, after all; this was my first venture in the wild, and I was not dressed for the region . . . and I was lost. I inquired from the merchant at the store there where we were — the store was the post office and the hotel and everything, and the owner said to me, You'll have to wait 'till next week. You've just missed the postman who travels from here to the ranch. So this was pretty dreadful; but Mr. Vermandeer said, "Well, I have this car and after all I've always wanted to see how this Water Hen country was, and there's lots of time, so we'll drive you there. He didn't know himself that there were two rivers to cross and that we had to carry our own canoe across one island from one river to another, but we got on the island, way out at the end of the world. By then I was so lost that I didn't know just where I was, and it was almost night by the time they landed me there. Mr. Vermandeer said, Now do you really want to stay here? Because if you want to come back, you know, I wouldn't think the less of you. But I had my pride, and besides I'd given my word to the school board, and so I said No, I'll stay. Little did I know then that a book would come out of all that. . . . I was so lonely that I set out just living with the children and with nature and with the rivers, . . ."[21]

IN SEPTEMBER 1937, Gabrielle landed in London "in a very divided frame of mind."[22] She enrolled in the Guildhall School of Music and Drama, and spent every spare moment visiting art galleries, museums, and, most of all, the theatre. When she returned to her room at night she was so stimulated by everything she found that she could not sleep. She studied for six months at the Guildhall School; it was long enough for her to decide that the theatre did not hold her future: "I saw people giving everything they had to the job of acting — so that they could repeat someone else's words. Acting is an interpretative art; I suppose that I prefer the creative one. I had enjoyed amateur theatre in St. Boniface because of the good fellowship; professional acting is not like that. It is very hard."[23] She was also advised that her voice was too light for a theatrical career.

She had made one decision; but she was still not ready to go home. First of all, there was everything to see in Europe. She travelled back and forth between England and France and took a walking tour through the Côte d'Azur and Provence — beautiful countryside which she responded to with characteristic intensity. Her one year away was stretching into two. It was then that she made her second decision. "I was in England when the desire to write came to me so strongly that I couldn't put it aside. Now what was I going to write? and in what language? because, although French was my native tongue, I had a certain knowledge of English, and perhaps if I had worked very, very hard I could have become an English writer."[24]

She started, however, in French, and sent two articles about Europe back to the St. Boniface paper, *La liberté*. They were published, and so, with a little more courage, she sent three articles on Canada to a well-known Parisian weekly called *Je suis partout*. They were accepted. The publication of these three articles was the signal Gabrielle had been waiting for. She would be a writer, and a writer in the French language. Although the moment was a significant one, she says now: "My writing of this period is poor, unimportant — I would have given part of my life to hide it forever. It is not even worth mentioning — the first stutterings of one who knew nothing yet about the craft of writing, let alone artistic value. Even the articles in *Je suis partout* do not amount to much. I just had the good luck to submit them at the very moment, I imagine, when they were sort of on the look out for something on Canada. But the acceptance of my little 'compositions' by so important a newspaper did boost my morale considerably, as I had published almost nothing until then."[25]

In early 1939 it became evident that Europe would soon be at war. Gabrielle's slender savings were running out, and she was exhausted by the rigours of travel. What of her ambition to write? ". . . I didn't feel any possibility of it in France. Especially for a French-speaking writer, coming from the west, it seemed just hopeless."[26]

She sailed for home.

THE NEWS OF Gabrielle's arrival in Canada was greeted with relief and joy in St. Boniface. The old job at the Provencher Institute was waiting for her, or, if she preferred, plenty of jobs were available in the Manitoba Civil Service. Gabrielle, landed in Montreal, hesitated. Then she wrote home to say that she had decided to give up her career as a teacher. She would like to stay in Montreal and try to make her way as a writer.

Surely not! her mother wrote. In Montreal she knew no one. She would be lonely — and poor. To struggle as a writer — a hopeless career — would be to submit herself to unnecessary hardship. Everything was waiting at home.

Nevertheless, Gabrielle rented a small room on Stanley Street near the bus depot and Windsor Station. At first she wrote short articles for two Montreal periodicals, *Le Jour* and *La Revue Moderne*. They were articles about Europe — for example, the quaint ritual of the tea hour in England. Her payments were sometimes as low as three dollars.

In the spring of 1940 she went to see the editor-in-chief of a large magazine called *le Bulletin des agriculteurs*. She offered her services as a reporter. "Can you write?" asked the editor. She showed him the three articles she had written for *Je suis partout* in Paris, and was hired. Thus began a five-year association with *le Bulletin des agriculteurs*, during which time Gabrielle wrote over sixty articles, mainly for *le Bulletin*, but for other publications as well.[27]

The articles were of two kinds. One was about the people of Canada; she travelled widely across the country and wrote about the Hutterites, the Mennonites, the Jews, the Ukrainians. The other was about growing industrialism, mostly in Quebec, although she also went to Ontario, the Peace River and the Alaska Highway. Visiting the mining and mill towns of the Saguenay Valley, Granby, Drummondville and Sherbrooke, among others, Gabrielle saw Quebec on the march, entering the twentieth century, participating, at last, in global progress.[28]

It is easy to understand her pride in Quebec's development — although she warned that American and English-Canadian money was being used too extensively, and that Quebec would find itself owned by outsiders. Traditionally, French Canada, both in Quebec and Manitoba, had existed in small backward farms. To some degree the Church had been responsible for this. It had hoped that the French-

Canadian culture could survive by remaining apart, on the land, instead of in cities where it might be absorbed. Gabrielle believed that Quebec kept itself at a disadvantage by remaining outside modern development. She thought that technology would bring freedom.[29]

However, her living quarters soon gave her another view of industrialism. She had moved to Dorchester Street where she had a flat in a building which was bordered on one side by the wealthy district of Westmount, and on the other by the slum tenements of St. Henri. Sometimes, in the evening, she strolled through St. Henri and she was appalled by what she saw. These people were not beneficiaries of industrialism, they were its casualties. They had come from farms to find jobs, but the Depression had trapped them in poverty. With four articles she wrote about Montreal in 1941, her journalism took a radical turn. She described that city, not as an example of progress, but as a nightmare of sprawling disorder that no one cared about. Writing of St. Henri, she said, "The nature of neighbouring industry pollutes this quarter; there is poverty, absence of hygiene, and vermin which spread rapidly to other areas."[30] The network of "sinuous and magnificent" highways linking the industrial towns of the north were reduced to "furrows" in the streets of St. Henri.

From the time that Gabrielle wrote the four Montreal articles, she was never again able to view growing industrialism with the optimism which had marked her début as a journalist. In fact, she says now that she wishes her first articles could be relegated to "the shadows."[31]

While she was still working as a reporter, her activities expanded into other areas. She wrote a play which was performed by the Montreal Repertory Theatre and she had a part in a radio serial called *Vie de famille*. She began to write short stories, one of which won a two-hundred-and-fifty-dollar prize and was published in *La Revue Moderne*, and another of which was dramatized on Radio-Canada. By now she was recognized as a capable writer. *Le Bulletin des agriculteurs* paid her increasingly higher fees. She moved to an apartment between Greene and Atwater streets, but it too was on the borderline between a wealthy and a poor district.

Gabrielle's walks through St. Henri changed more than her journalism; they changed her life. She began to walk there when she first came to Montreal: "I was very lonely in Montreal. I practically didn't know a soul, I was a penniless free-lance writer, selling articles here and there, just enough to pay my room and eat somewhat. For human warmth I used to roam the streets, walk and walk and walk. I landed in St. Henri one spring night and it was just pulsing with life, because poor people, when the weather is fine, they're out on the sidewalk. They had no galleries or verandahs, they were all sitting right on the sidewalk. They brought their chairs out and they sat there and they talked about life, so much so that if you walked in those little streets you picked up bits of conversation here and there and in the end you had it all, without much pain, so to speak."[32]

Listening to the talk of these people in the early years of the war, Gabrielle was struck by a pitiful irony. The war, with its destruction, death, and heartbreak, was rescuing these people from the inactivity and poverty of the Depression. The men had been out of work for ten years, while the women struggled against terrible odds to keep their children and homes together. Young men, hanging around restaurants, had never worked and were cynical and listless. The war, which was to kill many of them, seemed to offer security. At least it offered money, which they had not had before: soldiers were able to send allowances back to their families, and these small allotments were fortunes to people who had had nothing.

In the summer of 1941, at the same time that her four articles on Montreal were published, she began her first novel. "Suddenly, one day it was all there — characters, theme, meaning — as a huge, hazy mass, yet with a sort of coherence already."[33] She took a holiday at Port Daniel in the Gaspé Peninsula and began work. She allotted three months a year to the novel; it was still necessary to earn a living as a journalist.

If there had ever been any doubts that Quebec was her spiritual home, they were dispelled by the compassion which she felt for the people of St. Henri: ". . . I linked my life at one time with the Québec people and it was *really a link*, you know, deliberately, and with love, and understanding, because when I discovered the world of *Bonheur d'occasion* [the novel's title], it was for life. I felt tied. Although I'd been born in Manitoba and travelled all over Europe before I found myself, when I landed in Montréal and I discovered

St. Henri, as it was then, along the old Lachine Canal, I discovered the people that was my own, and its tragedy, and its sadness, and its gaiety too. Since then, I have tried to give it expression. But I couldn't forget the rest of the country which is also part of my heritage, so I alternate."[34]

The years in Montreal were good ones: "They were tremendously difficult and tremendously exhilarating." By 1943 her first novel was growing and she was earning a good living as a freelance writer. Always, in the back of her mind, she looked forward to the day when she could hand her mother her first novel. It would justify her departure and explain it. It would be a gift of thanks. Then, in 1943, Mélina Roy died.

Her death came in the nature of things. She was seventy-six years old and in the past few years had weakened markedly. Gabrielle blamed herself for her mother's rapid decline, as though her going had taken the desire for life from the spirited and courageous lady. In a muted two sentences near the end of one of her stories, she wrote: "My mother failed very quickly. No doubt she died of illness, but, as so many people do fundamentally, of grief too, a little."[35]

Many critics have commented on the rich mother-figures found throughout Gabrielle Roy's work. She sees mothers not only as sources of life, but also as perpetual wellsprings of love. Her fictional mothers are based on Mélina Roy, a woman who cared and worried endlessly over her large brood of children, always provided support, and, more than that, insisted that life was splendid. Sadness and misfortune were challengers, not destroyers. She was not a particularly affectionate mother, according to Gabrielle,[36] but she was a never-to-be-forgotten source of inspiration. Many of Mélina's own dreams remained unrealized. Although she found great satisfaction in her family and home, she longed to travel, as though, like Gabrielle, she expected to find something radiant "out there." Gabrielle recognized her mother's longings and has said that her own drive to achieve was in part a desire to compensate for much that Mélina had missed. Her first novel came too late.

The novel, *Bonheur d'occasion*, was published in 1945 in French. It had taken three and a half years to complete, and it was one of the most successful ever written in Canada. One day a friend called to say that she had sent a copy to her brother-in-law in New York. He was a partner in the publishing firm of Reynal and Hitchcock, and she thought he might be interested in publishing it. She hoped Gabrielle did not mind. "I had no objections and no hopes," said Gabrielle Roy. "I didn't think that Americans would be interested in a Canadian story."[37] Reynal and Hitchcock was extremely interested, and in 1947 the book was published in English, with the title *The Tin Flute*. It was then published in Toronto by McClelland and Stewart. "I remember a year in that exciting decade . . . ," said Hugo McPherson in his introduction to the paperback edition of *The Tin Flute*, "when people kept asking each other: 'Have you read *The Tin Flute*? It's Canada's most devastating novel'; or, 'Who *is* Gabrielle Roy? She must have lived through a lot to write a book like that.' "[38] Journalists by the score interviewed the author, and the success of the book was trumpeted by the press: "*The Tin Flute* is one of the most satisfying adult novels yet to appear in Canada," said the *Canadian Forum*.[39] The Literary Guild, an American book club, chose it as their May 1947 book, with a printing of 750,000 copies; and Universal Pictures in Hollywood bought the film rights, although the production floundered in the complicated machinery of the movie industry. An independent edition of the novel appeared in Paris, and further offers to publish came from Switzerland and Germany. Soon after, it appeared in England, Spain, Denmark, Czechoslovakia, Sweden, Argentina, Romania, and Norway. In 1972 it was published in Russia.

The Tin Flute, or *Bonheur d'occasion*, was given the Governor-General's Award for fiction in Canada and the *Prix Fémina* in France. Gabrielle Roy received medals from the French Academy and from the French-Canadian Academy. She was the first woman to be elected a member of the Literary Section of the Royal Society of Canada.

The author herself was quietly beginning a new story in her room when the news of the Literary Guild selection came to her by telegram. "Its success surprises me greatly," she said to one reporter, "for I wrote a simple story about people and a way of living evident to all."[40] "In fact, all the time I was writing it I was afraid that someone else would do the same story. It seemed so obvious."[41] Then she added, "I have an idea that it takes more character to withstand success and what it brings, than to face the hardship of a struggle at the beginning."[42]

The book was dedicated to Mélina Roy.

What was this book — a first novel by a new writer — that it aroused so much attention?

Gabrielle Roy's *The Tin Flute* swept away the myth of the French Canadian as a peaceable, contented farmer living either in a slow-moving village or on a family farm. It revealed him as he had never been seen before — as the urban dweller of St. Henri whose life is rendered desolate by poverty. *The Tin Flute* does not appeal to the sentimental; although it is filled with compassion for human beings, it offers no comfort. There had been other realistic novels about Canada, but this was the first to take a straightforward look at the Montreal slums, districts considered quaint by tourists. If the truth had seemed all too obvious to Gabrielle Roy, it had escaped most people. A reviewer wrote: ". . . with its realism it showed French Canadians that they had been living psychologically in a false world. They had been imagining themselves as living outside the twentieth century in an abstract world of their own, but Gabrielle Roy made them discover that most of them are living in despair and squalor. It was a condemnation of the ruling French-Canadian bourgeoisie. . . . it can be argued that the transformation of French Canada started with the publication of *The Tin Flute*. . . ."[43]

In this novel, Gabrielle Roy describes the people of St. Henri with uncompromising force by concentrating on one family with eleven children, whose surname Lacasse in English translation means "breakage," "damage," or "trouble." In particular she focuses on the eldest daughter, Florentine, a thin, pretty girl, who works as a waitress in a dime-store restaurant yet dreams of being rescued by a romantic young lover. However, she miscalculates the attention of an ambitious, cold young man, Jean Lévesque, who has no intention of saddling himself with a poor girl from St. Henri and abandons her after she becomes pregnant. With the ruthlessness of the poor, Florentine then marries another young man who is in love with her, who thus legitimizes her expected child and leaves her with enough money to live when he goes off to war. Each person in the Lacasse family has a dream — the kind of dream everybody has about romance, financial windfalls, or a successful career. The dreams give them hope, but they have such a fragile basis that the whole book is invested with the tragedy of the impossible. "Indeed without hope life would not be a tragedy," Gabrielle Roy has said.[44] Both French and English titles convey the idea of desperately grasped straws of joy. *Bonheur d'occasion* is difficult to translate into English, but it means something like "bargain happiness" — at least, joy which is only mocking. The English title, *The Tin Flute*, draws attention to the cheap toy of Daniel, a little boy who is dying of leukemia. This tin article is all that he has in the world, yet it makes him happy — a flimsy basis for joy.

While almost everything in the lives of the Lacasse family is pinched and squalid, there is one pervasive, bountiful force: the strength and love of the mother, Rose-Anna Lacasse. Every year, as the Lacasse family faces inevitable eviction, Rose-Anna trudges about to find another home. She worries, she sews, she scrounges; and although despair is her constant companion, her fruitful motherly qualities never falter. Poor Rose-Anna also has a dream. She longs to visit the sugarbush farm where she lived as a child, and, most of all, to experience the comfort of her mother, who still lives there. When, one day, her husband, Azarius, in a borrowed truck, takes her and the children on a visit to the farm, this dream crumbles. Her mother is cold and disapproving: Rose-Anna cannot hide their poverty; her children are heartbreakingly pale and thin beside the robust, country-bred offspring of her brother; and she is not even able to visit her beloved sugarbush because of her mother's disapproving remarks about her "condition" — Rose-Anna is, of course, pregnant again. There is no room for dreams in these lives, and Rose-Anna returns home to face once more her grinding struggle. In many of Gabrielle Roy's works, we find an attempt to recapture innocence by travelling to an Eden-like setting, but never with such devastating effect as in *The Tin Flute*.

There are two opposing sets of values presented in this book: one is the humane love of Rose-Anna; the other is money. Because the lack of money has stunted their lives, the characters see money as the answer to everything. The people of St. Henri drift along glittering Ste. Catherine Street, staring into shop windows, and gazing with envy at the well-fed people they see. In their simplicity, they believe that all these people are happy. Florentine's loveless marriage is made for money and security, but we sense that when her husband returns from war, there will be little joy in such a marriage. The book ends as the men of the family leave for war, and of course they do so for the sake of financial salvation. Even Azarius, Rose-Anna's husband, joins up on a foolish impulse, believing that this will relieve Rose-Anna of himself and provide her with a livelihood. Rose-Anna is heartbroken; it is not money she wants, it is him. Her life is rooted in love, and without it, nothing remains.

The Tin Flute is a painful book to read, made more so by the ironical indictment of society which it contains. As one of the characters says, "Yes, money. . . . There was never enough for old age insurance, never enough for the schools or for orphans, never enough to give everybody a job. But look here, there's money enough for war. They've got money for that!"[45] The indictment was too strong for some sectors of the society. While the book was acclaimed throughout the world, it struck a nerve-ending in Quebec. A priest appeared before the executive committee of the Montreal City Council and denounced Gabrielle Roy for giving St. Henri "bad publicity." Oddly enough, he himself had come to complain about the smoke, the lack of playgrounds, and the poor lighting in the district; but it had not occurred to him that *The Tin Flute* supported his own argument.[46]

There is pain in all Gabrielle Roy's books. The pain which the reader experiences, however, gives him an intense feeling that he has touched life and other human beings. Gabrielle Roy has said that without pain we cannot know joy; and the great success of this book is the mixed pain and joy of coming to understand other people. "The work of the novelist," she has said, "is to bring more knowledge, more sympathy, more love."[47]

THE YEAR 1947 was a momentous one for Gabrielle Roy. It was the year of the English translation of *Bonheur d'occasion* and all the honours which followed. It was also the year she married. She had gone back to St. Boniface for a visit, and was hailed on all sides as the local girl who had made good, a celebrity whose sensational first book had brought her fame and fortune. Invitations came from everywhere; newspaper interviews and photographs appeared. One photograph from newspaper files of the time shows a beautiful girl with long brown hair, brilliant, widely-spaced eyes, and a high forehead. It has glamour, but it does not capture the eloquent, tragic sense apparent in her later portraits. Gabrielle Roy has never liked it: "too Hollywood," she says.

In actuality, Gabrielle had not returned home for happy reasons. Two of her sisters, Anna and Clémence, were quite ill and in need of care. She was not much in the mood to attend all the festivities in her honour. One of the invitations came from Le Cercle Molière, the theatrical group with whom she had acted for several years: "I received a formal invitation from the president, Dr. Marcel Carbotte. I very much hesitated to accept. Finally, for the sake of the times when I had shared so much with this group, I accepted. I met Dr. Carbotte who took me home after the dinner and suggested right then little trips around the city, pilgrimages, as it were, to sites of interest which I might like to revisit. So we went to the locks on the Red River, the old ferryboat crossing on the Rouge (all gone now), to St. Norbert and many villages I had a longing to see again. Quickly we also found interest in each other as well as in my beloved vista of prairie land. Unconsciously, I was looking for a true friend in the world. So was he, very likely — and this we became to one another."[48]

Gabrielle Roy and Marcel Carbotte were married soon after in a small church in St. Vital, near St. Boniface.

Shortly after their marriage they went to France, where Dr. Carbotte continued his studies in gynaecology. They lived in Paris and St. Germain-en-Laye for three years and during that time travelled widely throughout Europe. Fame followed Gabrielle overseas, where *Bonheur d'occasion* had been published in several countries, including France. In 1947, while living there, she was awarded the *Prix Fémina*, an honour that was bestowed only after some odd and nerve-racking experiences.

She and Marcel had been in Paris only a few days when M. d'Uckermann, literary director of Flammarion, the house which had published her novel in Paris, paid a call. After a lengthy, polite conversation, he announced that a jury of distinguished French women who awarded the literary *Prix Fémina* was considering her as a recipient. He advised her to go and meet the ladies. Gabrielle protested that she did not see why she should call on women whom she did not know. M. d'Uckermann lost his affability for a moment and then pointed out that she represented Canada, implying that she had certain duties toward her country. Gabrielle, taken aback "by the great weight of responsibility placed upon my shoulders," recovered enough to announce firmly, "In Canada we do not make visits of solicitation."

"No! No! You misunderstand me," cried M. D'Uckermann. "It is simply that it would be polite to shake the hands of these ladies."

"Well," countered Gabrielle, "is the *Prix Fémina* a prize for a book or for politeness?"

"But you are French, also," he went on, evading her question. "One hundred per cent French. However, your existence appears uncertain to the ladies. They ask, 'Who is this Canadian author? Is she a real person — or perhaps a myth?'"

"Ah well," said Gabrielle, "tell them I am a myth and let us have peace."

Monsieur d'Uckermann, however, persuaded Gabrielle and Marcel to join him for lunch, where the fourth member turned out to be a juror for the *Prix Fémina*. She told Gabrielle that she admired her book very much, but that she also liked the book of a sailor-explorer and could not make up her mind between the two.

The next day Monsieur d'Uckermann telephoned to say that the juror had been much impressed by Gabrielle. The sailor, it seemed, was losing out. However, another French author, Emmanuel Roblès, was now being considered. The committee was divided into two factions: one wished to honour Canada; the other thought that there were enough French authors without importing a Canadian for the *Prix Fémina*.

Gabrielle was given hour by hour accounts of the sway of opinion. One elderly member, too old to leave her home, was said to be an assured vote for Gabrielle because once, a long time ago, she had paid a visit to Canada and had planted a cross on a point of the Gaspé Peninsula. The competition had become like a horse race. "The Canadian is in the lead . . . alas, the next day Emmanuel Roblès passed me by a nose . . . I regained first place; I fell back to second; to third." Newspapers took up the argument — should a Canadian or a French woman be honoured? After all, Canada's granaries held millions of tons of wheat which France needed, and this author came from the plains of the West. Perhaps, if the Canadian government heard that she . . . .

The tension began to tell on Gabrielle: "I considered fleeing back to Canada and hiding in a remote cabin." When she was near collapse, the decision arrived. The telephone rang and Gabrielle thought with relief that the whole affair had died "a beautiful death." Not at all. She was informed that she had captured the *Fémina*. She was asked to go to receive her prize and to be photographed by the newspapers. All the ladies embraced her, even those who had voted against her. " 'Vive la France! Vive le Canada!' everyone cried, as if we had reconquered the Plains of Abraham."

Marcel and Gabrielle decided to celebrate her award with a festive dinner together. "Alas, my *Fémina* had ruined my stomach. I feasted on a quart of Vichy water and a biscuit . . . . Little by little I recovered from my *Fémina,* as from a long and perilous illness . . . ."[49]

While the nuances of the final decision may have been complex, the *Prix Fémina* is a high award and one given for merit. Because of it, the Ambassador, General Georges Vanier, and Mme Vanier held a reception for Gabrielle at the Canadian Embassy in Paris. Both Gabrielle and her husband began to feel a little overwhelmed by the amount of attention she was receiving. When *Bonheur d'occasion* had first been published, Gabrielle had naturally warmed to the praise. Now she was beginning to sense that it was dangerous — "like an opium." Warnings from her father, about the world and its opinions, came back to her. After this reception, Gabrielle became much more reticent about making further public appearances and playing the role of celebrity.

During the few hours spent at the Embassy, Gabrielle met an influential new friend who was to have long-range effects upon both her life and her writing. A strange man wearing a priest's collar approached her and congratulated her on the award. He was the Jesuit priest and palaeontologist Pierre Teilhard de Chardin whose writings became widely known after his death for the faith they held that science and religion could be reconciled. His religious order did not allow him to publish his books during his lifetime and he did not attempt to do so; consequently, his ideas were not widely known at the time Gabrielle met him.

He had a strongly compelling appearance, mostly because of his eyes, which while immensely alert and intelligent were also hauntingly sad. As soon as Gabrielle saw his priest's collar, she expressed to him her doubts about her religion. When she had first gone to Europe, in 1937, she had stopped practising it: "One of the principal reasons which had led me to abandon my religion when I left for Europe was a sort of discrimination of which the priests were too often culpable. This attitude incited me to revolt. A sort of latent revolt which had been burning in me for a long time. . . . I had heard whole sermons preached against the Protestants . . . to the point of intervening in the question of race, of peoples. I had heard some priests identify the English as people who could not achieve salvation."[50]

Teilhard's response to her objections was "Good for you." He had strong ecumenical beliefs and could not accept an exclusive salvation any more than she could. He also believed that all man's works on earth are part of God's plan, including the work of the artist, which was reassuring to her. Describing Teilhard later, Gabrielle said, "From his viewpoint there was no question of being passive. Every person collaborates and helps the creation of the world. The world is on the march. To participate in creation is to participate in the work of God. There is no work which is totally lost. It is the same for all of us as it is for those who choose the religious life. The simple work of man is sister to the work of God. The work of the artist, for example."[51]

Gabrielle asked him how the war atrocities of the Nazis could be the work of God; Teilhard had no answer to this. He was as troubled as she. However, because of their friendship which continued for many years, Gabrielle did return to her religion, and the essentially hopeful message of his teaching is evident even in her most tragic novels. The humble people about whom she most often writes are each illuminated by a radiance which says that each one is important. Her portrayal of Rose-Anna Lacasse had already contained this feeling, but it was not so directly realized as in her later books. The significance of Teilhard's influence upon Gabrielle Roy was that he clarified feelings which she already had.

The destruction caused by war troubled Gabrielle greatly. Living in Europe, the damage and the suffering were very apparent. On the streets of Paris, the shabby French women cast backward envious glances at Gabrielle's Canadian fur coat; she stopped wearing it. Perhaps the thought that troubled her most was that the superb old civilization of Europe, one which she admired, had somehow produced the supremely uncivilized war. In a kind of horror at what the old had produced, her imagination fled to a place which was new and untouched — the Water Hen country in the far reaches of Manitoba where she had once taught. Her next book was the direct result of her search for freshness and innocence. She said that the book began one day when she and Marcel with two friends visited the Cathedral at Chartres. In the car her friends chatted about Gothic architecture and the beautiful things which had survived from old cultures, while Gabrielle, half-listening, was, with the other half of her mind, far away: ". . . my imagination was pleased to return to the land of the Little Water Hen, intact, set apart among the dreams of the creator. There, I told myself, chances of human hope are nearly whole; there, people are perhaps still able, if they wish, to begin anew. But alas, I also thought with a certain sadness, it is only very far away, at the end of the world, in a very little known human community, that hope is still truly free."[52]

A little later, Gabrielle went alone to England, where she stayed with friends in a village in Epping Forest. The peace there reinforced her imaginative conception of a good life close to nature. She had been writing stories while she was in France — stories set in that country — but for some reason they did not please her. She is not sure why, and she has never submitted them for publication. Now the new novel, set in Manitoba, engrossed her completely. It was about a large family, the Tousignants, with a mother, Luzina, whose pure, motherly soul is the personification of the goodness Gabrielle wanted to convey.

The novel, *La Petite Poule d'Eau,* was published in 1950, the same year Gabrielle and her husband returned to Canada. They lived for a year at Ville LaSalle and then finally settled in Quebec City. The novel was translated into English the following year, as *Where Nests the Water Hen.* Gabrielle had now gained enough confidence to insist that a Canadian do the translation. *The Tin Flute* had been translated by an experienced American, Hannah Josephson, who in spite of her ability was unfamiliar with Montreal street language;

thus there were errors which Gabrielle had not been able to catch in the twenty-four hours allowed her for checking. Harry L. Binsse, who now became Gabrielle's translator, had a fine ear for the rhythms of language, and he and Gabrielle got along well. She was somewhat amused by his mild eccentricities and his casual manner of dress, with buttons hanging loosely from jackets disinterestedly arranged about his rotund frame. He finished the final chapter of *Where Nests the Water Hen* in her living-room while she kept him supplied with coffee and cigarettes.

Gabrielle Roy described *Where Nests the Water Hen* as ". . . life such as it might have been, or could have been, or could be. It's the beginning of all time, almost, . . ."[53] It has a dream-like quality, partly achieved by a past and present melting of time, so that sometimes we progress forward in time as we read, and then we find ourselves back a little farther. On the surface it is simple — funny, endearing, full of innocent charm. But it is not a simple book, and while it expresses our deepest longing for peace, it is pierced from time to time by reminders of the real world.

The large Tousignant family live on an island, and would seem to be isolated from the world, but not so. Manitoba had been settled by myriad nationalities, as Gabrielle was well aware from her father's work, and they are all in this book. It is as though Gabrielle had scooped up all the troubled ones she had seen in Europe and set them down in paradise, saying, "There, start again in peace." More than that, the action of the book does not remain on the island. It is set as three parts, or *volets,* in a triptych, and describes three kinds of journeying out into the world.

The first *volet,* "Luzina Takes a Holiday," is about the mother's annual trip into the outside world, just to a few neighbouring villages. However, in Luzina's mind it is a high adventure; and indeed, travelling over treacherous spring roads and catching rides with whoever is willing to carry her, does lead to anxious moments. Among the varied people she meets are a dour Ukrainian postman, who is her first chauffeur, and a Jewish merchant who is none too happy to have her as a passenger. Although these people are not particularly pleasant, they fall under Luzina's motherly spell: "Such was Luzina's power. She disposed people to become aware that they had reasons for being happy."[54] It becomes clear that only a perpetually loving spirit, such as Luzina's, can bind the peoples of the earth together. One stormy night, Luzina and one of her drivers are taken in by a poor Icelandic family. These people do not understand Luzina's language, nor does she understand theirs; nevertheless, this does not deter her from her happy chatting and laughing, nor from distributing presents among their children and generally having a good time. The idealistic spirit prevalent in the United Nations at the time when this book was written, a time when we hoped and tried to believe that all nations, in spite of language and cultural barriers, would come to love and respect each other, is expressed in this sequence. When Luzina returns to her family on the Little Water Hen, she brings the present which has been the purpose of her "holiday": another new baby — the most hopeful note of all, for life goes on.

The second *volet* of the triptych, "The School on the Little Water Hen," is an intellectual journey. While Luzina is happy with her family on their island, she does not wish her children to be ignorant; after some amusing correspondence with the mighty government in Winnipeg, she arranges that teachers shall be sent to educate her children. The first is a young French-speaking girl, Mademoiselle Côté, who reinforces the family's French heritage with glorious tales of the French heroes who explored the new land and fought their battles like gentlemen. However, since teachers are appointed to the island only during the summer, in October the beloved mademoiselle leaves. All winter the family waits agog to find out what sort of teacher the Government will send next. Mademoiselle Côté's successor turns out to be a grim, Protestant, Anglo-Saxon old maid, who knows not one word of French and makes no effort to learn it. Gabrielle Roy is a little sensitive about this character, Miss O'Rorke, who expresses a French-Canadian's scornful conception of his English-speaking compatriot. Miss O'Rorke's approach differs greatly from Mademoiselle Côté's — she tries to instill reverence for His Majesty the king and insists that a British flag and flagpole be made so that the flag can be raised and lowered each day. Worst of all, she speaks scathingly of the French heroes whom Mademoiselle Côté had taught the children to love. Miss O'Rorke is not liked, and the children try to run away from school, but Luzina believes that all learning is full of riches and she is pleased that English is taught by this strange woman. The story is told with good humour, but underlying it is an awareness of the disunity which troubles Canada today. Emphasizing the potential dangers embodied by the first two teachers is the third, who turns out to be a man, and one who is armed to the teeth. Armand Dubreuil is a hunter. Up at dawn to shoot the game which abounds on the Little Water Hen, he begins school late, and ends early. The flag is often at half-mast for holidays which he invents so that he can spend days shooting. He is the god of war whose bloody tracks Gabrielle had seen strewn across Europe. However, the spirit of Luzina and the Little Water Hen is incorruptible, and Armand, perhaps sensing that he has no place here, leaves before his term is up. Although he himself cannot remain in the Little Water Hen, he seems to have glimpsed its perfection: when he leaves he advises Luzina to forget the school and to concentrate on being happy, suggesting that eating the fruit of knowledge will lead to the evil ways of the world. But for Luzina, and for Gabrielle Roy, paradise is not built on ignorance, nor in isolation from mankind; learning is one of our responsibilities. Although, after Armand, the Government ceases to send teachers, the desire to learn has been caught, and one by one the children leave the Little Water Hen, one to become a nurse, one a teacher, another to study literature, and so on. Luzina is finally left with her last "surprise package," little Claire-Armelle, whom she hopes to keep with her always.

Luzina is distressed to have her children leave and blames Mademoiselle Côté for first kindling the dangerous spark of learning; but when Josephine, the teacher, writes back to her mother, it is Luzina whom she thanks for having sent her off into the world: "Dear Mama, when I went into my classroom this morning and I saw the children's faces turn towards me, I certainly thought of you. This happiness I in large part owe, dear Mama, to your spirit of sacrifice, to your devotion. . . ."[55] Genuine culture springs from the love of Luzina; it is mutilated by war.

In the third *volet,* the emphasis shifts from Luzina and her family to a Capuchin priest, Father Joseph-Marie. If Luzina is the loving, motherly spirit of mankind, this priest is the father. Although his name contains both those of the father and the mother of Christ, he is a re-creation of St. Joseph, his favourite saint.

"Everything about the life of Jesus' foster father was made to order to please him; his most chaste function as guardian and protector; . . ."[56] Father Joseph-Marie travels far and wide; he is a multilingual European and therefore he encompasses all cultures. Although he embodies internationalism, it is his ecumenicalism, which had been expressed to Gabrielle Roy by Pierre Teilhard de Chardin, which provides his chief message. Father Joseph-Marie is, of course, Catholic, but his spirit is such that a Jew somehow finds himself donating towards a statue of Saint Joseph; one Presbyterian lady gives her harmonium to his church, and another, the best musician in the neighbourhood, is persuaded to play it; and the president of the Canadian Pacific Railway, a Scot, gives him a train bell for his belfry.

The book ends in the peaceful spirit of all men joined in goodwill. At a dance set in a small grove of poplars, Father Joseph-Marie sits on a bench, smoking his pipe and watching Luzina and her husband, Mademoiselle Côté, and several others dance to the Red River Reel: "Above his head shone billions of bright stars; in the grass fireflies emitted their brief sparks of light."[57] Glory exists not only in the heavens, but also on earth and in our momentary lives, if only we have the grace to achieve love and peace.

Gabrielle Roy, in this book, had been wrestling with her own conflict over the respective values of the old world and the new. The last two sentences give each its due, as she reflects the thoughts of Father Joseph-Marie:

> To him also the old civilization seemed faraway, loveable, gracious.
> The farther he had gone into the North, the more he had been free to love.[58]

Every reader has his own mental picture of characters, as Gabrielle Roy discovered in 1972 when an exquisitely produced folio edition of *La Petite Poule d'Eau* was published in Paris, with illustrations by her friend, the French-Canadian painter, Jean-Paul Lemieux. Lifting her own copy, in its large heavy box, down from a shelf to show some friends, she remarks on the painter's vision, which was slightly different from her own. There is the apple-cheeked Luzina, her happy face shining under a kerchief — "Perhaps more like a peasant than I had imagined." The purse-lipped Miss O'Rorke fits everybody's notion of an angular old maid; but the portrait of Father

Joseph-Marie was a surprise to his author-creator. Jean-Paul Lemieux
has shown him as a thin man, striding purposefully forward. Somehow, although Gabrielle had not described his figure, she had thought
of him as a stoutish priest; but Jean-Paul Lemieux pointed out that
the priest is always taking long strides and, besides, he eats very little,
so of course he would be thin. She conceded his point and, in any
case, had respect for his individual artistic view. The magnificent edition gives her great pleasure. It has become a collector's item.

THE TIN FLUTE had had a dazzling commercial success; it was a
hard-hitting social documentary, highly relevant to its time. The
books which followed, including *Where Nests the Water Hen,* although they never achieved the phenomenal market-success of the
first novel, showed increasing artistic power and confidence, appreciated by a continuing, faithful audience. While there was some bewilderment when the idyllic *Where Nests the Water Hen* was published by a writer who was supposed to be a harsh social critic, it
brought Gabrielle a new wave of attention. By now, though, she was
determined to defend her energies and her privacy. "If I speak to
students about my work, how can I write it?" she once asked in
consternation. One gentleman who met her at a party said, "I felt
that out of good fellowship she would like to know how to talk the
rubbish of the world, but she has a great natural horror of banalities.
. . . She seems to nourish a great dread of crowds."[59]
    A legend began to grow that Gabrielle Roy is a shy recluse. This
is not so. With her friends and relatives, of whom there are many,
she is vividly extroverted, warm, and affectionate. She has her
mother's dramatic gift for storytelling, and while relating one of her
anecdotes, she strides up and down, gesticulating vigorously. Her
lovely face with its blue-green sorceress eyes is extremely mobile in
a highly French way. She can reduce small audiences to helpless
laughter when she describes blind officialdom, a continuing target
for her ironic humour. While she has the artist's flexibility of attitude,
she is no bohemian. Her convent education and her mother's sense
of elegance are apparent in her fastidious good manners, her grace-
ful appearance, and in the charming, comfortable apartment where
she and her husband live in Quebec City.

Underlying the warmth and gaiety that she can bring to her friendships there is, however, a kind of sadness, an anxious maternity. She is without children, and instead pours her natural motherliness over everyone she meets. "Poor child!" is a constant exclamation, even though the child be particularly robust, or the person not a child at all. Laying a gentle hand on a rosy child's head, she seems to be foreseeing that life will be much harder for him than he suspects. She believes that all humanity is pitiable and has said, "Every life is a tragedy."[60] Her pity extends even to herself. Rifling through some early pictures of herself as a young girl, she said, "I don't feel as though I have any connection with that girl; I only feel a great pity for her, thinking of all she will have to go through."[61]

GABRIELLE ROY IS a writer of striking contrasts. In individual stories she uses opposites to dramatic effect; for instance, in her short story "The Two Negroes," a negro boarder always gives white presents to the members of the white family in the house — white gloves, white stockings, white scarves, and so forth. On a larger scale, she is capable of concentrating fully on one aspect of society in one novel, and then in the next of making an abrupt change to thoroughly investigate its opposite. *The Tin Flute* and *Where Nests the Water Hen* are about as different as two books by the same writer could be.

In her third novel she made an equally astounding reversal from the gentle idealism of *Where Nests the Water Hen* to the desolate realism of mechanized citydom. Her story of Alexandre Chenevert, a bank cashier running on a treadmill which offers no rewards or satisfactions, is almost unbearably painful. Published in French in 1954 as *Alexandre Chenevert*, it was translated into English by Harry Binsse in 1955 as *The Cashier*.

Every aspect of Alexandre's life is drained of joy: his drudgery at the bank offers no advancement; his wife is stupid; his daughter has married a shiftless man who has left her and her child; he lives in a dreary apartment where there is nothing but the daily bombardment of disaster from his radio. Alexandre's appearance is as pinched as his life — he is a thin, stooped, balding man in his fifties.

Gabrielle Roy makes it clear that he is only one of many. "Every morning at a set hour he walked down a thousand staircases at once, running from every corner of the city toward bulging streetcars. He crowded into them by the hundreds and thousands. From tram to tram, from street to street, you could see him standing in public conveyances, his hands slipped through leather straps, his arms stretched in a curious likeness to a prisoner at the whipping post."[62]

The people like Alexandre are not robots, however, no matter how they are treated. Alexandre is convinced that his life must have greater meaning than seems obvious, that he was born for some purpose. The book is about his search for purpose in an apparently purposeless life.

In his pain, Alexandre makes two wishes, which, if granted, will relieve him, or so he thinks. One night, as he is going home through the medical district of Montreal, he sees that all the care in the world is poured out for the sick, not the unhappy. He wishes to be sick, to be coddled, protected, and looked after like a child. A little later he makes his second wish, to be happy. Both wishes are granted.

He finds one day of happiness when he goes away for a holiday to an idyllic spot called Lac Vert. In this Eden he meets an Adam and Eve, and their children. The Le Gardeurs are the Tousignant family re-created for Alexandre's benefit, and through them and his one happy day, he finds that joy is possible on earth. However, having discovered this, he comes to another conclusion which sends him back to his apartment in Montreal before his holiday is over. Happiness, he concludes, as it is revealed to him through the Le Gardeurs, comes from self-sufficiency; but this independence from others is limiting and somewhat irresponsible; neither is happiness our true quest. This realization on the part of Alexandre is an admission from Gabrielle Roy that the secluded world of the Little Water Hen is an evasion of responsibility, an awareness which motivated Luzina's children to set forth into the world.

Alexandre goes back to Montreal to find that his second wish — to be ill — has been granted with a vengeance. He has terminal cancer. During his last days in his hospital bed he finds, too late, the purpose for his life: to touch and to know other human beings. It is true that he was greatly concerned by the miseries of the world which he heard about through his radio — as Gabrielle Roy says, "Alexandre is a sounding board for all the communications which bombard us."[63] Still, it is ironic that while Alexandre suffered for the victims of earthquakes and for the persecuted Jews, he had limited sympathy for those close to him. He and his wife shared little; he loathed his neighbours because the blare of *their* radio pierces his thin apartment walls; and he was grouchy with his clients and fellow workers at the bank.

Now, lying in his hospital bed, Alexandre finds that he misses the bank. He wants to be engaged in life, not removed from it: "More even than to be happy, more than greatness, he wanted to be back in his cage."[64]

He struggles to come close to God, but, as he confesses to a priest, he believes in God but he does not think that God loves him. When the priest leaves, Alexandre is disturbed by the man who shares his room and who has just come back from an operation and is suffering pain. Alexandre rises from his own bed and goes to comfort him. "And suddenly he knew that he was less alone before God."[65] In reaching out to another he has come closer to the deity.

Now, pitifully, Alexandre finds that his co-workers at the bank seem to be fond of him. They send fruit. An elderly lady client travels by a complicated street car route to see him. He and his wife, Eugénie, recognize their attachment to one another: "And then they looked at each other, almost unhappy to discover, at this moment, so late, that they loved each other."[66]

At the end of the book, Alexandre dies. He has been a sacrifice to society; his illness had been caused by the worry about social problems and the quality of life around him. It is ironic that technological society made him ill and then poured all its resources into trying to prolong his life. There is some sort of recognition from his friends that he died for their sake; his name, after death, is still pronounced at times with affection.

Alexandre Chenevert haunts us. He also haunts his creator. She says, "It seems to me that Alexandre Chenevert is one of the most complex characters that I have created. I am far from knowing all about him. It seems to me that I know more about Florentine, for example. Everything has not yet been said between Alexandre and I."[67]

DRIVING TO QUEBEC City, the visitor finds himself on the outskirts of what might be any booming North American city. Everywhere there are ugly scars on the earth where meadows or old buildings have been ripped up to be replaced by superhighways, bridges, and multi-storey buildings. Traffic is confusing and noisy. Truck drivers shake their fists and shout threateningly in French. With perseverance and great courage, however, a driver can fight his way through the endless suburbs until he comes to the old, walled city of Quebec. Blessedly, it is another world, with narrow streets winding among the stone façades of buildings erected three hundred years ago. It is here that Gabrielle Roy and her husband, Marcel Carbotte, live in a formal, brick, apartment building on the Grande Allée. Quebec City is not only the capital of Quebec, it is also the heart. Within walking distance of Gabrielle's apartment there are reminders of both the pride and the humiliation of the French — the Citadel, the Plains of Abraham, the elegant Legislature. She and her husband are Québecois by choice.

Gabrielle, however, is from another French community, the one in St. Boniface. In her next book, *Street of Riches,* she became one of the few spokesmen that community has had. The book is a collection of memories from her girlhood, partly fictional, but resting on known places and personalities. She named her heroine Christine.

It starts with a story called "The Two Negroes," describing a time when Christine's mother and the mother of her friend each take in a negro boarder. The story is not about negroes at all, but about the dependence of the two women on each other's opinions. They form the total of society for one another; here Gabrielle lets us know that her setting is a small, enclosed place, St. Boniface in the early years of the century. Indeed, the French felt themselves to be living on a small island, and perhaps still do, even in Quebec.

One of the most famous stories in this book, which reveals the loneliness of Christine's father, is "Petite Misère," the nickname given Gabrielle Roy. Christine's father, in a momentary burst of anger and thoughtlessness, speaks harshly to her: "Oh, why did I ever have any children!"[68] For Christine, this is not a passing mood, but sure proof that she is not wanted and that no one loves her. She flees to her attic hideaway, and stays there all day, refusing calls to meals or shouts from the neighbourhood children who want her to join in their play.

While Christine suffers from her father's hard words, he is filled with regret for his unintentional cruelty. When the long day is nearly over he tries to make it up to her. Struggling clumsily with ingredients and pots and pans, he bakes her a rhubarb pie. He goes to the attic stair and calls her to come down and eat it. In a moment of sudden understanding, Christine sees that her father's sadness is even greater than her own: "How could I have uttered an answer! What was the sorrow that all evening had kept me from my usual games compared to the sorrow which now held me in its grip! Was it then the same with sorrow as with the mysterious paths in my book of *The Thousand and One Nights,* where each led on to a broader avenue and disclosed ever-widening vistas?

"I heard my father sigh. So slowly did he close the door that I barely was aware of the click of the latch. He went away.

"Those slow, disheartened footsteps!"[69]

Christine smooths out her wrinkled clothes, rubs away her tear smudges, and then goes downstairs to her father. In the kitchen she finds a white cloth spread, and in its centre, the pie, and "far removed from each other, our two plates." Her father cuts two large pieces, and they each try to eat; but the pastry is leaden and their feelings more so. That night Christine has a severe attack of indigestion, and her mother scolds her father: " 'To have her eat pie at ten o'clock at night! Have you lost your mind?'

"With a sad smile and without pleading any excuse, he bowed his head; and later, when he came to bring me a dose of medicine, his face was suffused with such grief that, often, I think it immortal."[70]

Christine is never able to eat rhubarb pie again. We know that it is not the pie which is hard to take, but the revelation of her father's pain, forever associated with that particular food. She began by being immersed in her own grief; she ends by suffering for the sake of her father. It is a step in growing up.

"My Pink Hat" is about a lonely child's need for attention. Christine has jaundice, and to comfort her, her mother buys her a candy-pink hat. The hat is not entirely appropriate; Christine is still bright yellow from her illness and the dress she is to wear it with has a red collar.

The outfit is to be worn when Christine goes to the country to stay with her aunt and cousins, to hasten her recovery. Leaving home where she is coddled and spoiled because she is sick, she is put in the hands of a Grey Nun on the train, who looks after her until she reaches her destination. The nun likewise pampers her with candies and ice cream. Reaching her aunt's house, however, she finds things a bit different. The bed on which she is to sleep has not come from the neighbour who is to lend it, and she must sleep on a mattress on the floor. Missing her mother, she will not part with the pink hat and places it on the floor beside her. Her aunt removes it, and the child moans to herself. The exasperated aunt hands it back to her with the remark, "Silly girl."

Christine wears her hat from morning till night — at breakfast, at play, everywhere. Throughout the story we can see the little hat moving from place to place. She is not happy in this house. No one pays her any attention. Her cousins are dreary children who read the lives of the saints and are forever darning clothes or doing other useful tasks. The lonely child swings in the garden, and from high in the air she notices a pretty house with two old people warming themselves on the porch "like two cats." Christine senses that there is comfort in this house. When the old man goes out to shop she trails after him until he asks, "Wherever are you going?"

"With you,"[71] she says, and she runs up to him and puts her hand in his.

Christine spends the afternoon on the porch with the man and his wife: "We were very well pleased with each other, all three of us together on the porch, looking at each other and laughing soundlessly, just with our eyes and the corners of our lips." Between the very old and the very young, there is mutual understanding of neglect.

Her aunt, however, has been searching for her all over the neighbourhood. "Have you see a little pink hat going by?" she asks everyone. It is nearly dark when she finds the child. She is carrying a small stick "and she looked like someone who wanted to use it." Behind the bushes she spies the pink hat: "Her face immediately relaxed. Her eyes were no longer in the least angry. Her pace grew auspiciously slower. The stick fell from her hands. . . . And as for me, I ran out to meet my aunt and thrust my hand in hers."[72] Her place in her aunt's house has been won; she has made her point that she is to be noticed. The pink hat, which she wears so stubbornly, is a sign of her mother's love which she clings to in her loneliness. It is also a symbol of importance that insists that she is somebody, even though a stranger and far from home.

The pivotal story is "The Voice of the Pools." The "voice" which

Christine hears from the pools is the singing of frogs on a summer evening. Their "strange music" cries out two messages to her, each tugging in opposite directions, symbolizing the two forces which will struggle within her for the rest of her life. One is the voice of her childhood, pulling her back to the warmth of family life; the other is a call to the future — to be someone of worth.

One night, as she listens to these voices, she conceives the idea of becoming a writer. She speaks of her ambition to her mother: " 'Writing,' she told me sadly, 'is hard. It must be the most exacting business in the world. . . . Is it not like cutting yourself in two, as it were — one half trying to live, the other watching, weighing?' "[73] Mélina Roy did not actually say this to Gabrielle Roy; she was more concerned with the physical hardships of poverty. These words are more truly the writer's analysis of her own condition.

The final story gives Christine a little respite before she thrusts herself into the real challenge of becoming a writer. "To Earn My Living . . ." is about her job as a young teacher in the little town of Cardinal. In this story, Christine is still close to other people. She describes how happy she is in the school room, snug and warm with the children, while a winter storm rages outside.

> And I did not fully realize it yet — often our joys are
> slow in coming home to us — but I was living through
> one of the rarest happinesses of my life. Was not all the
> world a child? Were we not at the day's morning? . . .[74]

From hints in "The Voice of the Pools" we know that this kind of happiness cannot last. Throughout the entire book there is a note of lingering regret for joys past, things lost forever.

The French edition of this collection, *Rue Deschambault,* was published in 1955. Translated by Harry Binsse, the English version, *Street of Riches,* appeared in 1957.

In 1958, *Street of Riches* won Gabrielle Roy her second Governor-General's Award for fiction. Out of fourteen works submitted, hers was judged to be the best. One of the judges called it "a product of the creative imagination and one of a very high order, in the field of fiction."[75]

A RESTLESS MAN, tall and lean, his eyes pulled into a perpetual squint after years of facing northern snow and sun, strode up and down Gabrielle's living room. His slender hands moved constantly as he described a canoe trip up the Churchill River.

René Richard was an old friend, met years ago at Baie St. Paul when Gabrielle was a reporter. Whenever he visited Quebec City he dropped in to see her, and there was nearly always a story or two about the days when he was a trapper, travelling by dog-sled over the tundra of Ungava or wandering through the Northwest Territories. His life was largely a solitary one, for he was not only a trapper but also an artist, a painter — an occupation which, as Gabrielle knew, was a lonely one. When he had finished his story, he pulled out a folio of his latest drawings and spread them out for her to see. There were hundreds of black-and-white sketches and some in simple crayon.

Gabrielle always loved a good storyteller, and Richard's descriptions of the North, his way of telling of the remote Indian and Eskimo villages, were particularly vivid. There came a point for her when the image of Richard, alone on the vast snowy tundra, painting in a remote shack, became more than a good story. It crystallized an idea which had been lurking in her mind for years.

She has always dreaded the loneliness of her own work. Even now, she says that the onset of a new book fills her with despair. It means cutting herself off from friends and even her conversations with her husband become absent-minded. Although her husband is a staunch supporter, and when a book is completed she considers seriously any criticisms he may make, while she is working she is her own only resource, a condition which she feels acutely. Gabrielle had poignantly expressed the isolation of the artist in one story in *Street of Riches,* but now she was ready to give it full attention. The result was her next novel, *The Hidden Mountain.* The book is dedicated to René Richard, or "R.R.," as he is identified. "My good fortune," she said, "was to have access, through this painter-trapper-traveller, to a tremendous store of distilled descriptions, images and short-cuts of great impact. From then on I gave myself complete freedom to use the material as I saw fit."[76]

Pierre Cadorai, the artist-hero of this novel, is an orphan. It is significant that in every one of Gabrielle Roy's novels there is an orphan juxtaposed with a large family. In *The Tin Flute* the orphan is Florentine's cold lover, Jean Lévesque, who accentuates his situation by setting himself apart from others. Father Joseph-Marie is the orphan in *Where Nests the Water Hen;* he is drawn toward the warmth of Luzina's family, but cannot participate in that sort of affection himself because of the nature of his calling. Poor Alexandre Chenevert is also a loner; his condition is clarified when he meets the bountiful Le Gardeur family. The orphan and the member of a large family are two opposing aspects of Gabrielle Roy's conception of her own persona.

Pierre of *The Hidden Mountain* is strongly tempted by the life of the "ordinary man," the family man; he too meets a large family who demonstrates all that he will sacrifice when he sets forth on his life as an artist. He has a friend, Steve Sigurdsen, who is another trapper; they live together in a shack and follow trap lines. One summer, Steve takes him to visit his family, a whole flock of cousins, aunts, and grandparents, all living together in a settlement on the edge of Great Slave Lake. Pierre spends a contented summer with these people. He has also met a girl, Nina, who, if he had chosen such a life, could have become his wife. Pierre, however, is in search of a subject worthy of his most splendid dreams. He knows that he must leave the family on Great Slave Lake, and even his single companion Steve: ". . . to fulfill himself, he must set out alone."[77]

After a long and discouraging search, Pierre finds the subject which will obsess him for the rest of his life. As he is travelling across Ungava in the glory of midsummer, a magnificent mountain appears before him. It is crowned like a king with snow and ice "that sparkled like a jewel."[78] The mountain seems to be demanding that Pierre recreate it on paper for others to see, for the job of the artist is just that. "Beyond all ordinary things I am beautiful; that is true, it was saying. As mountains go, I am perhaps the finest achievement of creation. Perhaps there is no other like me. However, since until now no man has seen me, did I in truth exist? As long as you have not been held captive in another's eyes, do you live? Are we alive if no one has ever loved us?"[79]

Pierre spends the remainder of the summer and dangerously far into the winter painting his mountain. So engrossed is he that he does not notice that he has run out of food, that the fish have fled to warmer waters, and that there is no nearby shelter. He is not even aware that he has almost run out of ammunition. Suddenly, hungry and cold, he sees the shadow of an old bull cariboo; he must kill it in order to eat. Firing a few shots, he wounds the animal, but then finds that he has run out of ammunition. Seizing his hatchet, he plunges forward and, with immense pity for the animal, kills it. "Pierced with cold, Pierre let himself slip down next to the dead cariboo, which gradually began to give him its warmth."[80] Pierre merges with the beast and becomes both the hunter and the hunted, Gabrielle Roy's image of the artist. She said, "The artist is a pursued hunter, a hunter who tries to drag up the greatest possible number of things which pass during his lifetime. He is pursued most of all by God, the creator, for whom he will immortalize creation and the time in which he lives."[81] Perceived this way, the artist also seems like a soul damned, pursued relentlessly until death by the demands of his gift.

In the last short section of the book, Pierre goes to Paris to learn technique and to observe the great works of art there. However, his teacher insists that he paint Paris, not his mountain. Pierre tries, but fails; all his paintings of the Seine have "the wild appearance of the rivers of the North."[82] He has learned that, finally, the artist's greatest contribution is his own individuality, his unique view. Even his paintings of the mountain portray not the real mountain, but one reborn in his imagination.

With a premonition that he has not much time left, Pierre secludes himself in a tiny room, lighting a wood fire like those in faraway Canadian shacks, and devotes his last days to the supreme effort of capturing the spirit of the mountain. He breaks away from it long enough to paint a self-portrait: it is a haunted, strange picture; above his head grows the hint of antlers. He is still the beast pursued. On his last day, through a fog of pain, his true vision of the mountain comes to him. He works feverishly, the painting forms, but too late. He crumples and dies. His story ends with two sentences:

> The lofty mountain faded away.
> Who, in the mists, would ever find it again?[83]

Pierre has failed inevitably. Speaking of him and of writers, Gabrielle Roy said, "I think a writer dreams, as Pierre of *The Hidden Mountain* hoped, of putting all the subjects, briefly, in one undertaking. Of course he never arrives there, and that is why there are always writers and always artists. They're all chasing the one thing. Mauriac had a very beautiful expression: he said that he was always striving to write the one book that would dispense him from writing others. Fundamentally what we hope is to get it all down in one book, or in one picture, or in one song, but of course always something is left out. That's why we start again."[84] Pierre's apparent failure, however, raises the question of what failure really is. Is it to aim high and miss the mark, or to aim low and succeed? Pierre's dream, although he failed to achieve it, invested him with nobility.

The Hidden Mountain has an austere, breathtaking quality, like the tundra of Ungava. Pierre is a man stripped of every desire except one, to catch an eternal truth in painting. Some critics have complained that the book fails because it does not develop Pierre as a character and because it does not show him in relation to other people. Gabrielle Roy has in the past given us character development, but it was not her intention to do so in *The Hidden Mountain*. This book is about a man's inner life and his relation to God more than to man. Nor is it intended to be a book solely about the artist: "It is about every man who aspires."[85] It is also a profoundly religious book. Speaking of Pierre, Gabrielle Roy said, "He is in the hands of the Creator. The Creator is always above him."[86]

It is not a cold book, but one with a deeply emotional inner core. In Gabrielle Roy's work, it is the un-named which conveys feeling. Her description of Pierre's painting of the mountain gives the precise effect of her own writing: "What invested the whole with meaning . . . remained as though invisible — or at least barely perceptible. Beyond the green rock there opened what might be called a perspective, a minute slit showing distant depth, even though the painting was not twice the size of a man's hand. You looked at this narrow opening — a crevice no thicker than a thread — on a distance invisible, luminous; and you held your breath, you were captured by quiet expectation; you could say to yourself, yes, this world is lovely and compassionate; this world is lustrous."[87]

She does not believe that the inner mystery can be defined. "It is in those things which escape the critic that a work lives in the most interesting way. . . . But also, and above all perhaps, in those things which escape the author himself, elements beyond knowing, beyond thought, deriving from the sure source of his dream."[88] When people try to analyze her work she says that she feels "pinned like a butter-fly."[89]

The Hidden Mountain was published in 1961 in Montreal as *La Montagne secrète* and was translated into English in 1962 by Harry Binsse.

BACK IN 1963 EXPO '67 was a gleam in the eye, and skeptics were staring dubiously at the St. Lawrence River, wondering whether the man-made island and the imagined buildings and displays would really materialize. Undaunted, eighteen experts gathered at the Seignory Club at Montebello to hammer out the theme "Man and His World."

There were architects, neurologists, lawyers, writers, painters, and scientists. Gabrielle Roy was one of the most active participants at the Montebello Conference. In the conference room, with the windows open to the fresh spring air, she argued that Expo should concentrate on man himself, rather than on technological advances. The splendour of man and his earth — a powerfully felt theme in her work — should be celebrated. By man, she meant all of us, for as she said later in the introduction to a book of photographs about Expo: "And who is to say which one is the most important in the final count of all the musicians who make up the orchestra? And how many in turn 'create' without knowing it? The child who invents his own game is creative; the mother who makes up a story for her sick child or a tasty dish for her harrassed husband is creative. The nameless man coming home in the evening from office or factory amidst the teeming crowds is creative when he can still learn to believe in himself once more and in the Earth, . . ."[90] Her convictions carried as the basis of the theme, even though technology was well represented. As Expo rose triumphantly out of a sea of mud and chaos everyone caught the excitement lying behind the central idea, but not many knew that the French-Canadian writer Gabrielle Roy had been one of its key creators.

GABRIELLE'S ELDEST SISTER, Anna, had become the centre of the family after Mélina Roy's death. She was still living in Manitoba and thus was a link with the old home. It was she who wrote to everyone about family news, and she whose house in St. Vital was the place where visiting members stayed. Several of the Roy children had died, including Germain, the next youngest to Gabrielle, who had been killed as the result of a car accident. Each time there was a death a tie was cut, and each time Gabrielle's thoughts returned to the early days. In 1964, while she was engaged in the planning of Expo, Anna died. It was a loss which brought back more memories to Gabrielle, not so much of Anna as of her mother.

Her next book has a sombre tone. *The Road Past Altamont* returns to her girlhood in St. Boniface in four, long, interwoven stories, quite different in mood from *Street of Riches*. Discussing this book, she said, ". . . *The Road Past Altamont* is the meeting of people after the present. It's a sort of narrowed circle, where you understand your mother when you reach the age when she said such a thing and you were not able to understand. You've reached that stage now, but she's gone now, and forever it's like that. You reach one another, but late in time, when you've reached the experience that this person had when she spoke such a word. Before, you were too young to understand it, but there comes a time in your life when you realize, Oh, that's what my mother meant! Yes, that's what she suffered — oh yes, that's what she went through. But it's twenty years or thirty years too late, and you can't go back and tell her, I do understand now what you said, dear mother; excuse me, I couldn't understand then, I did not have the age or the experience. But she went through the same thing with regard to her own mother. Every generation is blind and deaf until in time we meet those who are dead, and we say, Oh *now* I know. That's what *The Road Past Altamont* is about. It's a tragedy, but it's also a very beautiful thing, because *eventually* you get there."[91]

The anxiety which Gabrielle had felt about leaving her mother when she was twenty-seven is met here, and assessed as part of the never-ending human desire to strive for achievement. There is reference to the antiquity of the earth and within that long history humanity is perceived as both pitiful and splendid; pitiful because each one's achievement is miniscule in the whole, and splendid because in spite of this the desire to achieve resurges with each new generation.

The strange and inexplicable phenomenon of human life is evoked at the moment before sunset when the sun casts a red light over the Prairie — "that seems to extend its vastness and at the same time empty it of all human presence, as if giving it over to wild dreams of the time when it existed in utter solitude."[92] This is a terrible moment of desolation for Christine, again the heroine as she was in *Street of Riches*. She senses that the only way to overcome the feeling of alienation is to create.

The four stories in *The Road Past Altamont* each tell of a journey, but the last is the real journey, when Christine leaves her mother to go to Europe. The previous three are rehearsals for the final departure — preparations and foreshadowings of the moment when the tie between mother and child must of necessity be broken.

The first journey takes place when Christine is a little girl and goes to visit her grandmother in the country. Here she sees what it is to be old and past the stage of building anew. She also sees, although she does not know it, her mother in the future.

To overcome Christine's inexplicable sadness at the moment of sunset and her own sense of uselessness now that her children are gone, the old lady creates a little doll for the child. They spend enchanted hours together as the grandmother sews the doll from all the scraps left around the house by her departed children, as though bringing back her youth in this one small creation.

The grandmother's days of creativity are almost over, however. She is failing, and Christine's mother brings her back to their house to live. Here the old lady fades quickly, becoming like a child to her own daughter who must feed and nurse her. As her ways become those of a child, so do her thoughts, and she returns in memory to the place near the Assomption River where she was born, a recurring experience among the old people in this book who try to regain their youth by returning to places of memory.

The second story, "The Old Man and the Child," takes place shortly after Christine's grandmother has died. She is greatly saddened; but through friendship with an old man, she acquires a greater understanding of the old, and in this way, comes closer to her grandmother.

The old man and the little girl meet where the circle of life ends and begins. He catches a glimpse of youth through her, while she meets the future through him. He suggests that they take a trip to Lake Winnipeg together, to escape the heat, he says, but really for him to re-live a place he had known when young, and for her to find new experience. They do so, but underlying Christine's trembling excitement is her anxiety and guilt over leaving her mother, a warning of the sadness she will feel later: "My poor mother! I don't suppose I had even thought till then that she had never seen Lake Winnipeg either, though it is not far from where we lived. But, always the slave to our needs, when and how could she have yielded for even a day to the still eager desires of her own spirit . . . . And was she not beginning to realize that for her it was late now and not much time remained to appease those longings that, if not satisfied, leave us as if imperfect in our own eyes, in a train of nostalgic regrets?"[93]

Christine sees farther into the future than she wished. After lunch, Monsieur Saint-Hillaire falls asleep and reveals himself as a very old man about to die. His false teeth slip, and his hand falls as though dead. Christine, in a panic at what old age brings, thinks: ". . . I did not wish to grow old. I wished to know everything without growing old; but above all, I imagine, I did not wish to see others grow old around me."[94]

To pull her out of the despair into which these thoughts have plunged her, Monsieur Saint-Hillaire begins to describe all the splendid things which the future will hold for her. There will be travel to foreign cities, and to the country of love where he says, ". . . everything shone with a special light . . ."[95] Thus, he manages to distract her, as she says, "from the pain he had caused me by being so old."[96] Now the sky begins to darken, and her thoughts fly to her mother. She is not quite ready for these adventurous trips into the unknown, and she thinks of her mother "as of my one and final refuge."[97] When they return to St. Boniface late at night, she flings herself into her mother's arms, unable to articulate the strange voyage she has made into the future, and only cries: "I've seen it, Maman! . . . Beautiful Lake Winnipeg."[98]

In the third story, Christine makes a terrible journey into the real world, the world of *The Tin Flute,* where poverty, fatigue, and hopelessness are the constant elements. Here, Christine learns that all journeys into the world are not like trips to mystical lakes with dreamy old gentlemen. As a child, Gabrielle Roy knew a family whose father, on Saturdays, hitched up his horse and wagon to move the household effects of poor people. His small daughter usually went with him on these expeditions, and Gabrielle longed to join them, sure that they led exciting lives compared to her dull one. She never did go; but Christine in the story "The Move" does. She had already asked her mother for permission, but it was firmly denied. One Saturday morning, she runs out of the house before her mother is up and climbs onto the wagon with the rough-mannered father and his daughter. During the journey they go to a poor shack, pick up the cracked, filthy belongings of the family, and move them across Winnipeg to an equally dismal dwelling. There is nothing but ugly wrangling, crying, hungry children, and tired cruelty the whole way. When at night Christine returns home, exhausted, her mother is of course frantic with worry and very angry. Christine does not try to escape punishment; she only cries out: "Oh why have you said a hundred times that from the seat of the covered wagon on the prairie in the old days the world seemed renewed, different and so beautiful?"[99]

Her mother takes her in her arms and says: "Ah, so that's it! . . . You too will have the family disease, departure sickness. . . . Ah, poor you! What is to become of you!"[100]

In the last story, "The Road Past Altamont," Christine leaves home for good; but before she does, she takes her mother on a drive across the Prairie. Maman is now aging and, like her own mother before her, has returned in her mind to the places of her youth in Quebec, where there were hills. On the ride they become lost and drive through a mysterious place called Altamont, which afterward Christine can discover on no map. Near Altamont, they find themselves in some unexpected hills, and her mother, in one of her last attempts to recapture her youth, jumps out of the car as though she had suddenly found herself back in Quebec, and disappears from view. Christine realizes that when an old person tries to make the circle back to childhood, she is near death. When Maman returns to the car she begs Christine to remember the road past Altamont — she wants to see it again. However, on a second journey, they cannot find it — it is too late. Maman's youth has passed, and Christine's near departure is proof of it: "Maman was perhaps close to admitting that she felt herself too old to lose me, that there is a time when one can bear to see one's children go away but after that it is truly as if the last rag of youth were being taken from us and all the lamps put out."[101]

Christine goes away to Europe, and with her going Maman's tenuous hold on life goes too. She does not even travel any more, for she has lost the road to Altamont, the way to find her youth. She dies: "Her capricious and youthful spirit went to a region where there are undoubtedly no more difficult crossroads and no more starting points. Or perhaps there are still roads there but they all go past Altamont."[102]

La Route d'Altamont and the English translation, *The Road Past Altamont,* were both published in 1966. This time the translation was done by the Toronto writer Joyce Marshall, beginning a continuing collaboration and close friendship. Harry Binsse had accepted a full-time job with the Quebec government and has since died. The relationship between Gabrielle Roy and Joyce Marshall is distinguished by mutual respect and many arguments. Each accuses the other of being exacting; each takes a passionate interest in language. When they work, they keep a pile of dictionaries at hand to resolve disputes. Each word is weighed. The result is translations which are crisper and closer to English construction than those of Harry Binsse, although his were notable for their fine sensitivity.

GABRIELLE ROY IS fastidious about correct syntax. Writing a short biographical piece on her for the book *Great Canadians* published in Centennial Year, the novelist Brian Moore said that her writing "in the freestyle 1960's seems like an echo of Victorian propriety."[103]

She was not always considered so proper, for as she points out, "Many French critics deplored the kind of French I used in the dialogue of *Bonheur d'occasion,* describing it as a sort of jargon." Still, as she says, "I use that kind of language less and less now." In fact, she has some firm remarks to make about the current vogue for *joual,* a kind of French which is a combination of French and English words, and which some advocates of the new Quebec have said should be the recognized language of the people because it is the one most often used. "I do not like that dreadful *joual,*" she says. "There was a time for such expressions; they were tried out. Now, our efforts must tend to a French, partly our own, with its valuable particularities, but understandable to the world outside. There may even be a limited place left for the use of *joual* in our literature, but to use it exclusively would be disastrous and silly. It does not even correspond to reality, for the quality of French has improved immensely in Quebec in the last ten years. On the whole, this debased language is a dangerous tool. Sometimes it may simply hide lack of talent. Because it is colourful, in a sense, one may forget that it says nothing of lasting value. And where will it lead us in the end? — to poverty of words, poverty of thought, poverty of self. In any case, one must remember that this particular language is far from being representative. Damon Runyon used an *argot* in his books about New York, but he did not pretend that it was the language of the whole United States."[104]

THE PAINTER RENÉ RICHARD had given Gabrielle Roy a dramatic portrait of the Far North. With this, and with her own imagination, she created the cruel background which was the setting for her novel *The Hidden Mountain*.

She had another friend who knew the North. This man was a geologist who had worked in Ungava. Like René Richard, he spent several evenings recalling for her the people and the land. One evening, her imagination thoroughly stimulated, she said, "I would love to go and see it!"

"Nothing could be easier," replied the geologist. "I will arrange for you to go by plane. There is a hotel of sorts at Fort Chimo where you can stay."

In the summer of 1961, Gabrielle flew to Ungava, landing at Fort Chimo. There she found a strange new world, something as she imagined the moon to be, swept clean except for the few human inhabitants and the three elements of land, sky, and water. The white inhabitants at Fort Chimo were people employed in government and technical installations. The rest were Eskimos.

She saw the white culture moving in on the simple lives of the indigenous people, changing them, and not always for the best. The abrupt changes imposed on people by technological advance had preoccupied her for a long time, since the days when she had been a reporter, writing about growing industrialism in Quebec. She had shown the result in the starved lives of the people in *The Tin Flute* and *The Cashier*. In Fort Chimo, she saw changes taking place before her eyes. One enterprising young man, employed by the Bell Telephone Company, was installing telephones in the small huts of the Eskimo people. This struck her as somewhat mad and she protested to the young man, who replied: "But the Eskimos love telephones. I can hardly keep up with the demand. In fact, they want the most elaborate models. Princess phones are going very well." This disturbed Gabrielle Roy even more.

"But in these small shacks," she pointed out, "the people are poor. They can barely afford necessities and what need have they of telephones?"

The Bell Telephone man replied with great pride: "I have just installed a phone in a tent."

She saw a sick Eskimo woman being lifted by stretcher onto a hydroplane to be taken to a hospital farther south. The woman, she thought, must be frightened and bewildered, removed from the only home she had known. It was true that the medical advantages which the whites offered saved lives and prevented suffering. The Eskimos, however, had a fatalistic acceptance of illness and death. They believed that when a man's time to die had come, he should do so with dignity. In the old days, aged people sometimes walked away to an ice flow where they were allowed to die. This was not an attitude which the whites understood. Their efforts were to prolong life at all costs.

In contrast to the new ways which were coming, Gabrielle Roy had an opportunity to glimpse life as it had been before the white man came. She made friends with a policeman who offered to take her across the Koksoak River to Old Fort Chimo. The Fort Chimo she was in, it turned out, was Fort Chimo town. It had been built only recently when the white man came and was able to offer employment to the Eskimos who, one by one, left their homes in Old Fort Chimo to cross the river. On the old side she found the remains of a primitive village, with little more than a graveyard as proof that people had once lived and died there.

Gabrielle Roy remained in Ungava only one week, and in that short time absorbed impressions which were to result in a novel and three fine stories. "I didn't go with the idea of collecting material for stories," she said. "When I was there it didn't occur to me. I don't think stories are made that way, at least not for me."[105]

Nine years later, in 1970, the Eskimo stories were published. Three stories and a novel appeared in one volume titled *La Rivière sans repos,* but only the novel, called *Windflower,* was published in English, translated by Joyce Marshall. So far, English-speaking readers have not had the opportunity to read the three stories.

The first one, "The Satellites," draws on Gabrielle Roy's fleeting impression of the Eskimo woman being taken away by hydroplane for medical attention. In it, she challenges not only the assumption that medical advances always mean an advance in the quality of life, but also the notion that so-called civilized ways are superior to native ones. The Eskimo woman, Deborah, is forty-two and has cancer. She is weakening rapidly and is prepared to die, but the Protestant missionary who serves the district will not allow her to give up and urges her to make an effort to live. He tells her that if she goes away to a hospital in the south there is a chance that she will be cured. His arguments bring a simple question from Deborah — she asks him why the white people are so anxious to live for a long time and wonders whether it is because their lives are so much better than the Eskimos! Very often Gabrielle Roy uses simple people to ask profound questions, questions which a more sophisticated person would not ask because the point has never occurred to him. Deborah's inquiry leaves the missionary both startled and embarrassed, for when he considers it, he admits that white people have not yet learned to live in peace either with others or with themselves, and yet they insist on living for as long as possible. Deborah tells him of her old grandmother who went away to the ice banks to die, and this shocks the Reverend Hugh Patterson, who has used this very story in his sermons to illustrate how far modern Eskimos have advanced over their ancestors. Deborah does go south to the hospital, and here, through her eyes, Gabrielle Roy gives us a clever, ironic comparison of white and Eskimo ways. Deborah is, at first, very happy. The white people are kind to her and they mean well. She discovers two pleasures in her life at the hospital: one is the hot shower and soap — she washes her beautiful hair endlessly; the other is cigarettes. Gabrielle Roy makes it clear that civilization is a double-edged blessing: "Like others of her race, she had finished by taking from civilization two things which seemed contradictory: soap for brightness and cleanliness, tobacco to muddle her thoughts and stain her fingers."[106]

Deborah has somehow received the impression that white people have discovered the secret of eternal life, but at the hospital she finds that white people suffer as much as Eskimos and that they die. Her morale disintegrates completely when the leaves she has picked to take home to her village beyond the tree-line, and some oranges she has been given and put away to take home to the children, both rot. Of course, eventually, all living things die. She becomes so disconsolate and homesick that the authorities decide to send her home. When she returns to her village she finds that she is a burden on her community and on her household. Her old father, Isaac, speaks to her of the grandmother who went away to die on the ice banks. "It was a beautiful cold night. There were spirits in white tunics dancing all around and making a great tour of the sky. . . . The cold is good and compassionate." He describes the old lady, seated perfectly preserved in the middle of a pedestal of ice — "a white islet in the middle of an angry black sea — . . . in the last free waters of the earth, like the satellites of today, those curious objects, suspended in the sky, never more to descend. . . . That is what she became . . . a satellite."[107]

One night, Deborah slips out of the hut. Her footsteps are seen next day in the freshly fallen snow, showing that she often stumbled, but kept walking from ridge to ridge until she came to free water. She had chosen the splendour of death, as described by Isaac, instead of a life of uselessness.

The second story, "The Telephone," retells the senseless installation of the telephone in the Eskimo tent. The old man, Barnaby, who owns the tent, is at first delighted by his new toy. He phones everyone he can think of, from the Hudson's Bay Company to his busy neighbour, whom he can clearly see hanging out her wash. Finally, in exasperation, a priest advises him to go for a ride on the Koksoak River and think things over. He tells him that the telephone means servitude. Barnaby goes to the river, realizes that he has been foolish, and decides that he will return to the old village where his people lived before the civilized new one was created. He leaves his telephone with all the other junk he has collected during his brief sojourn among the white men. "Far away, on the shore, among the twisted old iron and debris of the abandoned camp, the telephone, already half buried in the sand, rang and rang."[108]

"The Wheel Chair" is about old Isaac, the father of Deborah who died on the ice flow. He is now paralyzed from head to foot as a result of a seal-hunting accident and cannot speak. A mysterious philanthropic organization sends him a wheel chair, which is dropped out of the sky by an airplane, like many other strange things which come to the Eskimos.

Isaac, however, is totally dependent on the care of others, and having lost all dignity, wishes to die. He would like to go off like Deborah, but with her death the white people had asked a lot of embarrassing questions: "Had she been depressed? . . . Why do you think she did this?[109] Isaac dreads causing so much trouble himself, but one day he can bear no more. Without anyone noticing, he finds that he can manipulate one of the wheels of his chair by himself. When no one is looking, he manages to push himself to the edge of the water, only to be snatched back in the nick of time by Esmerelda, the Eskimo woman who cares for him. She understands very well how he feels, and somewhat puzzled herself, tries to explain to him why he cannot go off to die. "You saw what happened with Deborah. 'They' arrived with all their questions. 'They' wanted to know why. 'They' made us ashamed."[110] Isaac is condemned to life.

The novel, *Windflower,* is Gabrielle Roy's fourth Eskimo work. It is about a simple Eskimo girl, Elsa, who is attacked by a young American soldier stationed at Fort Chimo, and bears a child of mixed blood. As a result of this actual and symbolic rape, Elsa and her child, Jimmy, live in a no man's land between the two cultures. The message of the book is that the indigenous culture is becoming a no man's land as a result of invasion by the white world.

At first, Elsa decides that the white world is the best and that Jimmy should be brought up in its ways. She goes out to work in order to keep Jimmy in beautiful clothes and toys. She mimics the cleanliness taught her by a nurse, and each day gives Jimmy an elaborate, ritual bath, to the amazement of the entire Eskimo community. Finally, the local pastor chides her for her extravagance and warns her that the child may grow up to be ashamed of his mother and her people. Elsa, in a panic that the white man will somehow take Jimmy away, decides to cross the Koksoak River and live in Old Fort Chimo, in the old Eskimo ways. There they live a serene and contented life with her uncle Ian, a stubborn holdout against civilization. The shadow of the white man is never far away, however. A policeman turns up to tell her that, by law, she must send the child to school. She protests that she is already teaching him to read. The policeman's rejoinder is, "Don't make it necessary for me to come and get you by force."[111]

Elsa and her uncle Ian decide to run away to escape the white man. They pack a few necessities on a dog sled and travel over the tundra, building an igloo each night for shelter. The child loves the adventure, but pampered and protected as he has been, he cannot withstand the hardships and develops a burning fever. He is so ill that Elsa knows that she must take him back to the white hospital. She does so, where he is almost immediately cured with penicillin. Now she is trapped in the new ways, or perhaps more truly, seduced, for she accepts a Quonset hut to live in, an unbelievable luxury for an Eskimo woman. Her Eskimo nature is further eroded by the gift of a sewing machine, which she uses with true work-ethic industry to earn their living by manufacturing an endless assortment of little Eskimo dolls, animals, and parkas made out of Hudson's Bay blankets. The irony is that by making Eskimo objects, she is able to maintain Jimmy in white-man style.

Elsa has one more opportunity to live as an Eskimo and to have an Eskimo husband. She meets a young widower, and they are attracted to each other; but Jimmy, seeing his mother's attention caught by someone else, makes a pest of himself, and the widower sadly goes away. The white man who has given Elsa his child has also indirectly robbed her of her chance to have an Eskimo husband.

All Elsa's gifts do not make Jimmy happy. In modern parlance, he is a "disturbed child." He accepts the values of his white playmates and snubs the Eskimo children, but he is troubled because of his dark-skinned mother. One day he asks her whether she is really his mother. Had there been a mix-up in the hospital? Elsa, taking her courage in her hands, tells him the story of his birth. She does not even know his father's name.

The boy, already cynical and bitter, turns in hatred against his mother. He stows away on an airplane and disappears. He is found, but he runs away again, never to return. His mother knows that he has gone to the United States, a place which seemed like paradise to him.

With all reason for effort gone, Elsa falls into sloth. She stops working and sells her sewing machine for food. She leaves her splendid Quonset hut, which now represents slavery, and moves into a shabby, abandoned old hut. Here she lives, sleeping in her clothes, selling what she can for food, beer, and cigarettes, working as a cleaning woman when it becomes necessary.

When the war in Vietnam begins, Elsa knows instinctively that Jimmy is one of the G.I.s who has gone to fight there. She imagines some young Vietnamese girl who may have gone into the bushes with Jimmy, and given her a grandchild.

Elsa grows old, looking much older than her years. In the summer she can be seen wandering along the banks of the Koksoak, the local eccentric, followed by the eternal wreath of her cigarette smoke. Poor wraithlike Elsa is the image for wasting Eskimo life — lost, confused, without conviction.

The story ends with one of her wanderings. She picks a little windflower growing with its fluff of white seeds. She breathes on it and watches the seeds "rise and scatter into the evening."[112]

The windflower, emphasized in the English title, suggests the seed of all the peoples who will scatter their children about the earth. Jimmy was a product of a scattered seed, and he may also have had a child by a Vietnamese girl, as Elsa thinks. These Eskimo stories not only describe the world in which we live, where people move quickly from one corner of the globe to another, but also forecast the clash of cultures in the future. Gabrielle Roy does not foresee much happiness, nor does she provide easy answers. The Russian writer Chekhov said that it was not a writer's job to give answers, but to ask the right questions. Gabrielle Roy leaves us with this question: "Will not primitive peoples disappear from the world leaving us with a terrible loss?"[113]

The French title, *La Rivière sans repos,* makes the unanswered question more troubling. It implies the whole stream of human life, travelling endlessly on a restless quest.

THE AUTHOR OF *Windflower* is in many ways, a world citizen. She is a cultivated woman of wide knowledge and interests. The French

Canadians, however, are happy to claim her as their own. They are possessive and proud of her, as well they might be. Her books have been translated into fourteen languages. Besides her two Governor-General's Awards, she has been given the *Prix Fémina* (1947), the Lorne Pierce Medal, the Canada Council of the Arts Award (1967), the Order of Canada (1967), and the *Prix David* (1971), Quebec's highest literary honour. She is a member of the Royal Society of Canada and a Knight of the Mark Twain Society.

Some of the more militant French Canadians would like her to use her talent and prestige to promote political ideas. She says, "My main concern, I think, is the human condition. Naturally, I will study the human condition in those nearest to me by blood and presence — therefore, the French Canadians — sometimes the Quebecers, sometimes the French Canadians of the West that I alone, perhaps, of writers, am familiar with and to whom I have given voice. They too should be spoken about. It is through fiction and in my own way that I speak for people. I don't think that I would have achieved more by direct use of political ideas. Possibly much less. Ideas often last but a day; feelings, dreams, almost forever."[114]

"My great hope would be that Québec would realize itself fully as a distinct part of Canada, and stay Canadian, bringing to Canada a part of its richness. Sometimes I dream that the French Canadians will be happy not so much when they themselves feel free and find their own identity, but when they find in themselves enough to give to the others and contribute to the others.[115]

YEARS AGO, WHEN Gabrielle was a young child, her pretty sister, Bernadette, had left the family to become a cloistered nun. Mélina and Léon Roy had felt her departure keenly because this daughter was truly lost to the family. Then, in the 1960's, the Catholic Church began to relax its rules. Gabrielle found that it would be possible for Dédette to visit her. In 1965, Dédette and Clémence, another sister, arrived at the village of Petite-Rivière-Saint-François, north of Quebec City, where Gabrielle and her husband have their summer house.

Dédette was a revelation to Gabrielle. By now she was an elderly lady, but one so full of vitality that it was difficult to keep up with her. It seemed that after so many years in a convent she could not get enough of life. Gabrielle had had some intimation of Dédette's humour and intelligence when they began to correspond after Anna's death; but Dédette in person turned out to be even more engaging than in her letters. Her black nun's habit could be seen fluttering up the hillside as she searched for birch bark. She quickly became friends with the woodsmen she met on her expeditions and wanted to know all about them and their lives. She loved Shakespeare and quoted him often. After a lively month spent together at Petite-Rivière, Gabrielle knew that she had found a friend after her heart in her long lost sister. They corresponded frequently; Dédette was the most sympathetic of friends; she was genuinely overjoyed by Gabrielle's success.

The friendship which had come to mean so much ended as abruptly as it had begun when, in 1971, Dédette developed cancer and died. There were now only three children of the family left — Adèle, living in Manitoba, Clémence, and Gabrielle.

In the summer of 1971, Gabrielle returned to Petite-Rivière-Saint-François. Its beauty struck her as particularly poignant. She recalled Camus' remark — he hoped that the tragedy of life would never hide the beauty, and that the beauty would never hide the tragedy.

She began to write a new book, a book about Petite-Rivière-Saint-François, its beauty, its animal life, and her friends living there. All the events described are gentle, but each one is transformed into a celebration of the earth. A triumphant note rings throughout as she describes beauty reborn, the miraculous rhythms of death followed by new life. *Cet été qui chantait* was published in 1972. "Every writer must eventually write his Ninth Symphony or give in to despair," she said.[116] Beethoven's Ninth Symphony is a ringing choral work.

The title means "that summer which sang," and the whole book reverberates with the sounds of summer, the cry of the birds, the mournful rustling of a solitary pine, the chiming of a chapel bell. Although the title refers to "that" summer, it is about all summers melting one into another, as though every summer is timeless and the same. It is the season when the earth flourishes and so it is a fitting period for her to re-find hope.

One story, "La Gatte de monsieur Emile," opens with a description of a damp, ugly field belonging to a poor farmer, Monsieur Emile. *Gatte* is his original and unusual name for his field; it means "manger," and it recalls the place where Jesus was born. However, at the moment, nothing beautiful or useful will grow there. Nevertheless, out of a feeling of tidiness, he builds a fence around it.

One day he has a great deal of trouble with a stubborn cow. To punish her, he shuts her up in the *gatte*. Here the restless animal plunges back and forth in the mud, uprooting the ugly couch grass which is the only thing which will grow, boring big holes in the ground with her feet, and meanwhile generously fertilizing the *gatte* with manure.

The following spring a miracle occurs. A little plant appears, the kalmia. The *gatte* suddenly becomes very gay. Children clamber through the pole fence to pick nosegays "which had the air of wedding bouquets."[117] But how did this marvellous flower suddenly appear in the sorry *gatte?* Did the wind carry the seeds from a faraway colony of kalmia? Did birds drop them? Or had the seeds always been buried deep in the soil, without a chance to reach the light? Perhaps the cow, when roaming through the mud, had brought the seeds to the surface. Very likely, the seeds had always been there.

The following spring the blossoms grow bigger and more beautiful than ever. All the windowsills of the surrounding houses hold bouquets arranged in mustard pots and peanut-butter jars. "But plants are like people. When one group finds a good place to live, everybody else follows."[118] Hardly has the kalmia established itself again when some blue iris appear, then buttercups: "The old *gatte* which had been all rose-coloured the previous spring was, this year, multicoloured."[119] In autumn there are asters and golden rod. Birds come and perch on the fence poles which Monsieur Emile has erected. Until frost, the tender life flourishes.

In winter a further miracle occurs. The *gatte* is at the foot of a mountain, and just before the sun passes behind the mountain it seems to pause: "At this instant, it illuminates the entire field, like a strange search light. The pale, lifeless snow becomes, at its centre, as pink as the kalmia, on the edges as blue as the iris, and here and there blazes like the flame of the dead golden rod. For three or four minutes each day, the poor field is radiant with the most marvellous colours of refound summer. Then the darkness of night falls."[120]

Not all the stories are joyful. Gabrielle Roy has slipped in a remembrance of death from long ago when she was a young teacher in Manitoba. The story is about the death of the Métis child in Marchand, and the visit by the teacher and children to see her and surround her with wild flowers. It creates sombre balance within the structure of the book.

IN THE SUMMER of 1973 after *Cet été qui chantait* was published, Gabrielle Roy made her annual return to Petite-Rivière-Saint-François. It was still beautiful, but she had written about it now, and somehow the fine edge of her feeling had vanished with the writing. She felt empty.

Early on a summer evening, she sat in her garden swing, waiting for the fire flies to appear. In her hand she held a small blue flower which she had discovered in the lawn near a cluster of birch — the blue-eyed grass. Her eyes moved from the flower to the trees at the edge of the cliff. She had had some conversation with her husband about these trees. She thought a few should be cut down to give the others more room — and more attention. Then her imagination began to travel. Suppose we cut them all down, all but the handsomest — sacrifice many in favour of one, just as in art we give up a hundred details in favour of the most revealing. Thus, we would have the perfect tree. But then, suppose the tree died? She lost herself in this thought for some time.

The flower still lay in her palm. Its fragility was heartbreaking; the stem no larger than a thread, the flower only as big as the little fingernail. But, as though to defy pity, its colour was a vivid and astonishing blue.

1. Grove with May, age five, in 1921. Cutter is similar to the one described in *Over Prairie Trails*.
2. One of Mrs. Grove's favourite pictures of her husband, 1921.
3. Grove, on holiday at Lake Winnipeg. Probably 1923.
4. Grove, May and Catherine, camping at Lake Winnipeg. Probably 1923 when Grove was working on *Settlers of the Marsh*.

Frederick
Philip
Grove

ROBERT FLETCHER, DEPUTY MINISTER of Education for the Province of Manitoba, looked up from his desk in his office on Bannatyne Avenue in Winnipeg to see an unusually tall man enter. The man's name was Grove; he had telephoned to arrange an interview and then had phoned again to say that he would have to come wearing overalls —that was all he possessed.[1] Fletcher saw a man with a long, sensitive face and slightly receding chin, haunted blue eyes and reddish-blond hair combed neatly back. His overalls, work shirt and boots evidently embarrassed him. It was late in the fall of 1912.

Fletcher had been particularly eager to see Grove, who was fluent in both German and English. Although most of the multitude of one and a half million immigrants who had flooded into Canada since 1896 had come from the United States and the British Isles, there were 594,000 from non-English-speaking European countries. In Manitoba, the government had promised bilingual schools to help them adjust, but promising was easier than providing: bilingual teachers were scarce. Here was a man who said he was a teacher; his credentials had been lost, but that was not unusual among recently arrived Europeans. Several whose papers had vanished were working on permit; they could take the Normal School teacher-training course later and receive permanent certificates.

The Deputy Minister may not have realized that besides speaking German and English, Grove knew Latin, Greek, French, Italian and Spanish. Even if he did know, he was probably impressed by more than Grove's education and stature — everyone was, although not always favourably. Arthur Phelps, head of the English Department at Wesley College in Winnipeg, who met Grove later at a teachers' convention, put it this way: "It was not his height, not the slight stoop and thrust of his shoulders, not the head, nor the eyes. It was an aura, an emanation. He was different and formidable. He towered. Physique seemed to have nothing to do with it. Grove was separate."[2]

Robert Fletcher was the first Canadian we know of to set eyes on the man who at that moment called himself Fred Grove, and he was to remain his staunch supporter. He arranged for him to be hired as a teacher, although Grove was privately dismayed at the low salary — only fifty dollars a month. But he was penniless, and glad to have any job; besides it was important to him at this vulnerable stage to prove that he could take a job and succeed at it. Fletcher, wishing to encourage a man who was plainly outstanding, told Grove that if he passed two Grade 12 examinations the following summer and attended Normal School for eleven weeks, he would be given a provisional certificate for better paid high-school teaching — and perhaps even a position as principal. Grove was elated at this, and before long, having exchanged his overalls for suitable teacher's garb, he was speeding across the wintry prairie on a train towards his post in a tiny village.

Early in January, 1913, he stood before a class of twenty children, Grades 1 to 6, in the white, one-roomed Kronsfeld School[3] in Haskett, a place of about fifty people within walking distance of the United States border. He was a good teacher. Besides, he knew a great deal about the progressive ideas on education which were now emerging everywhere. His nature study class could be seen trailing across the fields to collect specimens, because Grove believed in visual education. He began to ask for playground equipment, because he thought that play was an important part of learning.

Grove was considered rather strange by the German Mennonites in the neighbourhood. They were awed by him, of course — anybody learned enough to be a teacher drew their admiration — but . . . well, he had an unusual reverence for natural life. He fed the coyotes who wandered down from the Pembina Hills; nobody else liked coyotes. His room was alive with mice he had rescued from the cold, with insects in bottles and with a great variety of common weeds. At the school picnic in June some boys found a nest of snakes and set about trying to kill them with sticks. Before they knew it, Grove himself was standing in the middle of the snake nest, intervening forcibly. "Before you kill another snake, you kill me!"[4]

There were several people, however, who had cause to be grateful for Grove's energy and imagination. One of the kindest things he did was to take a special interest in boys who could not attend school because they were needed for farm work, and to tutor them privately at night in his room. His sympathy had been caught by these boys and, years later, the plight of a brilliant boy caught in crushing pioneer circumstances became the story of his novel *The Yoke of Life*. In an early stage the book was called "Equal Opportunities," an ironic title, for Grove felt that their opportunities were far from equal.

There was one Mennonite who did not find Grove odd, but intelligent and interesting. John Warkentin was the twenty-six year old principal of a school at Winkler, fifteen miles away. He and Grove became good friends, sharing strong ideas about new teaching methods. When Warkentin decided to go to Germany to study, he made a recommendation that Grove take over as principal. Grove was not qualified, but in the summer he wrote Grade 12 mathematics and history exams and attended Normal School for bilingual teachers. In the fall of 1913 he was promoted, and became principal of the four-room, two-storey Winkler School with an enrollment of one hundred and sixty pupils.

GROVE TURNED EDUCATION in Winkler upside down. When he arrived he found, first of all, that two of the four teachers were not properly qualified and had no opportunity to take the required training. There were other teachers in the district working under the same handicap and if the supply of teachers increased they would be replaced by others with more education. Some of the permit teachers had not even progressed beyond Grade 9, so Grove opened a night school especially for teachers and taught them Grades 10 and 11.

The Winkler School itself did not offer courses beyond Grade 8, and the Mennonite and Jewish families in the neighbourhood were anxious for their children to be well educated. With the encouragement of the school inspector, Grove began senior classes, teaching all high school himself. This caused some juggling of the lower grades who had now to be spread among the remaining three teachers. The heroine of the transition was the primary teacher, a Miss Katrina Wiens, known as Tina, who assumed a double class without complaint. "A pedagogical genius," Grove noted.[5]

High school courses required chemistry and physics equipment — the school had none. Grove bought the equipment himself and installed it in the basement. In a burst of enthusiasm, he decided to add wood-working courses for students who were not academically inclined and bought more equipment. He was in no position to buy expensive classroom tools and soon found himself in debt. Luckily, two inspectors arrived from Winnipeg and were so impressed by his innovations that they gave one hundred dollars to the School Board to help pay expenses. Grove reported later that he had some trouble extracting this money from the Board and that even when he did his debts were considerable.

That was not all. He decided to help the farmers too. In the local paper, the *Morden Times,* an announcement appeared. It said that seed tests for grain and garden products would be held at the Winkler School to determine which seeds were best. Principal Grove would supervise these tests at no cost to the participants, but small contributions would be welcome.[6] As it happened, the Department of Agriculture was already carrying out seed tests and not asking for money, but Grove didn't know this. He meant well.

Grove had flung himself at reforming Winkler like a cyclone. Inevitably, there were a few who felt bruised by the onrush and, by Christmas, Grove found to his bewilderment that he was not the object of the wholehearted admiration which he felt he deserved, but of a certain amount of criticism. He had demoted some students whom he thought had been pushed ahead too fast; the School Board began to rumble threateningly, no doubt prodded by angry parents. Grove wanted to provide as much education as possible for everybody and when he found that one of his teachers had turned away some students from outside the district, he was furious. The extent of his anger is made clear in a letter he wrote to John Warkentin: "I went after those people again — poor farmers whose only chance is with me. And I told the trustees that if they did not think it worth their while to discuss school affairs with the principal instead of one of the assistants, said principal would not think it worth his while to go on with his work beyond the next pay day."[7] Grove's letters to Warkentin at this time reveal a man who could not endure to be challenged — the irascible Grove was to become familiar to acquaintances later on. With criticism, his buoyancy collapsed like a pricked balloon — and soon after Christmas, he wrote again to Warkentin, hinting at another cause for his despondency. He told his friend that he had planned to be married in Arkansas. During the holiday, he had gone there to see a girl whom he told Warkentin he had known for five years and who had been a pupil of his. She, evidently, had turned him down. "As for my marriage, that has gone to smash. . . . I don't blame the girl — I merely don't understand her."[8] The mysterious love affair has never appeared in any other account of Grove's about himself.

He did not suffer long. Spring came, and he found himself very taken by the "pedagogical genius" who taught the primary classes in the school. Tina Wiens was twenty-two, tall and slender, with blue-green eyes. She was obviously quite taken by him too: "He was 42 years old at this time, and I was quite awed in front of this tall, aloof somebody from another country. In the spring of the year I think he came to my room at recess time to talk possibly a little oftener than would seem necessary as far as the actual principal's duties were concerned."[9]

By the time school ended in June an invitation had come from Tina to visit her at her parents' farm near Rush Lake, Saskatchewan. Later accounts by Tina and Grove of this invitation vary somewhat. Tina claimed that he insisted on an invitation, while his story was that she had made the first suggestion. In any case, a trip to Rush Lake would announce to the world that he had serious intentions. He had a case of the nerves, but while waiting to visit the family he wrote to her regularly. These letters are hardly passionate declarations of love — they all begin very properly, "Dear Miss Wiens." He went so far as to say that he would only be interested in returning to Winkler if she were there too, but beyond that the first letter makes only hesitant references to his proposed visit.[10] The second contains an indirect argument against marriage — Grove disapproved of the marriage of one of his friends.[11] The third and fourth letters, however, make specific arrangements for his appearance at her home.[12]

He spent two weeks at Rush Lake. Tina's family had originally consisted of fourteen children, but four had died. In this large family, Tina was known as the girl with a mind of her own. Her father, Johan Wiens, was a Mennonite who had emigrated to Canada from Germany in 1888. He had gone to Plum Coulee, Manitoba — where Tina had been born — and become a farmer and a miller. He had built the first large flour mill at Emerson, a business which was to become the basis for one of Grove's novels, *The Master of the Mill.*

Somewhat to Tina's chagrin, Grove appeared to ignore her for most of the visit. He showed foresight, however, by spending his time chatting in German to her father. Johan Wiens was as awed as everyone else by Grove and he had enormous respect for his education. Without inquiring deeply into the background of his daughter's suitor, he indicated his approval. Near the end of the visit, Grove proposed marriage to Katrina Wiens and she accepted him.[13]

They were married in a quiet ceremony in the Anglican Church in Swift Current, August 2, 1914. In less than two years, the totally unknown and rootless Grove had become a school principal, an awesome if slightly abrasive force in local education, and had acquired a wife and a substantial family of in-laws. Grove had chosen his wife well. Although he commented later that her family "were not exactly wealthy,"[14] Tina came from a solid, God-fearing, closely-knit family who were not so poor either. She possessed invaluable qualities of resourcefulness, strength and devotion.

Grove gave some puzzling information about himself on his marriage certificate. He said that he was forty-two years old; recent research into his life indicates that he was only thirty-five. Why did he represent himself as older? He also said that he was a widower; there is no indication in his autobiography that he had married before. His nationality was not stated — it was not demanded by the marriage form, only place of birth. Grove said that he was born in Moscow, but he was surely not Russian. Everyone assumed that he was German because he spoke the language. His religious denomination was given as Lutheran, suggesting either a German or Scandinavian background. He stated that his parents were Charles Edward Grove and Bertha Rutherford Grove.

IN THE CLEAR LIGHT of an early Saturday morning, neighbours could see the gaunt figure of the school principal fastening a mechanism from the roof of his apartment. Grove was putting up a pulley clothesline for Tina, a device not commonly used. Whispers passed among the neighbours: "Was he planning to send messages to German spies? He was German wasn't he?"[15]

Tina and Philip (as he was now called, having dropped "Fred") were living in an apartment above the local hardware store in Winkler. They were both busy teaching and Grove's nights were still spent in extra tutoring, so they had little time for friendly visits with neighbours which might have alleviated some of the hostility about Grove's nationality. Wartime was not a good period to be German in Canada. It was the time when the German settlers of Berlin, Ontario, decided to change the name of their city to Kitchener. In Winkler, the school was split between the German Mennonites, pacifists by religious conviction but passionately Canadian, and the other Germans. Tension grew, but Grove was inclined to treat the whole matter as a joke — the rumours over the clothesline were patently ridiculous. Entering a classroom one day he found two groups of students at loggerheads over the war and he asked, "Who's for Germany?" Two children raised their hands and Grove remarked defiantly, "Then it is the three of us against the world!" But he had always praised German science, German literature, German music and German education; he continued to do so.[16]

The atmosphere had its effect upon him nevertheless. Whenever he found himself in hostile surroundings his behaviour became erratic and he began to tell odd stories about himself. He taught as well as ever, but now his classes became even more vivid as he told colourful tales about his past life, tales that nobody exactly believed. He said that he had been with the German Embassy in Greece digging for artifacts; he had been a tobacco farmer in Kentucky; when his wife's ear was bitten off by a horse he had sewed it back on. This former wife was alluded to from time to time, as were one or more sons who were in the United States. At one point, he said that his name was not Grove at all, but Gropfe. "There was never a dull day at school with Mr. Grove,"[17] one former student said. His story-telling might have passed as an amusing eccentricity except that he also became haughtily autocratic ("bossy," as people said), another characteristic that emerged when he felt uneasy. He was dogmatic in his criticism of religious faith and he encouraged Mennonite children to question doctrine. Winkler was a religious town; the other teachers held religious exercises in class, he did not. The School Board had had enough: Grove was not asked to return the following year. His dismissal came at a bad time; Tina was going to have a baby in August.

Luckily for him he was rescued by his old friend, Robert Fletcher. He saw to it that Grove was offered the position of master of mathematics at the Collegiate Institute at Virden, west of Brandon. In fact, the situation was far from discouraging: he was given a raise from $1,000 to $1,400 a year and he was told that the Virden principal was near retirement; if Grove succeeded at his job the principalship might be his.

But Winkler had cast its shadow. Grove was never again to fling himself quite so wholeheartedly into the role of responsible citizen.

His foray into "civilization", albeit in only a small town, had taught him (once more, it would seem) that the ways of man were dangerous. He continued to teach well and also to improve his qualifications as a teacher, but the next years were characterized by irritability and restless moving from town to town.

WHEN PHYLLIS MAY GROVE was born in the hospital at Virden, Manitoba, on August 5, 1915, her father found himself torn by a private conflict. He adored the little blond child who, as she grew, came to resemble him closely. For both him and Tina, May, as she was always called, was the centre of solicitous affection. Grove, who was in many ways a despairing and pessimistic man, found hope in her young life. He wrote, ". . . ever since the little girl was born, there had been only one desire which filled my life. Where I had failed, she was to succeed. Where I had squandered my energies and opportunities, she was to use them to some purpose. What I might have done but had not done, she was to do. She was to redeem me."[18] His devotion to his family demanded that he provide a stable home for them, that he be a responsible breadwinner.

But the bitter experience of Winkler had disillusioned him about worldly endeavor. When he had first gone to Haskett he had been determined to prove that he could succeed and he had thrown every ounce of his energy into his work. The results had not been what he had hoped, and in disgust and anger at the hostility which his supposedly German background aroused, he had given up trying to fit into the small town mould and began to think in other terms. Grove had always hoped that once he established himself financially he would be able to pursue his real ambition to be a writer. Tina had no knowledge of the thoughts which lay close to his heart.

In the struggle, the claims of his family won out. Grove enrolled as an extra-curricular student at the University of Manitoba so that he could raise his qualifications and improve his position. Besides studying, he carried his full daytime load, and also took on the extra night-time teaching which he had done at Winkler.

The strain was too much. Grove became bad-tempered and impatient in class; he continued to indulge in fanciful stories about his past which did not strengthen his position in the school. On the streets he was aloof and cold; Grove was not liked in Virden. Tina was under pressure too. Besides having a large house and a new baby to look after, she had been harbouring ideas of returning to teaching, which she had dropped when the baby was imminent; under Grove's direction she now studied Grades 10 and 11, preparing to write Grade 11 exams. There were also financial pressures. As a newly married couple they had had to buy furniture and did so on the installment plan; out of a salary that was not large, furniture payments were taking a large chunk.

In January, Grove's health collapsed. He lay ill and delirious with pneumonia for five months. He recovered, developed pleurisy and lapsed again.

A weak, cranky Grove struggled back to school in late spring. It was made clear to him that it would be a relief to all if he would leave — and he did, made more bitter by the belief that poor health had ruined his chances.

However, he applied for the position of principal at Gladstone and he was duly appointed. He and Tina prepared to move again, but before doing so, Grove, with his characteristic grit, went off to write his second-year university exams. Despite his weak physical condition, he made a remarkable showing, with top marks in German and French. Oddly, English prose literature and composition was his weak point — he received only 48 per cent.[19]

GLADSTONE WAS A DISASTER. It was one of the oldest communities in Manitoba, peopled largely by settlers from the British Isles. Grove was inordinately sensitive to their acceptable British background — and to his alien one.

Debts nagged. During his illness, when he had not been paid, they had run up bills amounting to nearly $1,000. Practising the utmost economy they managed to pay back $800 during the first year at Gladstone; on a salary of $1400 it wasn't easy. However, Grove persevered with his university work and in his third-year exams he won first prizes in both French and German.

One day, Grove showed Tina something he had written. For her, this revealed a totally new aspect of her husband. "He did not talk to me about his writing until after we were married. I had no idea he was a writer."[20] How did she react? According to Grove, she said, "A man who can write like that should not waste his time teaching."[21]

Grove, without directly expressing his thoughts, began to search around for some means to free himself from his present job and from the town he hated. Because of his good academic record, the University of Manitoba was prepared to allow him to write his fourth year exams in the summer, which, if passed, would give him his bachelor's degree without another year of study. But Grove had put those ambitions behind him and instead, pleading shortage of money, he took a teaching job in an idyllic little place called Leifur, on the shores of Lake Winnipeg. For him, it was the realization of a dream: a place where he might live in peace and write — although the grim life of principal at Gladstone would return in the fall.

To help pay their debts, Tina, who had passed Grade 11, decided that in the fall she would go back to work. There was no job for her at Gladstone, but Grove learned from the inspector that schools were being opened in newly settled areas. There, many of the children could not speak English and Tina's knowledge of German from her Mennonite family would be a godsend.

One day Grove set off with the local inspector to find Tina a school. As they drove north through the lonely forests his spirit expanded. This was what he had come to Canada to find. The roads in some places were hardly more than trails; the landscape, fragrant and fresh with poplar, aspen and spruce was untouched. The school they found was in a German district near Falmouth, close to the end of steel on Lake Winnipeg. A cottage was provided for the teacher. It was as desolate as Grove could have wished; the nearest farm was a mile away. He saw it as a place where he could live and work — even though it was Tina who was to live there. What she would think of it didn't occur to him. He returned home in a glow of excitement, describing it as a haven of peace and beauty. He neglected to mention that wolves howled around the place at night, but then, he liked wolves. Tina, at that point, was only worried about the distance from Gladstone, where he would be teaching all winter. It was thirty-four miles as the crow flies — farther by road. Even Leifur, where Grove would be teaching for two months of the summer, was twenty-six miles away. He reassured her: he would get a bicycle, and then when the snow came he would get a horse. He would visit her every weekend.

For Tina, life in the wilderness all week was terrifying, especially when winter arrived. There was bush and dense forest all around her, swamps, into which men and horses had been sucked never to re-appear, and traces of devastating forest fires. The wolves came close to the cottage at night looking for food. She lived for the week-ends, sitting up late Friday nights with a lantern in her window, waiting for her husband.

But at school her terrors were hidden. Every morning she waited, little May at her side, as twenty-eight children, aged five to fifteen appeared out of the swamp. She was a kind of angel sent to these people; they responded with gratitude and affection and brought her eggs, milk and meat.[22]

Grove, meanwhile, was supremely happy, at least during his long drives and his snug week-ends with his family. He abandoned his bicycle when the snow fell, and bought a horse and buggy. Then he bought a second horse and a small sleigh called a cutter. He loved his rides and never failed to reach the cottage, fighting his way through blizzards and fog. Writing about this year in his autobiography, he said, "Today, it seems to have been the happiest year of our lives."[23]

At Gladstone, however, things were going from bad to worse. He became more contemptuous, the people more hostile. At last he could bear no more, and on March 1, 1918, he resigned as principal of the Gladstone School. The School Board promptly accepted his resignation and hired somebody else at a higher salary![24]

It was not difficult to get a new job and Grove moved to Ferguson, only four miles from Falmouth. He lived in the cottage with Tina and May and drove the few miles to his own school in the morning. He relaxed; he was not called an alien here — everyone was German.

His own pupils, like Tina's, struggled out of the bush every morning to school — and Grove's imagination was caught again, as it had been by the boys striving to learn at Haskett. Len Sterner, the youthful, struggling hero of *The Yoke of Life* was growing clearer in his mind. The Big Grassy Marsh country near Falmouth and Ferguson was to become the setting for several novels.

IN THE SUMMER of 1919, Philip and Tina were faced with a decision. Grove had had a serious accident with the horse and buggy. A dog had leapt at the horse's nose and bitten it, the horse had bolted, the buggy had rolled into the ditch and Grove's back was injured. He was in bed thereafter for months at a time, suffering intense pain and recurring paralysis. He feared permanent disablement and both he and Tina wondered how much longer he would be able to teach. Her temporary certificate was about to expire. If she attended Normal School she would receive a permanent certificate.

With reluctance on both sides at the thought of further separation, they decided that she should go to Winnipeg for five months to attend the Normal School. This meant that Grove would look after May; it also meant that he had to find a school close enough to Winnipeg so that Tina could visit them from time to time. He eventually decided on one at Eden, where he was appointed principal of the Consolidated Intermediate School. Eden was a tiny village in the foothills of Riding Mountain on the road between Dauphin and Neepawa. Even there commuting from Winnipeg was difficult; the nearest railway station was at Neepawa, eleven miles south.

In August, a depressed family set out for Winnipeg to install Tina in a boarding house. When they said good-bye at Union Station, four-year old May wept inconsolably.

For Tina, it was a time of bitter loneliness. She remembered later, "Eden was far enough from Winnipeg that I didn't get home as often as I would have liked to. And I was so desperately homesick; I could have died of homesickness. And I would walk down the street and ahead of me I'd see some tall, slender, good-looking man, and I would always say, 'Oh, that looks like Phil,' just to find out that it wasn't he.[25]

Grove, meanwhile, had installed himself and May in a shabby, run-down house which he disliked intensely. A kind neighbour came to his rescue and looked after May with her own child during the day. After school he would come to call for her and they would go home together. Early in the evening, after he had cooked supper and tucked May into bed, Grove was left to himself. He wrote.

ONE WEEK-END in early fall, Tina came home for a visit. Her tall husband greeted her happily. He showed her the first three chapters of a book which he called "Seven Drives Over Prairie Trails," a

collection of essays about seven of the trips he had made from Gladstone to Falmouth during the winter of 1917-1918. It was to become
his first published book, *Over Prairie Trails*. Tina returned to Winnipeg in better spirits, confident that her husband's writing career had
begun.

Grove worked feverishly in her absence. By the end of November,
Over Prairie Trails was finished and he had already begun work on
another collection of sketches which was to become *The Turn of the
Year*. In early December, Grove sent *Over Prairie Trails* to the publishers McClelland and Stewart in Toronto. On December 19 they
replied. They wished to publish the book the following autumn.

There was great excitement in the Grove household. Tina completed her Normal School course at Christmas and decided that she
would take on the support of the family while Grove wrote. Besides
being totally caught up in his writing, he was still suffering from the
crippling pain resulting from his accident and it was difficult for him
to endure standing in the classroom. He resigned his position at Eden
and in January, 1920, they moved to Ashfield, twenty miles north of
Winnipeg. Tina became the breadwinner.

McClelland and Stewart were greatly interested in Grove's work.
They wanted to see his next book of sketches, but instead, he sent
them part of a huge manuscript, called "The Immigrant," about his
early years wandering through North America as a salesman, hobo
and farmhand. Their reply on receiving this was more than encouraging: "We think you have a very important book in this, and shall
be glad to receive later on any additional chapters."[26] By the end
of April Grove had finished "The Immigrant" and sent it off.

Grove's health always improved when life itself seemed better. His
back ceased to trouble him. He began to work on three books: *The
Yoke of Life; Our Daily Bread,* his study of a patriarchy using some
details from Tina's family at Rush Lake; and *Settlers of the Marsh,*
a book suggested by a lonely white house he had seen on his drives
from Gladstone to Falmouth. But when summer came the bottom
fell out of the world. McClelland and Stewart wrote to say that they
would be unable to publish *Over Prairie Trails* because of sudden
financial difficulties. They returned "The Immigrant," unable to find
an American publisher. Grove was to learn that American publication
was necessary for large scale distribution of a Canadian book.

Grove was not only devastated by the disappointment, he was ashamed that he had failed his wife. He made another attempt to sell "The Immigrant," sending it at Tina's suggestion, to the magazine *The Saturday Evening Post*. It was returned. Grove's back seized up again, leaving him in excrutiating pain. There were doctors' bills and growing debts.

It became clear that Grove must go back to teaching. Both he and Tina applied in Eden; Grove was appointed principal of the new high school and Tina teacher to the upper public-school grades. They would be able to find their financial feet on combined salaries of a little over three thousand dollars.

Grove took steps towards a practical future. In December, 1921, he became a naturalized Canadian. He returned to his studies and in May, 1922, received his Bachelor of Arts degree from the University of Manitoba. But while he had been conscientious about making the right moves, his emotional state was working against him. Depressed by the blow to his writing ambitions, he was at his dour worst in Eden. He and the School Board were soon at odds and he resigned his position before the end of May.

Rapid City, north of Brandon, was Grove's next home and was to remain so for seven years. Grove became high school principal at a salary of twenty-two hundred dollars and Tina, who would from now on use the Anglicized, adult version of her name, Catherine, became teacher of the senior public-school grades. They were relatively rich and bought a Ford car. Rapid City was a place of beginnings and endings; the last prairie town where Grove lived, the culmination of the western experiences which were to result in the novels that created his reputation.

HARDLY HAD CATHERINE and Philip settled into their new jobs when the galley proofs of *Over Prairie Trails* arrived from McClelland and Stewart. The book was to be published after all!

A small printing of one thousand copies appeared in the fall of 1922 and sold out. There was a second edition in the fall of 1923 which didn't do as well, but for all its limited sales *Over Prairie Trails* announced the arrival of a compelling new writer.

The book is permeated with joy — the only book of Grove's to have this quality. It comes from his delight in the nature he observes from his sleigh and from the loving detail which he applies to its description. But it must also be admitted that a good deal of his happiness is due to his weekly, Friday night departures from Gladstone. The town is not mentioned much, but it is always there, the force that makes nature seem so pure by contrast. The book, for all its charm, is a revelation of Grove in flight. The dangers of fog that shrouds the world and leaves him directionless, or snowdrifts so deep that one covers the treetops, are as nothing compared to the dangers of man and all his works. Indeed, there is exultant masculine triumph in his descriptions of the manner in which he overcomes natural hazards. Will he make it to the little cottage where his wife and child wait? He always does, and there is much tenderness in his descriptions of his arrivals, when the little girl climbs out of bed in her nightie to sit on his knee.

Of all the animals and birds he lingers over, it is a lone wolf, who takes to waiting for him at a familiar corner, that stands out. Grove saves scraps of bacon from the sandwiches which his wife has made and drops them from the sleigh, turning to watch the lean outcast, as though he sees a reflection of himself.

Over Prairie Trails was widely reviewed; it was applauded as a genuinely original book, one which caught the mood of the prairie landscape and hinted at the lives of the settlers. It was a portrait of the land which every prairie dweller recognized as authentic and which had never before been rendered with such loving attention.

IN THE LIBRARY of Wesley College in Winnipeg, the doughty Scot librarian, John McLean, made his way across the room to Arthur Phelps. He placed a book firmly in front of him. "Ha'e ye read the buik?" he demanded. Phelps, startled, said he had not. "Read it nuw," said McLean.[27]

Phelps read *Over Prairie Trails*. He was head of the English department at Wesley College, a shrewd, kindly man in his thirties. He and his friends in eastern Canada formed an influential network in the Canadian literary world, and they were always on the alert for Canadian writers. They, like many Canadians, had begun to feel a new, proud nationalism. This was largely the result of the war, for

Canada had played a significant part. Half a million men had fought, many of them in frightful trench and gas warfare. With this kind of contribution behind her, Canada was demanding greater autonomy in commonwealth councils and Quebec was making even stronger claims for greater independence from London. In painting, national awareness had produced the Group of Seven, artists who brought a brutal landscape alive. Poetry in the twenties was marked by the appearance of major figures — E. J. Pratt, Dorothy Livesay, and the Montreal group: A. M. Klein, F. R. Scott, Leo Kennedy and A. J. M. Smith. Fiction remained strangely lonely. Morley Callaghan emerged as the shining light — and Grove. Grove, with his persistent view of himself as the neglected artist, never saw that with his first book he stepped onto an almost empty stage before a waiting audience.

In March, 1923, a short time after the publication of *Over Prairie Trails,* Grove attended a teachers' convention in Winnipeg. Arthur Phelps was one of the speakers and he made it a point to meet the author of *Over Prairie Trails*. It was not difficult to find him. ". . . there was a tall man towering over the shoulders of his fellows, with an austere look on his face as if he were self-distinguished from the group, a little stooped. And I went over to him and I said, 'Is this Mr. Grove?' And with an accent, he acknowledged that he was Grove. When I talked to him I found him friendly; it was probably natural that he should be interested in one who was interested in him because at that time he was an unknown writer, and he was, I suppose, sensible of his own literary isolation. There was a quality of maturity about him; he was no tyro; he was no boy among those teachers. He was very much a man, and *the* man."[28] Arthur Phelps introduced Grove to Watson Kirkconnell, his colleague at Wesley College and a distinguished scholar and poet. These two would later move heaven and earth to help him.

Meanwhile, McClelland and Stewart, pleased by the critical acclaim which had greeted *Over Prairie Trails,* was urging Grove to send them the companion volume, *The Turn of the Year*. In January, 1923, he did so. McClelland and Stewart did not like it. There was too much detailed description of nature and it lacked the dramatic suspense of the traveller struggling to reach home which had brought *Over Prairie Trails* alive.[29] Grove rewrote *The Turn of the Year* which, as we know it, is an exultant celebration of a wildly vivid nature; it introduces man, however, and is therefore a step closer to the novels which were to follow.

Three of the vignettes in the book describe a humble farming couple. We see them first in the shy rapture of courtship; then as parents of young children in the full vigour of young adulthood, loving each other and the honest farming which they do from dawn to dusk; and finally as old people, their children gone, sitting in the sun and holding hands while still mourning the death of a son who was drowned years ago. There is naïve charm in these three sketches; they are sentimental but they reflect Grove's search for an ideal. Farming was to remain Grove's conception of man's noblest occupation.

Interwoven around these figures and others, including Grove and his family, there are descriptions of nature — a nature that is often violent. Thunder roars like "a hundred lurching freight trains",[30] the northern lights are imaged as "a great stir and commotion going on in the heavenly halls."[31] Even though nature calms down from time to time, as in the blossom season, man is fairly swamped, and survives, one feels, only on sufferance. He is the humble observer; nature is the star.

The Turn of the Year appeared in November, 1923, with an introduction by Arthur Phelps which offered the first public information about Grove to curious readers. It contained the germ of the Grove legend which was to persist for years until recently questioned. Phelps said that Grove was born in Europe (he didn't say where) in 1872 and had travelled widely. He had been in Canada in 1893, had left and returned in 1896. "He has been writing for more than twenty-five years. . . . His manuscripts — novels, stories, sketches, poems — lie piled in his desk. . . ."[32]

EVERYTHING HAD BEEN going so well. He had published two books. True, they were hardly best-sellers — *The Turn of the Year* did not sell well although it was sympathetically reviewed — but, they were a beginning. Even better, he had another book, a novel, which was such an advance on the tentative steps of the essays that he was gripped by excitement whenever he thought of it. It was to become *Settlers of the Marsh*.

Furthermore, now that he had his university degree, he could look forward to an advancing career in education, and at the moment he and Catherine were making a decent living between them. Catherine was as usual arousing admiration for her work and she had started a Wolf Cub Pack. Even he was fitting into the community and had directed a play for the Anglican Church.[33] Then there was little May — delightful, sweet-natured and clever. At seven she was perhaps rather grown-up in her ways — the close companion of adoring parents. It pleased Grove that she knew the Latin names for all the botanical specimens which he still lovingly gathered. Even his back no longer troubled him.

But Grove was growing deaf. He had been aware for some time that his hearing was poor; now he began to feel as though he were drowning in a sea of deafness. Whenever Grove felt that fate had struck him an unfair blow, he grew cantankerous. He had a dispute with the School Board over a discipline problem; angrily he resigned on November 11, 1923. Another man was hired who proved incompetent and Grove was re-hired in January to complete the year. It was his last term of full-time teaching.

Catherine had made up her mind that he should give it up. He wanted to write and his hearing, like his back, was a decided handicap in the classroom. In September, 1924, she was appointed principal of the public school in Rapid City; now, with effort, they could live on her salary until his books began to sell. *She* had no doubt that he would soon be a successful writer and she was a woman to stick by her beliefs. Arthur Phelps described her as "one of those women who comes into a room and stands in her own right, if you know what I mean? And I think there was constantly operative devotion between those two. She was committed to the idea that her man was a great writer, and I think he tended to assume that there was something in that."[34]

The book which now engrossed Grove was an early version of *Settlers of the Marsh,* which he called "Pioneers" or "Latter-Day Pioneers." In the summer of 1923 the family had gone off for a holiday to a remote beach on Lake Winnipeg, taking two tents and the manuscript of "Pioneers" in their Ford car. Every morning Grove had retired to a clump of willows and struggled with his book. At the end of the holiday, two parts of what was to be a giant three-volume panorama of pioneer life were complete.

In January, 1924, he sent the manuscript to McClelland and Stewart who rejected it. They had lost money on the second edition of *Over Prairie Trails* and *The Turn of the Year* and they were not prepared to try again. Grove sent it to Macmillan, who liked it but wanted it shortened considerably. Grove was not certain that this was advisable, so he appealed to his friend Arthur Phelps, asking him to read it. Phelps was greatly impressed, but he too advised strenuous cutting. Convinced, Grove did so and was ready to try again.

Meanwhile, the ever-helpful Phelps was laying elaborate plans for the publication of *Settlers of the Marsh*. He arranged for Grove to address a meeting of the Canadian Authors' Association in Winnipeg — a meeting which by great good fortune was to be attended by Lorne Pierce, editor of the Ryerson Press and a leading figure in Canadian publishing. With Phelps expertly handling the backstage action, Dr. Pierce was well and truly caught. His own description of the way the book came to be published reveals his awareness of being manipulated: "In 1924 I stopped off in Winnipeg on my way to the west coast, in search of authors for the Ryerson Press. At a lecture in Wesley College, Professor Arthur Phelps introduced me to Grove and told me that Grove had a novel that he would like me to read. I said that I would very much like to see the manuscript, but suggested that it would be wise to send it out to my office since my crowded schedule would not permit me to give it the attention at that time that it deserved. The next day I was invited by Professor and Mrs. Phelps to have afternoon tea in their charming home. The fireplace was blazing merrily, and we were having a happy reunion, when in walked Grove with a large manuscript under his arm. He was very tall and frail looking. I remember best his eyes, which were sad and searching. There was nothing that I could do under the circumstances but agree to look at the manuscript briefly before resuming my trip to Vancouver. I got into bed in the Fort Garry and as a matter of duty reached for Grove's manuscript. I read on forgetful of time. The phone rang very early in the morning and wakened me. Grove had asked me if I had had my breakfast, if not he was coming down. We had it served in my room. I told Grove I had been unable to lay down his manuscript and had read it on into the morning. I was so deeply impressed as a matter of fact, that I assured him of publication. He seemed pleased but not unduly elated, especially when I told him that the great length of the manuscript would require drastic cutting. There was an episode in the story that did not seem to me essential, and I felt that those few pages would cause more trouble than they were worth. Some people would read this incident, and miss the strength and excellence of the whole book. Grove was white with anger, and with surprising vehemence declared that he would vouch for its accuracy. He gave the impression that he had either been personally involved or knew intimately a similar situation. He made it seem that his integrity was at stake. I said that an editor was bound at some time or other to fight for his life, but he ought to make sure that he chose the battle ground himself and that no one else chose it for him. Since he felt as he did, I would accept it, and go the full distance with him."[35] More was to be heard of the famous "episode" when *Settlers of the Marsh* was published in the summer of 1925.

It is the story of an innocent young Swedish immigrant, Niels Lindstedt, who comes to the marsh country of Ferguson-Falmouth. Niels has left poverty in Sweden, and a widowed mother forced to support her children by gathering wood and scrubbing the floors of the rich. The image of his mother, work-gnarled and devoted, has given Niels a straightforward conception of good and evil.

What will become of this innocent who goes to work in the Eden which Canada promises? At first, his qualities of strength, honesty and capacity for hard work serve him well. He clears land, acquires livestock and erects buildings which are as strong and straight as he, and he grows rich.

He runs into trouble when he encounters women. There are two in his life — one, the pristine Ellen Amundsen; the other, the temptress, Clara Vogel. Ellen, whom he dreams of as the mother of his children and the mistress of the fine house that he builds, turns him down for a horrifying reason. Her mother had been brutalized by her father, forced to slave on the farm and eventually dying a withered, wasted shadow as the result of one pregnancy after another — but not before extracting a promise from Ellen that she will never marry. Ellen not only tells Niels this but also tells him how she overheard her father force himself upon her unwilling mother. The resulting children are deliberately destroyed by her mother with her father's encouragement; before each birth her mother forced herself into crushing work and all the babies were stillborn.

Grove believed this to be the pioneer woman's plight. Later, in his autobiography, he said, ". . . it is the fact in pioneer countries. There, woman is the slave; . . . It is an unfortunate arrangement of nature that the burden of slavery, for such it is in all but name, should be biologically aggravated."[36]

Niels, sent away by Ellen, is now putty in the hands of the flirtatious Clara Vogel. She seduces him, and for a man of Niels's straightforward morality, there can be only one follow-up to physical intimacy — marriage. To Clara's surprise, he weds her the next day and takes her home to the farm.

This drastic mismating brings misery to both. Clara had married Niels because she believed that he loved her. Niels does not, and when Clara realizes this, she retreats to her room to read. Bored to distraction on the farm and desperate for companionship, she tries to attract his attention by making dubious trips to the city. Niels, quite sure that he has done the honorable thing in marrying her, is resentful because she will not help in the house. When he discovers that she is renowned as the local whore, his peasant pride is outraged, and he shoots and kills her.

Niels gives himself up to the authorities, expecting to be hanged. His solid character is to his advantage, however, and there is so much sympathy for him and so many witnesses to his up-until-now blameless past, that the murder charge is changed to manslaughter and he is sentenced to ten years of labour. After six, he is released for good behaviour. In a scene that suggests new maturity and the creation of a less fervent life based on his former achievements, he walks back to his farm. The old marsh, which had been a raw wilderness when he came in the strength of his young manhood, is now settled. Even his own farm reflects the investment he has made — not only in hard work, but also in human kindness. Friends whom he had helped have maintained it and he is richer than ever.

Alone in his house, he decides to go to Ellen and offer her at least friendship, for he senses that she is his true mate and that he must have some degree of intimacy with her. He finds a middle-aged woman with greying hair, quietly knitting in her kitchen. In a muted ending, which conveys the less exciting but more peaceful compromises of maturity, Ellen tells him that she has been wrong to reject him. She still longs for children and she consents to marry him.

On one level this is a book of wrong-doing and atonement. Niels sinned in allowing himself to be seduced by Clara; he has been cleansed by long years of suffering, finally becoming free to make a peaceful *détente* with fate. But Grove's message has more complex overtones. He projects a great deal of sympathy for Clara in one powerful scene when she shouts at Niels: "At the time I thought you were really in love with me, you really *wanted* me, you really wanted *me!* Not only a woman, any woman. Do you know what you did when you married me? You prostituted me if you know what that means. That's what you did. After having made a convenience of me. When you married me, you committed a crime!"[37] Clara is not especially admirable; she is shoddy and pitiful, but there is more to her than Niels guesses. She was victimized by his heavy-handed innocence and by his egocentric insistence on being honourable, when he married her without regard for her individuality or feelings. Niels has been guilty of cruelty, which he only dimly suspects, but he is also a victim, not so much of Clara, but of his own nature.

Settlers of the Marsh is an examination of the fate-ordained forces which shape our lives. We are manipulated not only by our natures which we cannot control, but by our environments which are equally unmanageable. Niels has been shaped by a simple peasant's background and the image of his mother. He was in no way prepared to be the husband of the sophisticated Clara. The long estrangement of the true mates, Niels and Ellen, was caused by the cruelty of Ellen's father to her mother, and by the backbreaking pioneer environment. All these things were beyond the control of the central characters.

When *Settlers of the Marsh* hit the bookstands, however, it was not the themes which made the impact, but the scene in which Ellen describes the crude sexual attacks of her father upon her mother. A tempest blew up in the teapots of respectable society: the book was declared "unfit for sixteen year old girls to read"; Catherine and Philip Grove were cut socially in Rapid City; it was rumoured that the book was banned from public libraries. Lorne Pierce, who had taken responsibility for publication and who had expressed nervousness over this very scene when he first read it in the Fort Garry Hotel, described the rather terrifying reaction: "When the book appeared in 1925, the roof fell in. . . . The publishing house was invaded by angry mail, and by delegations of various sorts, condemning us unsparingly. Dr. Fallis, head of the house, was enraged by it all, and I believed that my time had come. Then one day he walked into my office, and laid a letter before me having the Canadian Coat of Arms embossed on it. It read roughly as follows: 'I congratulate you on having the literary insight to recognize a work of art when you see it, and on having the courage to publish it. Yours truly, Arthur Meighen, Prime Minister.' The war was over."[38]

The Prime Minister was not the only one to come to Grove's aid. J. F. B. Livesay, General Manager of the Canadian Press and father of the poet, Dorothy Livesay, wrote:

March 19, 1926

Dear Mr. Grove:

You don't know the writer from a barrel of apples, but it is a fact that for a number of years I did the literary criticism for the Winnipeg Telegram. I am glad to note that "Settlers of the Marsh" has been banned from the Winnipeg Public Library — the best kind of advertisement for a young author. Toronto Public Library lets it out only to mature people of good character. I think it the finest contribution to Canadian literature of the past fifteen years and in my mind I set it alongside Turgenev.

Very faithfully yours,
J. F. B. Livesay,
General Manager,
Canadian Press.

Unfortunately, in spite of the book's fame, or ill-fame, *Settlers of the Marsh* did not sell well. The reviews were another matter, and Grove was to find that his books were lauded in the periodicals and ignored in the book stores. The power of *Settlers of the Marsh* was much admired.

There were, however, reservations about his writing style. The book had been cut strenuously and the version we know is full of dots, indicating removed passages; many people have complained that the effect is jerky. Besides, English was not Grove's first language. In his autobiography he wrote: ". . . in the attempt to set down my vision, I realized that I had at bottom no language which was peculiarly my own. In a way this was an advantage to me; I had half a dozen of them instead. But in another way, it was a disadvantage and even a misfortune; I lacked the limitation which is best for the profound penetration of the soul of a language. I ground my teeth in my struggles; and, for the moment, all my struggles were with words."[39]

Grove continued to struggle with words. His prose is formal; to the modern ear it sounds a little old-fashioned, as though he wanted to be absolutely sure that he was using correct English. His dialogue in particular sometimes sounds stiff, and unlike the language we hear spoken on every street corner. Grove is nearly always defined as a "realistic" writer, that is, a writer who uses detail, including dialogue, exactly as it is seen or heard. Grove was not realistic in this sense. His detail was selected to convey a truth as it was perceived from his point of view, and his dialogue reveals subjective, not objective, truth.

Grove was bitterly disappointed over the sales of *Settlers of the Marsh* but Arthur Phelps was hard at work again on his behalf. Both he and Watson Kirkconnell liked Grove's novel "The Immigrant," which was to become *A Search for America*. Grove had tried hard, without success, to have it published, and by this time the immediacy of the book had left him. "It seemed very juvenile to me, full of garrulity and even presumption. . . . The book impressed me like the ghost of a man who had died three decades ago."[40] He much preferred *Settlers of the Marsh,* perhaps because it was newer and closer to him. In any event, Phelps was pushing "The Immigrant." His summers were spent at Bobcaygeon, Ontario, with a coterie of his literary friends — W. A. Deacon, Literary Editor of *Toronto Saturday Night;* E. J. Pratt; Hugh Eayrs, president of Macmillan; Lorne Pierce. This time he turned his powers of persuasion on W.

A. Deacon. Deacon recalled the way in which Phelps manoeuvred him: ". . . he said that he had something very important to show me, and I was to come over and sit by the fire and he would show me this thing. And what he had in his hand was an enormous manuscript (I don't know how many pounds it would weigh) — *A Search for America,* and he wanted me to read the whole thing to impress me. I said, 'No, I'm not going to be nailed down to doing professional work here when I'm on holiday.' And I said, 'You read me one chapter.' And he read me one chapter and I said, 'Okay, that's fine,' I said, 'Now what is the problem?' He said, 'Grove can't get this thing published. His original publisher, McClelland and Stewart had not done well with *Over Prairie Trails,* and I think *The Turn of the Year* also came from them. They couldn't meet expenses on it and didn't want to go ahead, and he hadn't any other publisher.' And I said to Phelps — I said, 'I can get this published easily enough — there is no trouble about it at all. It's first-rate stuff.' And I sent it down to Miller at Graphic whom I knew, and the covering letter was the shortest that I ever wrote. It contained two words. I simply said, 'Print this,' and he did. He thought as highly of it as I did."[41]

Not knowing all this, Grove was in a state of gloom. He had had another accident — this time falling off a woodpile while trying to reach a door key which lay on a windowsill. He was in bed, being attended by doctors who exasperated him and did not help.

There was one encouraging note. *The Winnipeg Tribune* asked him to write twenty-six short stories for their magazine section. They were all published between October, 1926, and April, 1927, bringing Grove twenty dollars a story. Grove, as he said, "ground out" these stories while lying in bed. Some of these, with other short stories, were published after his death in a volume called *Tales from the Margin.*

In February, 1927, Phelps and Kirkconnell came to visit him, hoping to cheer him up with news of the acceptance of *A Search for America by* Graphic Publishers in Ottawa. Grove was not especially enthusiastic and thought it needed rewriting. Lying in bed, he again cut it enormously and by June, somewhat recovered, he had finished it.

Then he and Catherine set out with May on a short motor trip to southern Manitoba and to Winnipeg to see Arthur Phelps. They were surprised when May, who loved travelling and was a good companion, suddenly asked to be taken home.

MAY GROVE WAS nearly twelve years old. She had passed Grade 6 with honours and she and another little girl in Grade 8 had received the highest marks in the school sewing competition. Her mother had photographed her with the rest of the class in the embroidered apron she had made.

She died very suddenly just before her twelfth birthday in 1927, shortly after the family returned from Winnipeg. She had developed acute appendicitis, been rushed to the hospital in Minnedosa and died under the ether.

May was buried at Rapid City, in the cemetery on a hilltop east of town. Watson Kirkconnell, who was standing beside Grove, remembered his grief: ". . . he was asking me with insistence what it all meant. How this calamitous bereavement that had overtaken their home could possibly have meaning."[42]

May's gravestone bears the lines, adapted from Shelley:

> She is a portion of the loveliness
> Which once she made more lovely.[43]

Grove wrote a long poem at this time called *The Dirge,* with the line: "My roots are growing down into a grave." Catherine flung herself into her teaching in an attempt to keep busy.

IRONICALLY, GROVE'S CAREER now blossomed into its greatest success. *A Search for America* was published in the fall of 1927, and became far and away the most acclaimed of his books, both critically and commercially.

A Search for America is about a young European immigrant's struggle to find a place where he can fit in the new land. Passing through it, he observes the values held in America. For Phil Branden, it is necessary to discover lasting values with which he can exist, because a return to Europe is not an alternative. His once wealthy family has squandered its money, both his parents are dead, and he is socially cut at home by his erstwhile friends because, in Europe, without money or position, one is not accepted. The legend of America proclaims that every man can find his niche on merit. It remains to be seen whether the legend holds up. Branden, eager and hopeful, believes that the true spirit of America was embodied in Abraham Lincoln, and it is his noble ideal which he seeks.

When the book appeared, there was great curiosity about whether Phil Branden's story was Grove's, for it was known that Grove had spent time in the United States before coming to Canada. He was asked so often whether *A Search for America* was autobiographical that finally, for the fourth edition, he wrote a preface explaining that fact and fiction are inevitably mingled in imaginative literature. The preface did not do much to satisfy the curious.

Certainly the sketchy account of Branden's early life in Europe before arriving on American shores contains the germ of the Grove story which appeared full blown in his autobiography, *In Search of Myself*. He tells of a giant, six-foot-five father and a "Junoesque" mother who swept across Europe in a series of tours with her son in her wake. The boy attended universities at Paris, Bonn, Oxford and Rome, and mingled in fashionable, artistic circles that included Gide and Régnier. When his mother died and his father's money had vanished, the boy cast his fortune with America's. The description of the culturally satisfying though restrictive Europe is used as a dramatic contrast to the raw America with its supposedly wide-open opportunities. There is more than a hint of homesickness in the early part of the book, although it is mixed with a sense of excitement at being independent and adventurous.

Landed in Toronto, the only job the shy, formal-mannered Branden can find is as a bus boy in a second-rate restaurant on Yonge Street. The dining room is a smooth scene of white tablecloths and deftly served meals but, below stairs, the staff washrooms are grimy and smelly; the kitchen is a grease-spattered nightmare of crashing dishes and obscenity where a waiter spits into the soup of a patron as a joke. One wonders whether the restaurant is Grove's metaphor for America; efficient on the surface, squalid beneath.

Leaving the restaurant for New York and the eastern United States he takes on one tacky job after another — mostly for fraudulent book companies. Finally sickened (and in a typically Grove reaction), he flees civilization and sets out on foot, heading west, following the myth of the frontier like many before him. His battered spirits are nursed back to health after close solitary contact with nature, and especially during a trip down the Mississippi River on a raft, like Huck Finn. The river's healing powers are so great that he begins to feel the first faint stirrings of a need to rejoin man. When he meets his first human in months, he is able to reach out to him with help — a move which will lead him back into the world. He saves an old man from drowning and then follows him to his shack to live with him for a few days. This hermit does not speak; he lives without reference to progress, education or culture. The simple outer life suggests a rich inner one, and Branden, now refreshed and more balanced, leaves to find his way back to the world of man.

In the centre of America he finds the spirit of Abraham Lincoln, the justification of all his suffering and privation, and a hope for the future, which will sustain him. Staggering up to a poor farmhouse, ill with pneumonia, he is taken in by a poor young couple who, with a devoted old doctor, nurse him back to health. Good men, it seems, do exist.

Grove, in his autobiography, was to say that he had spent some time as a hobo and an itinerant farmhand. We do not know if this is true, but in *A Search for America* he describes a great swarming mass of homeless, wandering men, living in camps, huddling under railways and living a rootless life. They are like a current, eddying and swirling around the rocks of the middle class. He uses this remarkable section to make some caustic comments on the place of the immigrant in American society, for although not all the hobos are foreign speaking, many of them are, and together they represent those people who do not fit, either because of circumstance or by choice. The immigrant, Grove shows us, is not only cruelly ignored, he is also discriminated against by those who have been established for a few scant generations and who are now scornful of the most recent arrivals. Although many of the tramps say that they are proud of their free lives, Branden, who is essentially middle class, views them as the casualties of the new world; by now he is ready to give up wandering himself and settle down. He has "a craving for peace with society, a desire to take root somewhere and to fit myself into this scheme of life in the western hemisphere as a cog which furthered its design in some definite way."[44] Before he does so, though, he catches a glimpse of privilege in America and it leads him to think that some of Europe's worst traditions have been transplanted. He goes to work for a rich man who owns a huge farm, acquired through his father's lucky purchase of cheap land. His house is called the White House, a smaller version of the American president's mansion. The outspoken Branden tells the millionaire farmer that he is like the European nobility, ruling land which by rights should be spread among many.

Branden has assessed America. He has found scurrilous evil and simple nobility; on balance he believes that the ideal lives, and that he will work towards its realization. He decides to become a teacher to immigrants. "I wanted to assist them in realizing their promised land."[45] To do this, he goes, as it happens, to Canada, but it is the entire North American culture which is embraced in his optimism.

After absorbing this strongly positive ending, the reader is startled to find a footnote near the end of the book, inserted by Grove just prior to publication. "I must repeat that this book was, in all its essential parts, written decades ago," he states. "I have since come to the conclusion that the ideal as I saw it and still see it has been abandoned by the U.S.A. That is one reason why I became and remained a Canadian."[46]

What happened? Something certainly. *A Search for America* is the most hopeful of Grove's books; it is the only one which shows the fulfilment of a dream. Although it is generally thought that Grove did not write his story of the immigrant until 1920, he had always claimed that it was the first he had written in North America and that it was drafted even before he came to Canada. The youthful, optimistic tone suggests that he may have been speaking the truth. The footnote and all his other more pessimistic books give some evidence that he went through a faith-destroying experience after writing *A Search for America*. Since his life in the United States is part of the Grove mystery, no one knows what this crushing experience may have been, although no doubt somebody will find out one of these days.

A Search for America received rave reviews and the book thrust Grove into the next stage of his career — lecturer and public figure.

GRAHAM SPRY READ *A Search for America* with more than the interest of a reader for a good story. He was the newly appointed Secretary of the Association of Canadian Clubs, an old organization, but one which had taken on new vitality with the rebirth of Canadian nationalism after the war. Its purpose was to stimulate Canadian awareness by arranging speaking tours across the country. As Spry read *A Search for America,* it struck him that Grove would make an ideal lecturer. He wrote to Arthur Phelps and asked him whether Grove could speak as well as write. He proposed three tours, the first to include sixteen lectures throughout Ontario, paying twenty-five dollars a lecture. Phelps of course knew that Grove was a good speaker and was elated at this opportunity for his protegé. He was sure that the publicity created by the tours would sell Grove's books.

Grove was just as pleased by the offer and accepted at once. As he prepared for his first tour, a new side of his personality emerged. He had lived austerely in Canada, but now it seemed that he was greatly interested in clothes and wished to be perfectly dressed for his public appearances.

He went to Winnipeg to stay with Arthur Phelps while he shopped. His appearance in faultless tailoring gave the shrewd Phelps cause for reflection: "He found out by some means, I don't know what, a tailor who in Winnipeg was reputed to be *the* tailor for *the* people, and he got measured and fitted, and one day the parcels came to our house at 72 Eastgate. A full outfit of beautifully tailored clothes: a dress suit, morning coat, striped trousers, everything. . . . Grove set out to try on his clothes, and we had a merry time making Grove walk back and fro and do his poses and pretend that he was before the Canadian Club offering his lecture, his opening remarks; and after it was all over Mrs. Phelps and I wondered whether Grove was slipping back into something with which he had been, all his life as a young man, familiar, or whether he was materializing a dream. And to this day I don't know."[47]

ON FEBRUARY 27, 1928, a tall, distinguished man, impeccably dressed, stood before his first audience in Portage La Prairie. He spoke on "Nationhood," and he urged Canada to strive for her own unique character and forget the chase after wealth. ". . . Greece decayed when it grew rich; . . . Rome never developed that indigenous culture of which the republic had exhibited the germs because it grew rich before it had done so. Wealth produces at no time true values."[48] Grove had a dramatic instinct for public speaking. He was still somewhat crippled by back troubles and appeared leaning on two canes — but the impression he made was, if anything, accentuated by this. His deafness did not seem to bother him at all.

He moved from triumph to triumph, crescendoing in Ottawa where a banquet was held in his honour by the executive of the Canadian Clubs. It was attended by bank presidents, newspaper editors, at least one senator and several millionaires. The American consul invited him to lunch and he was entertained by J. S. Woodsworth, who was the leader of the CCF party.[49] His second Ottawa address, to the Women's Canadian Club, was more than sold out and a larger hall had to be hired.

In addition to all the acclaim, several people seem to have hinted to Grove that various plum jobs might be his for the asking. In his daily letters home to Catherine he reported excitedly that a job in the Immigration Department had been suggested or perhaps a position as Professor of 'Moderns' or Classics in a university.[50] The people who made these casual suggestions seemed to have no idea just how much a steady income would mean to Grove. All the so-called offers vanished like confetti after a wedding when the excitement of the lectures had passed.

Toronto was as dazzling as Ottawa. He addressed five hundred men, including the best-known literary figures at the University of Toronto, and they "went frantic over my address,"[51] as he told Catherine. The poet E. J. Pratt entertained for him, and he met Hugh Eayrs, president of Macmillan of Canada.

Catherine, at home in Rapid City, teaching and living with memories of May, must have been cheered by his letters and the gifts of clothes which he sent her. From Port Arthur he wrote: "When I came to the statement of what I found in the west, there was applause after every sentence. . . . Financially I believe it will be our salvation. All these people who now know me will want to read my next book too."[52] From Toronto: "Newspaper men stood lined up when the train pulled in, to interview me. Photographers clicked their cameras."[53]

When Grove returned home at the end of six weeks, his financial situation was much improved and he settled down to prepare *The Yoke of Life* for publication — it had been bought by Hugh Eayrs of Macmillan as a result of their meeting, along with *Our Daily Bread*. He assembled essays to be published as *It Needs to be Said* and typed out the final version of the book he wanted to call "Chronicles of Spalding District" but which became *Fruits of the Earth*.

Summer came and Catherine's school term was over. To distract her from memories of May, Grove took her on a drive through lovely countryside in the Maritimes and then to eastern Canada where she met several of his friends.

At home in the fall, she returned to teaching while Grove prepared for his second lecture tour to western Canada, beginning September 9. He was troubled by the fact that she still had to work — he had hoped that his lecture tours would sell enough books so that she could retire — but so far they were a long way from financial security. The tour itself was a disappointment. The fame of Frederick Philip Grove had not caught on in the far west — at one place they called him Frederick Philip Cook — and he was discouraged and began to feel tired. At least, he wrote to Catherine wearily, the lectures were a way to earn money.[54]

However, *Our Daily Bread* appeared about the time he set off and, reflecting the glow of his public appearances, had become a financial success. It was published simultaneously by Macmillan in Toronto and New York, and Jonathan Cape in London.

Sometime about 1924, Grove had embarked on a trilogy about the family or, more truly, the disintegration of the family. Observing the changing times and particularly the movement away from the farms, he had come to the conclusion that the basic unit of society, the family, was about to disappear. Grove believed that living close to the land, in harmony with nature, man remains stable and noble. City living is synonymous with chaos.

Of the three books in the trilogy, *Our Daily Bread,* dealing with patriarchy, is the only one published. "The Weatherhead Fortunes," about a matriarchy, and "Jane Atkinson," about the children, were both turned down by publishers.

The patriarch, John Elliot, is one of the titanic, inflexible farmers who stalk through many of Grove's books. All Grove's heroes have a dream, which once conceived, turns into a relentless master. The protagonist is helpless to sway his course against the dictates of the dream. For John Elliot, the dream is to found a large family on his farm near Sedgeby, Saskatchewan, and then to see his children settled around him in his old age, engaged in the old life of the soil. The book is set in the short grass country around Rush Lake where Catherine Grove's family lived; there are strong similarities between the Elliot family and the Wiens.

John Elliot fulfils the first part of his dream; he and his wife, Martha, have twelve children. He has been fruitful and multiplied, like the patriarchs of the Old Testament who stand as his prototypes. He runs into trouble when he tries to force his children into carrying out his private ambition. He is surprised to find, as they grow, that they are not only combinations of his wife and himself, but they also have a third ingredient — themselves. He had not counted on this. All his children, and even his wife, rebel at being forced into the mould he has prepared for them.

The adhesive which holds all Grove's fictitious families together is the wife-mother. She, as in the case of Martha Elliot, acts as an intermediary between the stern father and the children. Essentially, she is on the side of the children, and she uses her power over the father to cajole him into a gentler parenthood. Unfortunately for John Elliot, Martha dies of cancer early in the book, and without her the family flies apart at the seams. The children are only too glad to escape his grim authority and while he admits sadly to himself that it was Martha, not he, whom the children loved, he blames two other forces for the family disintegration. One is the development of the sexual instinct which leads the children, one after another, into marriages — all of which John Elliot disapproves. The other is the lure of cities and towns, which in this phase of the country's development are growing and promise an easier life than the hard labour of the farm.

With his children gone, John Elliot is incapable of adjusting to the idea that the dream which has motivated his whole life will not be realized. Gradually he sinks into senility. He boards up part of his fine house and lives surrounded by dirt and disorder in the kitchen. He rents part of his land — the farm which had once been his pride. The only solution he can find after the flight of his children is to visit them one by one. He is hardly an easy guest, as he glowers with disapproval at all of them, and most of the children are happy to see him leave. He makes another attempt to gather them around him — he invites five who are in the neighbourhood to visit. None can be bothered; the truth is that they are afraid of their father. He waits day after day for a car which never comes and finally returns to the only activity he really understands: he ploughs his field.

In a powerful and moving ending we see the once proud patriarch reduced to a senile and demented Lear as he staggers on foot across miles of countryside towards his house after a last desperate visit to one of his children. Imagining that his comforting wife and the old ways are waiting for him there, he falls into his rotted old house to die. It is only after his death that his children finally gather around him again. Grove was to investigate the clash between the generations with greater and greater subtlety and insight in later novels.

GROVE WAS RIDING the crest of a wave. When he returned to Rapid City from his second lecture tour, *Our Daily Bread* was selling well; in the spring of 1929 his collection of essays and lectures, *It Needs to be Said,* would be published. Graham Spry asked him if he would be Associate Editor of the Canadian Club magazine, *The Canadian Nation,* and Grove accepted happily. He went off on his third and last lecture tour, from Montreal through the Maritimes, and repeated the brilliant success of his first tour.

A shadow fell with the publication of the essays. "*It Needs to be Said* has rather badly flopped," Hugh Eayrs wrote to him.[55] The book had seemed to be a good publishing venture, offering the reading public the chance to see what the smash hit of the lecture circuit had to say; but written, as most of it was, to be spoken, it contains a good deal of flourish and relatively thin substance. Grove, as a natural performer, knew that the personality of the lecturer is as important as what he says, if not more so. In the first three essays, however, even the personality comes through as a little uncertain, a combination of both arrogance and uneasiness, as though he were nervous that his credentials would not be accepted. Grove was a genuinely erudite man, but his insistence on his own sophistication undermines the effect in the book; obviously his powerful presence carried it on the platform. He preached that Canada should emulate the best in literature and embrace the simple life.

He continued to work on a revision of *Fruits of the Earth,* and he was working hard for *The Canadian Nation.* The May-June issue carried one of his short stories and besides, he was encouraging other writers to contribute. But his enthusiasm for the magazine was dashed in the summer of 1929 when the Association of Canadian Clubs decided to cease publication — it was too costly.

Grove was down, as only Grove could be. He wrote to Watson Kirkconnell: "I have done well last year; but there seems to be an end to it . . . I am tired of uncertainties. I am nearly 58 years old and want to look forward to a few yrs — if they are vouchsafed — of quiet settled life. It seems that Canada has nothing to offer me. There was talk of a salary in connection with lectures for the Canadian Clubs — of a sinecure in Ottawa — of editorial work for a publishing firm. Of all this nothing has come. I have a few thousand dollars in the bank (don't mention the fact); and I have 2 or 3 books ready for the press. . . . Mrs. G. has done her share; but I won't accept that any longer. . . ."[56]

PERHAPS IT WOULD be better to live in Eastern Canada. Grove was well known there so opportunities might be more plentiful and it would be an advantage to be near publishers. Besides, his spirit had been soothed by the adulation he had received during his lecture tour there. In Toronto he had stayed at the York Club and a valet had looked after his clothes; frankly, he had loved every moment of it. Who knew what splendours might appear in the future?

They were sure, at least, that they wanted to leave Rapid City. There, Grove said, ". . . every street and every corner was a reminder of May. If I suffered from tragic memories, my wife suffered from a mortal wound."[57] Catherine would be better away, but she suggested that they go, not to Eastern Canada, but to a shack in the wilderness where Grove could write and she could live in peace. There was one objection to this plan: they had decided to have another child, for without May, Catherine had said, "The terrible thing is that there is nothing left to worry about."[58] It would be difficult to bring up a child in the wilderness.

Then Hugh Eayrs wrote with exciting news. A reorganization of Macmillan was planned, and Eayrs was eager to include Grove on his staff. "I may buy this business entirely," he said. "If I do, I'll ask you to join me. If I don't I'll likely be able to make a proposal to you to come here and work editorially. I know the situation is urgent from your standpoint. All I can say now."[59]

The slender lifeline was enough. They abandoned all thoughts of going into the bush — although afterwards, when circumstances became difficult, Grove said that he always regretted it. On September 9, 1929, they packed their car and left the west for good.[60]

When Grove had arrived in Winnipeg seventeen years earlier, he had had a definite plan — to become a teacher and a writer. He had achieved both these aims, and found a happy marriage besides. When he left he had no plans whatever, except the vague offer from Hugh Eayrs. For the time being they had invitations to stay with friends; after that, "The Lord will provide."

So they spent a golden early fall in eastern Canada, staying with friends, and then came November with its chill air and the end of their brief, carefree days. They had nowhere to go. After leaving London, Ontario, they reached Toronto and Grove pulled the car up to the curb at Queen and Yonge. "What next?" he asked Catherine.

"Cross Yonge," she said.

They did, and drove all the way to Port Hope, where Grove asked again, "What next?"

"Turn towards Bobcaygeon," said Catherine.

By the time they reached Peterborough she had made up her mind. They would rent a cottage in Bobcaygeon, insulate it for the winter, and Grove would write.[61] They started work immediately, improving the cottage with hard-earned money from the lectures and successful books.

Earlier that fall, Grove had gone to Ottawa briefly at the invitation of Mrs. H. W. Cameron, a director of Graphic Publishers, the firm which had published *A Search for America*. During Grove's visit she had discussed with him a reorganization of the publishing company and the possibility of his joining it. In late November a letter came from Mrs. Cameron with a definite offer. Grove understood that he was being asked to become president of Ariston Publishers Ltd., a branch of Graphic Publishers. As nothing more had been heard of Hugh Eayrs' offer, Grove jumped at the chance. "I saw in a flash that here was an opportunity to make a certain amount of money by means other than writing."[62]

They moved to Ottawa in December, 1929, Grove bubbling over with enthusiastic plans. He and his staff would be courageous and publish Canadian books; Grove himself would edit a series of older Canadian books of historic interest. But money grew tighter and tighter during the Depression and without adequate funds many of the idealistic plans were curtailed or given up entirely. Grove discovered that his position as president was not as clearly defined as he had supposed; he complained that he did not have "a determining voice" in Graphic's affairs. Working in Ottawa was a more mundane experience than appearing as a lauded speaker. He was not lionized, and writing bitterly to Lorne Pierce later about his Graphic experiences, he said, ". . . in Ottawa, I lived in an isolation comparable to that of an Antarctic explorer. . . . How many of the Ottawa writers called on me or on my wife? Did Scott? Did Burpee? Did anyone? No, not one."[63] In truth, Grove was not altogether without friends, but by this time everything concerned with Ottawa had turned sour.

There was one bright spot, however. His son was born on October 14, 1930, and named Arthur Leonard after Phelps. They moved to a pretty house surrounded by an apple orchard on the Skead Road in Eastview, on the site of the present National Research Council. Grove, in spite of his discouragement over affairs at Graphic, was earning a salary of six thousand dollars and, feeling rather affluent, he could not resist buying a magnificent Chinese carpet. It was so splendid that it caused a certain amount of eyebrow raising among the more prosaic folk in Ottawa. One friend remarked stiffly that it seemed "to both my wife and myself, to be a little out of place in a summer cottage."[64] Leonard Grove has commented mildly that it was not a summer cottage: "It was our house. We lived in it."[65] Leonard still owns the famous carpet and it is as beautiful as ever.

There was another encouraging note and Grove was badly in need of encouragement. About the time Leonard was born, his seventh book and fourth novel, *The Yoke of Life* was published by Macmillan.

It had waited a long time for publication, conceived as it was during the days of Haskett and the happy time of Falmouth, Leifur and Ferguson. The barefoot children struggling out of the marsh to attend school were embodied in Len Sterner, the young boy of talent and ambition whose hopes were to be crushed by gruelling pioneer hardships. *The Yoke of Life* was the publisher's maudlin choice of title, replacing Grove's more straightforward "Equal Opportunities" or "Adolescence". Why Grove ever allowed the change is a mystery; he could be strong-minded enough when he chose.

Len Sterner is a boy born out of phase; his talents needed a more developed society, one in which his intellectual abilities could be nurtured. His younger brother, Charlie, is suited to the rhythmical, sane life of farming, raising a family, growing old — a life Grove still regarded as the best, for he has Len say, "We thinkers are rebels all; offspring of Satan. . . ."[66]

Like all Grove's men, Len is trapped by dreams which impose inexorable demands. With Len, Grove is able to show how the dreams are born in adolescence. The boy conceives three ambitions: the first is to "encompass all knowledge." A bright boy, he is encouraged by a school teacher to go on with his studies, and his ambitions are to become a learned professor. Then, typical of Grove's men, he senses that he needs a woman to complement his nature, and finds her while he is still an impressionable young schoolboy. Lydia Hausman is a pale, pretty girl, who is associated with the magic of the woods where Len sometimes meets her. Once he imagines that he sees a unicorn there, the symbol of purity, which as he stares at it disappears to become a common deer — all too symbolic of Lydia who runs away to the city to become a prostitute. Len, however, can never release himself from his vision of her as ideal woman. The third ambition is more spiritual. Grove often spoke of man's struggle between his "beasthood and his godhead"; it is his godhead which Len wants to realize — the best and the highest that is within him.

His attempts to learn are forever thwarted by the demands of the poor, stubbled farm where he lives with his mother, his step-father and his brother. Once a hailstorm destroys the crop and Len is sent away to work in a lumber camp to earn enough to pay the farm debt. Another time his step-father's horses are driven to their deaths in a swamp by wolves, and Len goes to work in the city as a coal hauler to make money to replace them.

Finally, after years of trying, he realizes that it is too late to encompass all knowledge, but at least he is still determined to achieve a certain splendour as a justification for his life. He decides that Lydia should be with him, and goes to the city to find her, wherever she may be. For months he haunts the theatres and night spots and, at last, one night when he is worn out and ill, he catches sight of her on the arm of an elderly protector. When he sees her, he collapses into one of those delirious illnesses which for Grove himself were always associated with emotional upheaval. For Lydia, after years of degradation, Len has become the embodiment of all that was worthwhile in the past. She becomes his devoted nurse and cares for him through months of semiconsciousness until spring, when he recovers.

Then begins a strange and, in its own way, a delirious ending. Len takes Lydia away to Lake Winnipeg, where they live in Grove's ideal surroundings, the pure wilderness which becomes a kind of enchanted forest echoing the Wagnerian crash of waves on rocks. The idyll ends, however, when Len forces a confession from Lydia about her life in the city. Faced with a horror that is too far from the dream to be endured, he takes the only possible course of action for a man of his high-minded temperament. In a boat during a storm, he lashes their bodies together with rope; the boat smashes into a rock and they are drowned together. The purified union is achieved in death.

Grove, however, does not leave us there. His purpose in *The Yoke of Life* had been to show that a person like Len is a sacrifice to the opening of new land. The next stage may be better for people like him, for at the moment of his death a child is born to his brother Charlie and his wife. "When, a week later, the new-born child was christened, he was given the name of Leonard, in commemoration of one who was dead and as a promise, perhaps, that he should have the opportunities which his older namesake lacked."[67]

The book received mixed reviews: on the one hand it was "a great novel" and "the way fiction ought to be written;"[68] on the other, Len's egomania was insufferable. Commercially, it flopped. The Depression was plodding along and four Grove books had come out in three years — perhaps too many for the market.

As a publisher, Grove was to find that his book was not the only one to fall flat. He had been responsible for the publication of *The Tide of Life* by Watson Kirkconnell and a novel by Ella B. Wallis, a writer whom he had encouraged when he was associate editor of *The Canadian Nation,* and neither did well. Then, Graphic Publishers, unable to pay their debts, went into bankruptcy.

Grove's fingers had been burned. His old forebodings that everything to do with cities and commerce meant trouble were justified. In March, 1931, he resigned from Graphic. From now on he would live as he had preached — on the land. With money that he managed to salvage from his investments and salary at Graphic he went out in search of a farm and bought one in Simcoe, Ontario.

ON LEONARD'S FIRST BIRTHDAY, October 14, 1931, Catherine and Philip Grove moved into their last home and the first that they had owned. The frame farmhouse was a handsome building, erected on the forthright, straight lines of the Ontario pioneers but embellished by a few bow windows. It was over one hundred and twenty-five years old; it stood on forty acres of fertile soil and was sheltered by a grove of cedar and spruce. Beyond, there were barns and sheds, more trees, a meadow and a little creek. Grove described it as "a loose-jointed, ramshackle affair of eight rooms, with floors of pine, two inches thick, which, in a century of hard use, under the hob-nailed shoes of pioneers, had been worn into a series of hills and valleys; with walls which had never been properly kept up but patched here and there as the necessity arose. The outside covering was of axe-hewn clap-boards hanging precariously on hand-forged, square nails which had rusted holes into the wood. Every breeze penetrated the worn-out shell. When I brought my fist against the bottom of the weather-boarding, a wave ran through the eaves; and of the last coat of white paint only the faintest traces were left. In places, one could see daylight through the walls from inside."[69]

House repairs would have to wait. Grove settled down to writing in the morning and farming in the afternoon. He bought six purebred jersey cows and, with his luck, the bottom immediately fell out of the milk market. Grove toiled on the farm, a man of fifty-two with a physique which had never been suited to hard labour. He hired a man, whom he could not afford, to help him. "Grove was no farmer!" a neighbour remarked. "He was a very impractical man. He depended on a man to do his farm work for him. About all that Grove got out of it was a rural place to live. You just can't farm that way, it's too expensive, and Grove didn't have the money."[70]

Catherine observed this for a few months and then took matters into her own hands. She opened a private school in the house in early 1932, beginning modestly with kindergarten, and then, when her younger sister Amanda arrived fresh from Normal School to help, she added a full public school curriculum. Catherine's retirement was over; for the remainder of Grove's life and until she was seventy-two, she kept house and taught. She was their main support for the rest of their lives.

Grove himself was scarcely an idle man, although in small town Simcoe the husband who sat on a lawn chair and thought, while his wife worked, was regarded askance. He taught French and Science in Catherine's school and he continued to produce and revise a stream of books. In 1933, *Fruits of the Earth* was published.

Grove had been fascinated by the way in which a pioneering district grows, from the moment when the first furrow is turned until it becomes a well-settled community. He was even more fascinated by the kind of man who can wrestle such a community into being. For the hero of *Fruits of the Earth* he created Abe Spalding, a titan and a natural leader. Abe has great capacities: he is powerfully built, shrewd, single-minded, hard, and driven to succeed. But he lacks sensitivity to other human beings and awareness of values beyond the material. In short, Abe is the masculine prototype. Grove's view of the division of human talents gave the feminine side an understanding of spiritual satisfactions. Many of Grove's men contain some of this feminine nature within them, and all but Abe search for a feminine counterpart to balance their masculinity. Abe possesses no feminine qualities, nor is there any real place within his scheme of things for a woman. Like all Grove's heroes, he is at the mercy of his nature. He builds because he must.

Unfortunately Abe marries, and his wife, Ruth, finding no place for herself in his headlong pursuit of success, grows listless, fat and dowdy. She and their four children live a life apart from Abe's.

Grove had no liking for the driven, hard type of man he portrayed in Abe, but he did have admiration for his ability. There is great zest in the writing as he describes Abe's struggles to create his farm, to accumulate more and more land, to buy livestock and to grow wealthy. Abe not only becomes the richest farmer in the neighbourhood, he assumes leadership. With calm authoritarianism, he steers through the first school and the first roads, and he becomes the first reeve. The community is named Spalding District after him.

The climax of Abe's creative powers is reached in the building of his magnificent house and barns. Nothing but the best will do, and for months his yard swarms with derricks and excavating machines. The electrical installations alone are a masterpiece of engineering. House, granaries, pigpens, hen house and yard are all electrified. One triumphant night the electrician switches on the whole system and a blaze of light bursts into the sky. Grove has created a superb scene of the tycoon who believes he has grasped the heavens when Abe drives across the prairie just so that he can look back and see the sky aglow. "That was the proudest moment of his life; and he raised an arm as though reaching for the stars."[71] Grove gives us an ironic comment on the real significance of the light which is not so far-reaching as Abe imagines. "It did not loom high but seemed rather to form a dent in the sky-line."[72]

Abe's pride is due for a tumble, and it comes through his four neglected children. His oldest son, Charlie, his favourite, has given him a glimpse of all that his ignored fatherhood has cost him when one day they go hand in hand to search for a bird's nest. Beguiled by the sweetness and imagination of the child, Abe has a momentary pang of loneliness, realizing that, in fact, he has always been lonely. But Charlie is sacrificed to Abe's driving ambition. Needing a man to drive a load of grain to town, he sends for Charlie, who is delighted to take on a man's work. He is too young for the task; the wagon upsets and the child is crushed beneath the wheels.

This is the turning point in Abe's life; it comes immediately after his proud reach for the stars. When he goes to vote on a school issue he is challenged by a sly opponent who proves that Abe, momentarily short of cash because of his house, has not paid all his taxes and is ineligible to vote. Humiliated, Abe strides from the voting station and in fury resigns both as reeve and chairman of the school board.

Without Abe's uncompromising leadership, the community falls into moral ruin. When a new school is built the old one becomes the scene of wild orgies. More disaster follows at home: Abe's second son, Jim, takes a job in a garage; who now will take over the magnificent farm Abe has built? The oldest daughter, Marion, tries to elope.

The shame of the final child, Frances, forces Abe back into his natural role as community leader. Frances becomes pregnant by a married man. In an earlier version of the book, Abe shoots the man;

he is chased by a posse, and jumping onto a haystack where all Spalding District can see his figure outlined against the sky, he is shot. Grove submitted this manuscript to the publisher and then changed his mind about the ending. Against the publisher's wishes, he wrote the far more adult ending which we have, avoiding the flamboyant operatics of shooting. Without killing anyone, Abe realizes that his daughter has been victimized because there is no moral leadership. In the last scene he stalks into the schoolhouse where a licentious party is in progress; he orders everyone out and locks the door. Abe Spalding has taken over again. He has been pushed, willynilly, into the role ordained by his nature.

Fruits of the Earth did badly in the bookstores although extremely well in the reviews. Grove was prone to complain that nobody in Canada appreciated his work; in fact, it nearly always received a good press. He had become a respected writer and in recognition the Royal Society of Canada awarded him the Lorne Pierce Medal for literary merit in 1934.

GROVE MIGHT HAVE been better pleased with honours if he had had enough money to live. Although Catherine's school never lacked for pupils, income in the 1934-35 session amounted to only two thousand dollars.[73] Enrolment was somewhat limited by the size of the building, and the fees, geared to depression incomes, were only ten dollars a month.

The school was, nevertheless, their livelihood. As Catherine remarked later when speaking of Grove's writing, "He could never have done it without me; and Phil knew it."[74] Phil did indeed know it, and the house, if it was to go on as a school, needed basic renovation, not only to meet fire and washroom regulations, but also because it was simply falling apart. Grove swallowed hard and went to the bank. He borrowed enough money to re-do the house. For several months they lived in uproar and confusion as the house was replastered, refloored, repainted and repapered. Once into the renovations, Grove thoroughly enjoyed supervising. He went himself to the lumber yard to choose wood for the doors and dining-room panelling, turning the sheets of wood back and forth in the light to catch the grain, so that matching panels could be installed to meet his aesthetic standards. In an extravagance of enthusiasm over the final effect of the dining-room panels, he said, "As they are today, they look, without imitating anything, like three symphonic movements from Beethoven's Sixth."[75] Their diverse attitudes towards redoing the house is an amusing commentary on the difference between Grove's and Catherine's temperaments — she wanted a workable school; he was carried away by artistic possibilities.

For all Catherine's basic practicality, her nature had a good deal of the child in it. Even when she was an elderly lady, somebody remarked, "She was like a young girl — she could laugh and laugh."[76] She put on a more formal face when she was required to play the role of wife of Frederick Philip Grove, the writer, but the real Catherine was affectionate and simple. The atmosphere in the school, described by Leonard, reflected the easy familiarity Catherine felt when she was with children: "I'd get up in the morning, and the car would bring a whole bunch of kids to play, you know — really what it amounted to. Also there was a certain amount of school work involved but, being an only child and having nobody around constantly, I was quite prepared for the condition that if all these kids were going to come and play with you, then you were going to have to play by sitting at a desk part of the time. Other people have told me about their troubles going to public school. I don't remember that at all. It all seemed like a holiday to me."[77]

The holiday atmosphere was part of Catherine's skill; she could work wonders, especially with children with learning disabilities. Her work was becoming known outside Simcoe, and in 1936 a twelve-year-old boy from Niagara Falls with a reading disability was referred to her by a psychiatrist. The child came to stay with them in the house and within a year Catherine had improved his reading ability from Grade 2 to Grade 8 level. From that time on, as other handicapped children came to her, she turned the house into a boarding school, specializing in the teaching of disabled children. She was indeed the "pedagogical genius" Grove had recognized when he first met her.

She was remarkable for sheer stamina alone. Leonard recalled one year when they had ten children boarding in the house: "My mother had thirteen people to feed and a house to look after. At night she cooked dinner, played with the children and put them to bed. During the day, she taught. She had no one to help her — except me."[78]

Catherine's life was never easy, but in recalling it, she seems not to have been troubled by the difficulties: "So much has been said, over and over again, about our economic affairs, as if they were the most important things in our lives, and they were not at all, at all. We were happy. We faced problems that arose. We solved them. We lived. We laughed. We talked. We loved each other. We were satisfied with each other's company. And these things — the economic, have never been as big a mountain to us as they seem to be to the public."[79]

IN 1939 GROVE was sixty: he was not well, and his doctor ordered him to give up farming. It was good advice for business as well as health reasons. The farm had never been a successful venture; some of the prize cattle had sickened and died. As Leonard said, "The principal product of the farm seemed to be annual deficits and after a few years we sold the livestock and the farm implements and so on and kept the farm itself, which we rented to a neighbour, and several years subsequent to that we sold the farm itself to the same man but kept only the house and the immediate ground surrounding it."[80]

Writing remained Grove's real occupation; he had done an enormous amount since the publication of *Fruits of the Earth* in 1933. One book was "Felix Powell's Career," the story of a cad. Grove had sent it to Lorne Pierce of Ryerson Press who said that it was "one of the most readable" of his books, but thought it too explicitly sexual to be published in Canada — probably he still had frightening memories of *Settlers of the Marsh* all too vividly in mind. Grove was disgusted. "It is a serious book which deals with a sexual problem," he said, "and it is written with a savage sort of frankness which should have convinced everyone of the sincerity of its purpose. I offered it. Publishers and agents alike failed to see its true import; they put it down as pornography."[81] Catherine, from a strait-laced background, and extremely sensitive to critical public opinion, did not like it; she certainly did not want to see it published. She may have felt that her efforts to run a respectable school in a small Ontario town would be undermined if her husband had a reputation as a pornographic writer, and perhaps she had other reasons too. She expressed herself so strongly that finally Grove handed her some copies and said, "It is yours; do with it as you please." Catherine burned the copies. A little later, young Leonard, sent to the attic on an errand, discovered one more copy pushed away between the insulation and the roof. Evidently Grove, unable to face the total destruction of his work, had hidden one away. Leonard, innocent of the controversy between his parents, and knowing only that manuscripts were precious, ran downstairs and gave it to his mother. Catherine took it outside to the backyard and burned it.[82] No known copies of "Felix Powell's Career" remain.

In spite of all the work that Grove had done — including a vast panoramic novel which he first called "Democracy" and then "The Seasons," and his autobiography *In Search of Myself* — he had published nothing except a few magazine articles in six years. He was growing anxious about money. There was another book, *Two Generations,* which Catherine did like and Grove decided to try publishing it. The trouble was that he was a little edgy about offering it to Macmillan, the Ryerson Press or McClelland and Stewart because he had quarrelled with them about previous books. So he tried to publish it himself by private subscription: he sent letters to his friends asking for money to finance the printing. One of these letters reached Lorne Pierce, who was now as concerned as Grove's other friends by his financial state. Pierce offered not only to publish *Two Generations* but to reissue *A Search for America* in its fourth edition. He also arranged for the publication of two of Grove's short stories in magazines.[83]

Two Generations: A story of present-day Ontario appeared in 1939. It is psychologically the best of Grove's novels about the battle between the generations, although it lacks the explosive strength of *Our Daily Bread*. The central tension is the same: there is the domineering father pitted against a large family of children, each struggling to achieve individuality. *Two Generations* differs in several important ways from *Our Daily Bread,* however. It is set in the easier, long-settled countryside of Ontario, so that Grove was able to focus on the psychological drama rather than on the revelation of early conditions. While John Elliot of *Our Daily Bread* emerged as incomprehensibly stubborn, Ralph Patterson of *Two Generations* is a believable sufferer. At the age of only forty-five, he is about to be pushed aside by his children, deprived of his parental identity and left without vital work. *Two Generations* is a study of middle-aged male crisis.

The mother, Di Patterson, is another Martha Elliot, cajoling and controlling her recalcitrant husband; but unlike Martha she does not die, and through her influence youth is served. Perhaps because of the final triumph of the children and the submission of the father, Grove called *Two Generations* his "pleasant book."

The two oldest sons embark on farming enterprises using modern business and technical methods. One of them proves so successful that he takes over his father's dairy farms with automatic milkers and phases him out of work. Ralph sees his children as rivals; as they succeed, he becomes futile — wandering sadly around his farm with nothing to do.

But it is the next two children — the team of Phil and Alice — who are the real thorns in Ralph's side. In Grove's view of the evolution of human society, they belong in the stage following rudimentary farming when there is enough money and leisure to pursue education and culture. These two want to study — Alice to become a doctor, Phil an astronomer. Ralph can well afford to educate them, but he refuses to do so. At this point his wife steps in; she threatens to leave him if he does not use the profits from a farm which she owns to finance both children through university.

Routed, Ralph now searches desperately for some means to repair his shattered masculine pride. He invests money in a business enterprise which, when the Depression strikes, turns out to be ruinous, and he is forced to sell his dairy farm to his son Henry. His wife rescues him, but by doing so causes him to accept her values and those of Phil and Alice. The farm she owns is sixteen miles from Ralph's former huge establishment with its heavily masculine brick house. Throughout the novel, it has been used as a refuge by the children when they are trying to escape their father. It is a gentler place, conveying the sense that it is closer to nature. The contrasting farm properties are symbols of the masculine-feminine dichotomy which recurs in Grove — and all his sympathies go towards the feminine. Di parcels up some of her land for each of her children, so that they will all have independent incomes and be free of their father's tyranny. She retains a hundred acres and the house for herself and she suggests to Ralph that they live there and farm the modest hundred acres.

Ralph accepts — there is nothing else he can do — and so abandons his domineering masculine identity and accepts Di's civilizing feminine one. For Grove, there is no place in developed society for the hard-nosed old curmudgeons like John Elliot, Abe Spalding and Ralph Patterson (they are essentially the same man). They are as much out of phase in civilization as Len Sterner was in the early period.

However, Grove's gift for creating supermen has given Ralph a vitality which one feels must remain uneasily confined within the environment decreed by his wife. He is the first of Grove's patriarchs to attempt reconciliation with the feminine side — even if perhaps a forced reconciliation. For all the understanding Grove applied to Ralph's suffering, the final submission rings a false note.

The public appearance of *Two Generations* repeated the dismal pattern of Grove's previous books: splendid reviews, wretched sales. W. A. Deacon in *The Globe and Mail* said, ". . . Mr. Grove has given us, in *Two Generations,* his best book; and that means one of the best novels ever written in Canada."[84] W. S. Milne in *Saturday Night* said, "I wish we had more Canadian novels on the same level."[85] Barker Fairley in *The Canadian Forum* praised it for its authentic flavour of Ontario rural life.[86] All very well, but when Lorne Pierce sponsored Grove for election in the Royal Society of Canada, the much-praised author could not, at the time, afford the twenty dollar fee.

GROVE WAS GROWING FEEBLE. Even his simple pleasures, like birdwatching with the Naturalist Club, were now a trial. His friend, Munro Landon said, "He couldn't hear the birds any longer. He couldn't get around. His back. His ears. He was too old for us to really have the good times we should have had. It all helped to make him bitter."[87] He still taught a little in Catherine's school, although impatiently. He listened happily to radio broadcasts of the New York Philharmonic orchestra, turning the volume up full blast so that the sound could penetrate his deafness. He continued to be a concerned though stern father. Leonard said, "When I was good he was 'Father', when I was bad he was 'Sir', and if that makes a Victorian parent, then clearly he was Victorian. One might disobey him once, but one certainly never did it twice."[88] Now, added to all this, was a certain crankiness. Outsiders sometimes thought that Grove was *always* cranky, but close friends and family knew another side of him. "He was always gentle with me,"[89] Catherine later told her daughter-in-law.

In 1943, feeble in body but strong in spirit, Grove took a fling into politics. He was friendly with J. S. Woodsworth, federal leader of the CCF, whom he had first met in Ottawa, on his eastern lecture tour. Woodsworth was exactly the kind of man Grove admired — distinguished and scholarly. Out of friendship for him, Grove agreed when the local CCF asked him to run as their candidate in the 1943 election. Catherine thought it was madness, but as Leonard remembered, there was little hope of his winning. ". . . I'm not positive of this, but I'm almost certain that I can recall the people who asked him to run as candidate assuring him that he couldn't possibly win and that it was perfectly safe for him to try."[90] Grove did lose — it was, after all, a traditional Conservative seat — but he was afterwards appointed honorary president of the local CCF. He enjoyed his political experience, but it didn't solve his money problems. In 1943, Lorne Pierce reported his book sales: *Fruits of the Earth,* 41 copies; *A Search for America,* 73 copies; *Two Generations,* 68 copies.[91]

At this, Grove went to work in a canning factory. Catherine was appalled, but for Grove it was one more experience — one which he discussed with Leonard, who remembers, ". . . during the war when there was a great shortage of labour and we were all called upon to do everything we possibly could, . . . my father worked for a period of time in the factory in Simcoe in the Canadian Canners. I don't recall how long this was, I know it was brief, and I know that every day was sheer agony for him to go down there to do this kind of work, not because he objected to the work itself, or to the kind of people with whom he was working, for whom I think in many cases he had a very high regard, but because the nature of the work was such that it was going to put money into somebody's pocket by virtue solely of the fact that he had been able to buy at one price and sell at another and was therefore reaping a profit without producing anything, either anything with or without value, and I think my father's views on the question of making a living were that as an author, he could justify making a living because for every dollar which he received he had in turn produced something which at least to him, had an absolute quality and merit."[92]

There is another story which is often told about Grove in the canning factory. He was surprised to find that one of his co-workers was a cultivated Englishman from Oxford. "What brought you here?" asked Grove. "Drink," replied the Englishman. "And what brought you here?" "Literature," said Grove.

Luckily, financial help was on the way. Over the years he had continued as an editorial reader for Macmillan, his old publisher. In 1944, Ellen Elliot, a newly appointed director of Macmillan, became interested in Grove's unpublished books and arranged to publish *The Master of the Mill*. Then in the same year, the Canadian Writers' Foundation was established to help needy writers and Grove became one of three beneficiaries. He received a cheque for two hundred dollars and thereafter a grant of one hundred dollars a month for the rest of his life.

Then, on April 14, 1944, there was "the appalling surprise." Guests had come for dinner and Catherine remembered, ". . . after they had all gone he went upstairs to his room to go to bed. I had noticed all evening that he was very quiet and didn't take part in the conversation as much as usual. When I came up a little later he was already in bed, and I could see at once that something had happened. I went over to the bedside and said, 'What's wrong, Phil?' and he was able to say, 'a stroke.' Which meant nothing to me because I didn't know what it meant, but I ran down to call the doctor who came at once. . . . The doctor hoped then that it was going to be a short illness, but it proved otherwise."[93]

Grove's right side was paralyzed — but he fought back. Next morning Catherine found him reading a manuscript for Macmillan; he typed his reader's reports with his left hand. By 1945, struggling manfully, he had learned to walk again with a cane.

GROVE WAS UNDOUBTEDLY bitter about his life. Effort it seemed to him, was to no avail. He had struggled, but circumstances always rose up to strike him down. By extension, he concluded that all mankind is helpless in the hands of fate. Most of all, we are caught in the relentless wheel of evolution; we participate in whatever phase we happen to be born in. Grove had investigated various phases in his earlier books, but in *The Master of the Mill,* published in 1944, he took on the mammoth task of tracing the entire history of man from the time the first simple tool is invented until automation takes over. Because of its chilling description of life during the automated period, *The Master of the Mill* is the Canadian contribution to the literature of future doom, along with George Orwell's *1984* and Aldous Huxley's *Brave New World.*

Grove accomplishes his sweeping survey by telling the story of four generations of a family, the Clarks, who own a flour mill. First is Douglas, who starts a rickety mill on the edge of the wilderness to help the farmers; second is Rudyard, who grows rich during the boom years following the building of the railway; third, and best of the Clarks, is Sam, the one who is able to receive an education because of his family's wealth. But Sam's enlightened, liberal time inevitably passes, and with his son, Edmund, we have the final stage when the machine takes over. Edmund is childless — Grove's implication is not only that automation produces sterility, but that mankind has reached the end.

The Master of the Mill is an ironic title; as Sam realizes, it is the mill which is the master, not he. Pitifully, however, the mill had begun as one of those fine dreams which ends as a monster because the dream is used for material gain. The original dream is evident in the opening, when Sam, now an old man, and through whose eyes most of the story is told, looks out the window of his mansion one night and sees the mill. It is huge and white, illuminated by a searchlight, a dominating, impersonal reality. It has, however, a mirror image in the lake, suggesting the perverted dream: "Its image lay on the mirror-smooth water like a fairy palace inverted; . . ."[94]

Sam is the hero of the book because he attempts to swim backwards against the current of progress. His private inclinations are to leave the running of the mill to someone else, to collect art and lead a quiet life. He discovers, however, that his father Rudyard had amassed enough capital to build the new mill by burning down the old one and collecting insurance based on a false assessment of its assets. In order to cover up the fraud, Sam must seize total control of the mill. His father has left him a heavy inheritance: plans already underway to build a mill so big that it will be "capable of supplying the needs of a continent."[95] The diabolical plan will, first of all, increase the number of labourers from two thousand to nine thousand, creating a small city; then it will switch to automation and the people will be cast adrift. Sam is so horrified that he tries to slow down the process, making social change at least less painful. It is not within his power to do so.

Sam is the only Clark with a conscience and the only real creator. As an engineer, he designed the machinery which increased the mill's productivity, but as a result its impetus for growth becomes so great that he is forced to buy up all the smaller mills and the Clark enterprise becomes a monopoly. Sam's conscience and creativity do not help — they only cause him to suffer, and they place him foursquare in the power of his ruthless son, Edmund, who finds it a simple matter to take power from his naïve father.

Edmund is even more lacking in conscience than his grandfather, Rudyard, and scornful of Sam's principals. "It is always the well-intentioned that do the most mischief,"[96] he says, believing economics to be the only force in human endeavor. The business interests of the Clarks, through Edmund, spread far beyond flour milling. Edmund boasts that he controls two-thirds of the industry of the country. With this kind of leverage, he *is* the country. Edmund argues that, as a result of automation, the workers will be freed of work and kept by the state. They will also, of course, be robbed of dignity and usefulness and they will be controlled by whosoever controls the economy — probably Edmund. Grove implies that technology and fascism go hand in hand. As a demonstration of the world to come, Edmund builds another mill called Arbala in Ontario. It is a stark, white structure, germ-free, set in a perfect, manicured park. There is a post office at Arbala, but no schools, no streets; in short, no life.

Edmund wants a strike at the home mill because it will eliminate all the workers who have been made useless by machinery. He cuts their wages; then, when the men strike, he calmly moves in the machines he has been holding in waiting. There is a riot, but in the riot, Edmund himself, in one of the most satisfying deaths in fiction, is struck by a stray bullet from a tank and falls dead instantly. There are few mourners at the funeral.

Sam is now flung unwillingly back into the leadership of the mill, although at this stage it doesn't much matter who runs the mill; it runs itself. Grove has drawn a bleak world, but in the final scene, he holds out faint hope. Sam has died, and after his funeral, three women, rather like the three witches in *Macbeth,* peer into the future. They foresee that man, kept by machines, will luxuriate in idleness, and deprived of purpose will become almost extinct. There will be no one left to oil the mill; it will rot and fall into disuse so that no food can be manufactured. But some man will be left; he will rise again, begin to till the soil, create a few simple tools and the whole cycle will repeat itself. It sounds futile, but one of the women breaks in to say that perhaps there will be "Some entirely unforeseen thing. Some development of which we cannot even dream yet. . . . I have come to place a great confidence in the capacity of the collective human mind."[97]

Contemporary readers, living with automation, respond to Grove's searching examination and his panoramic view of the stages of man's evolution. In 1944, however, the book fell with a dull thud: Grove was ahead of his time. *Saturday Night* described it as "unreal."[98] Grove's total royalties from the book were one hundred and nine dollars.[99]

FOR YEARS, GROVE, the raconteur, had been entertaining friends, pupils and casual acquaintances with amazing stories about his past. He had braved gales on the St. Lawrence; he had been on an archaeological dig in Greece when the house he was living in collapsed because hogs rooting in the cellar had undermined the foundations;[100] he had had a family in Kentucky with two sons who were now at universities but with whom he had lost touch. Grove's stories were both fascinating and well told. Mrs. W. E. Collin, wife of the writer, said, "He had a dramatic sense of telling a story, and I can remember sitting on the veranda of our cottage up at Wasaga Beach in the evening, listening to him all evening. Mrs. Grove finally said, 'You know, I have heard many of these before, so I think I will go to bed.' "[101]

The Grove legend jelled in 1945 and 1946, first when Desmond Pacey, a young professor of English at Brandon College, published a biography of Grove, and then when Grove himself published his autobiography, *In Search of Myself.*

The two accounts are similar; Grove sent Dr. Pacey the unpublished copy of his own manuscript as a biographical aid. Dr. Pacey was puzzled about Grove's birth date, which seemed to change from time to time in the autobiographical account. He asked Grove for clarification. Grove waffled considerably in his reply: "You can readily imagine that, in a life in which over 20 years are, as it were, taken out and thrown away [This refers to the twenty years Grove claimed he had spent wandering around the United States] chronology gets confused. I am not even sure any longer that I know in what year I was born. The only thing I have to go by is that my mother said to me, in a conversation I remember very distinctly, that the great event happened a year after the Franco-Prussian war. But whether she meant by that 1870 or 1871, I can't tell."[102] Dr. Pacey settled on 1871, but he was not the last to wonder about Grove's dating.

In Search of Myself is given artistic shape to illuminate the central question, "Why did I fail?" Still, it was labelled an autobiography, and its details appeared in all the biographical notes on Grove in encyclopedias and reference books for over twenty years.

It begins in the gloomiest possible way with Grove stuck in a quagmire — both literally and metaphorically. He had set off on a bleak, November day to fetch a young farm girl to help in the house. Since his car is stuck, he has a few moments to muse on his desolate frame of mind. It strikes him that it is not the present which depresses him, but memories of the previous evening. A friend had come bringing books, among them one by a brilliant Frenchman whom Grove had known and who is now a renowned author. (This man seems to be André Gide.) The contrast between his friend's achievements and Grove's poverty, isolation and rejection in the wilderness of Canada is more than he can bear. Eventually, when his car is dug out and the girl turns up, he drives home in the blackest of moods, forced to write his autobiography to find out why he has been "a traitor to my youth."

His very birth, it seems, had been followed by a disaster. "I was born prematurely, in a Russian manor-house, while my parents were trying to reach their Swedish home. . . . Incredibly, within an hour or so of the event, the hospitable house, belonging to friends of my parents, was struck by lightning and burned to the ground."[103]

The entire household escapes, however, and Grove and his parents proceed to their estate in Sweden. In *A Search for America,* Phil Branden's "palatial" home had been in "the fashionable residential district of a populous city on the continent of Europe. The exact localities are irrelevant."[104] *In Search of Myself* is more specific. The great estate is near the Swedish city of Lund. His father, he says, was of English-Swedish descent. His mother was a Scotswoman, the heiress of a distinguished family; Swedish was not spoken in the household. Grove had nine sisters, none of whom play any signifi-can role in the autobiography. The estate, called Castle Thurow, was the scene of a childhood spent on a fine property of two thousand acres near the sea among tutors, and splendid horses. Between times spent living in this magnificent house, the young boy toured Europe with his mother.

The father was the brutal giant familiar to every reader of Grove's novels. "My father was six feet seven inches tall, a personable man, the very devil with women. He rode hard, ate hard, and drank hard. *Me* he despised."[105] The parents are not happily married and when the young boy is brutally treated by his father once too often, the mother sweeps him off to live a whirlwind life in the capitals of Europe. Grove emphasizes the wealth, talent and brilliance which surround him at this period. He attends school wherever they happen to be: Boulogne, Odessa, Zurich, Budapest, Moscow, Florence — the list is long. Life is dazzling but erratic, and there is an undertone of longing for the more stable existence of a family containing a supportive father. Inevitably and significantly, the boy and his mother run out of money, and the brilliant company they had kept in more prosperous days (Grove says that he had met both Brahms and Mahler in his mother's salon) vanishes and is replaced by seedy bohemians.

A masculine figure appears to replace the father. "Uncle Jacobsen," a wealthy Danish ships' broker, is an admirer of the mother. He is a benevolent friend who turns up in times of trouble, and he guides the boy to some degree during his youth. He is, however, treated in a shadowy, hesitant manner, and although the boy's attitude towards him is not directly stated, we have the sense that his presence is disturbing, as though taste and jealousy over his relationship to the mother exists. She hopes that the Dane will take the boy into his business. But Grove is his mother's true son — he has her love of beauty, grace and the arts, and he has no more fondness or ability than she for the world of practicality and business.

Further disaster descends. The mother develops cancer and becomes swollen, disfigured and aged, and the father appears to take her home to Thurow to die. As we find out later in another story of Grove's life, the death of his mother was truly cataclysmic for him.

After her death, his father abruptly turns into a more satisfactory, concerned parent. Unlike the mother, he does not try to urge the boy into a business career but encourages him to study so that he may become a diplomat. Grove is sent to a gymnasium at Hamburg, a school which will ensure university entrance and lead to a diplomatic career.

At the gymnasium the boy does well. He has a natural gift for languages and excels in his classes. Hamburg, however, is a port town, a place where temptation is all too present. He is seduced by an "older woman," the wife of his chemistry professor, and the two carry on an affair under the husband's nose. When the school year ends, his mistress, Mrs. Broegler, tells him that she is pregnant; he, the father-to-be is only seventeen years old! Heroically, she sends him home to Thurow where he receives letters from her telling him that her husband is divorcing her, naming the young Grove as co-respondent in the suit. He is distraught but, ungallantly, immediately falls in love with Mrs. Broegler's opposite — Kirstin, a virginal young girl who is the daughter of wealthy parents.

In the fall he is ready to enrol at university in Paris. However, he comes across a man who is a Scottish relative of his mother's — an Uncle Rutherford. This man, whom Grove said was a famed explorer and author, is about to take an expedition into Siberia north of the Arctic Circle. Grove decides to go with him. There is a description of a meeting between the two travellers and a tribe of Kirghiz herdsmen on the lonely Siberian steppes which is one of the most famous incidents in Grove's writing, and justifiably so. It catches a ringing, surreal echo of Grove's inner self; it is the moment when he reaches the realization that he is to be a writer. As he and his uncle are travelling on horeseback across the bleak steppe, accompanied by Cossack escorts, they come across the tribe of herdsmen, driving their sheep and cattle. The men begin to sing — a melancholy, droning articulation of loneliness. Grove identifies with the singers: ". . . their song was eternal because, out of the stream and succession of generations, somewhere, somewhen, a nameless individual had arisen to give them voice. That voice was the important thing to me; for already I felt that one day, I too, was to be a voice; and I, too, was perfectly willing to remain nameless."[106] The matter of Grove being "nameless" is intriguing, since we now think that his name may not have been Grove at all. Furthermore, it appears that he never did make the famous trip across the Siberian steppes. It matters very little. As the statement of his commitment to a lonely profession it is superbly rendered.

He returns to Paris and university, and here we have an extended picture of the brilliance he knew in his life with his mother — careless wealth and stimulating intellectual companionship. He says that he was in touch with circles around Mallarmé, Verlaine, Rimbaud and Oscar Wilde, all dazzling names in the literary world. When the whim took him, he was off on quick trips to Madagascar and Biskra with a friend. He went to universities in Rome and Munich to study archaeology, and finally left for a grand tour of North America. Grove's story is that he arrived on the eastern coast in August, 1892, and made a coast to coast tour to California and back through Vancouver and the Canadian Rockies. When he arrived in Toronto, he received a cablegram; his father had died, leaving him penniless.

So ends Grove's account of his European life. One lady dismissed it brusquely as "romantic fiction" and there were plenty of others who frowned a little quizzically when discussing Grove's past.

The next twenty years of his life, from the time he was twenty to forty, are accounted for briefly in the autobiography. He spent his time wandering homelessly through the United States and Canada as a hobo and farmhand. The period had been dealt with fully in *A Search for America,* but as described there, it seems to cover two or three years at the most. Twenty years is a long time in a man's life, especially the years between twenty and forty, when most men are establishing a career and raising a family.

Grove tells us that he spent his winters writing in small rented shacks in Moose Jaw, Brandon or Winnipeg, or else looking after stock on farms. In May or June he headed south to Kansas and Colorado looking for farm work. All this time he was writing, not only *A Search for America,* but ten or twelve other books. He sent his handwritten manuscripts off to publishers all over the world, sometimes translating them into German or French. They were all returned.

To break the monotony, he made five return trips to Europe, where he enjoyed himself hugely. He met old friends, lived in fine hotels, escorted beautiful ladies to the opera and led wealthy tourists around Rome as a guide. The reader wonders why he always decided to return to North America — it didn't appear to offer much by contrast to Europe. The only reason he gives is that he had a fondness for the setting of his novel, *A Search for America.*

In any case, in 1912 he was in America. His life as he saw it had been wasted: none of his books had been published; twenty years had been spent wandering. He had no place in society, no family, no home. He was a man of education and ambition; he wanted to make a contribution — and he was lonely, as lonely as ever he had been when he first came to America, and just as poor. "Was I, to the end of my days," he wrote, "or at least of my working days, to go on being a hobo or tramp, a member of what, by-and-large, is the lowest social, economic, intellectual order?"[107]

It was as a writer that Grove wished to establish himself, for that was what he was. He decided that if he could save five or six thousand dollars he could invest it and live on the interest, which he calculated would be twenty-five dollars a month. Then he could write. He dreamed of the shack he would build in some idyllic setting near a stream and woods — perhaps the Pembina Mountains in southern Manitoba.

The means to earn the five or six thousand dollars was revealed to him by a stroke of fate. He met a Roman Catholic priest in a train station in Fargo, North Dakota, while he was reading Baudelaire's *Fleurs du Mal.* The priest, seeing the book, began to speak to him in French. The presence of a sympathetic spirit unloosed Grove's tongue, and he told the priest his life story and his present problems. The priest suggested that he teach. He should go straight away to Manitoba where teachers were badly needed and see Robert

Fletcher, the Deputy Minister of Education, whom the priest knew. Grove tells us that until this moment he had never thought of being a teacher, although later he was to tell stories about his previous teaching career in Kentucky. Grove promptly left the farm where he was working and walked to Winnipeg.

From this point on, the story is familiar — the interview with Robert Fletcher, the teaching posts, the money troubles which did not end. Grove's Canadian life has been subject to close scrutiny by academics, and it has been found that his own account of it is true, though he did heighten effects here and there and changed a few details to emphasize his role as the outcast artist.

The strongest impression that the book leaves is a pervasive anxiety about money. The autobiography reads something like an animated account book — at every stage we are informed of the exact state of Grove's pocketbook. "When school closed, we had nothing in reserve," but "my wife received a bonus of one hundred dollars for having stayed out her full year at Ashfield."[108] ". . . my earnings, plus the small balance of my savings . . . some seventy-five dollars in all . . ."[109] The book uses money as a scoring system for Grove's battle against the world — and he always comes out with a low score. His message is clear: there is no way that a person who is guided by the demands of the spirit and the imagination can adjust to the ways of the world.

As a vindication of his thesis, *In Search of Myself* did not make money. By now, however, Grove did not expect that it would, although it did win the Governor-General's Award for non-fiction. Grove was too ill to go to Vancouver where the awards were being given at the annual convention of the Canadian Authors Association, so W. A. Deacon, who was president, accepted the award for him and brought it back to Simcoe. He described in moving terms how he handed Grove his award: "It was after I brought the medal down to Toronto that I realized that the only courteous thing to do was to drive to Simcoe and hand it to Philip in person. It was then I had to sit down and write the acceptance speech, what I remembered of it, but it was a very much better speech than the one I actually made on the floor at Vancouver. Philip was delighted; I think he came nearer to humility as we sat at lunch that day than I had ever seen him before, and he was almost shy when he showed the medal to his young son with great pride. In fact for some reason, I don't know whether his eyesight was poor or something, he had me read the acceptance speech to him sitting out on the front steps. And Grove wept."[110]

The Governor-General's Award was the third honour in two years: in 1946 both the University of Manitoba and Mount Allison had given him honorary degrees. But by now Grove was seriously ill. He had had another stroke in 1946 and he was so helpless that Catherine rented a hospital bed which she put in the living-room so that she could watch him while she taught. Leonard, who had been away on a scholarship at St. Andrews College in Aurora, came home to look after his father.

The last of Grove's books to be published during his lifetime was his "Ant Book." He had mentioned it off and on over the years to friends as a book for which he had some affection, but which had not yet found a publisher. In 1945, Ellen Elliot of Macmillan gave him a contract with an advance of five hundred dollars for both his autobiography and the "ant book."[111] Published in 1947, it has the title *Consider Her Ways,* which Grove took from Proverbs: "Go to the ant, thou sluggard; consider her ways and be wise." *Consider Her Ways* is a fantasy about an expedition of 10,162 ants who leave the perfect civilization of their home in Venezuela for New York City to explore antdom and humanity. Their society is a superior one because they have chosen the pursuit of knowledge over the accumulation of possessions. As Grove had made abundantly clear in *Fruits of the Earth* and *The Master of the Mill,* materialism is a dead end.

The story is told by an amateur myrmecologist who signs himself F.P.G. He visits the formecary in Venezuela and one day becomes aware that an ancient and battered ant, who has evidently seen much of the world, is watching him intently. She hypnotizes him, and while he is in a trance conveys the tale of the ants' epic journey.

The book gives Grove the opportunity to satirize man's vanity. The ants believe themselves to be superior to man. Wawa-Quee (she of the hypnotic powers) has heard some ants say that man has the power to reason, but she doubts this: "Reason seemed to be such an incomparably precious gift that it was hard to imagine other creatures to be endowed with it, creatures remote from our own race which was by nature destined to rule the world."[112]

Consider Her Ways is also an adventure yarn. As the ants travel, they battle armies of enemy ants; they are attacked by a hen in a barn where they lodge for the winter; several of their number are wiped out by a car, and five hundred soldiers are killed by lightning as they cross an electric wire over the Mississippi River. To make matters doubly hazardous, there is an enemy in their midst. The commander of the ten thousand strong army, Assa-ree, has political ambitions — and the entire army is made up of her children. She is outwitted by Wawa-Quee, who on finding out about her proposed treachery, polishes off the army with one whiff of a death pellet which the queen has given her for emergencies. The army which had been brought along to protect the 162 scholars has turned out to be something of a nuisance anyway, and Wawa-Quee never did have much use for the military. Even Assa-ree had admitted: ". . . military gifts were necessarily associated with retarded mentality, capable of holding on to only one idea at a time; . . ."[113] Scholars are another matter. When Lemma-nee, geographer-in-chief, is scratched to death by a chicken "and one of the greatest scholars living was reduced to pulp," Wawa-Quee mourns, "What, compared to such a loss, was the death or the capture of a thousand soldiers!"[114]

As for man, he is both brutal and mad. With horror, the ants watch a farmer fondle his animals affectionately, only to murder them later for food. Proof of human degeneracy in the feminine eyes of Wawa-Quee is that in human society, the male, not the female, plays the dominant role. "This is against all reason," she states.[115] The outcome, she implies, is the human tendency to kill "without provocation or discrimination, all living things, sometimes at sight, sometimes after having enslaved them for a time."[116] However, she believes that in an earlier, superior period, humans possessed a matriarchal society, like ants.

Through the ants, Grove makes clear his attitude towards capitalism and all its works. One capitalist group are the Rubicunda whom Wawa-Quee and her band come across making forage raids into the formicaries of other ants and carrying off the eggs and larvae, partly for food and partly for slaves. The implication is that capitalists are parasites who rob others of their produce and keep the producers as slaves.

Grove also has a little, bitter fun describing the sad condition of some ants called "authors." These poor creatures contain honey —

Grove's metaphor for literature — which provides food for their fellows. They hang from the ceiling, where they are available whenever other members need nourishment. "Now authors were held in great esteem in the commonwealth; that is to say, they were ostentatiously honoured and secretly despised as unnecessary and unproductive members of society; yet it was the custom of inscribing their names on a roll of honour and thus conferring upon them a sort of immortality. . . ."[117] Authors may be honoured, but as Grove was aware, they were also likely to be starved. They "were first required to fast for a full year, or for a quarter of their lives, many of them dying during this period of their training."[118]

Afterwards Grove regretted some of his rancorous remarks in *Consider Her Ways*. In his autobiography, he said, ". . . it became harsh and bitter; it became a grumbling protest against the insanity of human institutions, it became a preachment."[119]

Still, it has its funny moments, as well as moving ones which result from the sad fate of ants whose personalities have become familiar to us. In the New York Public Library, Wawa-Quee's last place of sojourn before returning home, only three ants remain. Besides Wawa-Quee there is the zoologist-in-chief, Bissa-tee, and the chief signaller and recorder, Azte-ca. Bissa-tee spends most of her two years in the library performing reducing or "slimming" exercises; like many admirable ladies in Grove she is of enormous girth. Wawa-Quee, having a serious turn of mind, reads thoughtful books. Azte-ca, unfortunately, is frivolous, and cannot resist the fascination of detective stories. Alas, they are her downfall. Unable to tear herself away from the solution to a murder, she does not notice the army of cleaning women who appear to rid the library of ants, and perishes in the chlorine fumes which rise from the mop pails.

Wawa-Quee and Bissa-tee scamper away to safety and begin the long weary journey home. The period in the New York Library, however, has been the climax and the assessing point of their expedition. Their journey has been a pursuit of knowledge and the library is the storehouse of knowledge. For all Grove's respect for learning, he casts some doubts on whether a life devoted to books, as his was, is a substitute for living. Wawa-Quee observes that devotees to the library are rather unhealthy, pale specimens, and contemplating the books she comments distastefully: "Now all this human literature was mouldy; . . ."[120]

Furthermore, pride in knowledge is foolish, for when a being dies his accumulation of knowledge dies too. Sixty-six of Wawa-Quee's scholars have been flattened to death by a speeding motor car, and she cries out in frustration: "Sixty-six great scholars, every one a leader in her field, and collectively perhaps the greatest and most amazing aggregate of learning that had ever been assembled on earth, were reduced to a greasy smear on the highway! The futility of it all! The utter senselessness!"[121] Still *she* lives long enough to pass her story on to the amateur myrmecologist, thereby achieving a kind of immortality for herself and for her learning.

The allegory, *Consider Her Ways,* ended Grove's writing career on a surprise note. No one had suspected that he was capable of fantasy ("realism" was supposed to be his gift) or of the other un-expected ingredient — humour.

IN 1948 GROVE HAD SUSTAINED FIVE STROKES. When he developed pneumonia it proved too much for his frail body. Frederick Philip Grove died on August 19, 1948, at Simcoe. There was a simple service in the white house which he had loved so much. His body was taken to Rapid City, where he was buried in the cemetery be-side May.

The burial took place on a golden summer prairie day. The sky was brilliant blue. From the graveyard on the hill, with its shelter of spruce trees, the cluster of mourners could see a rich river valley below. The stooked fields were ready for harvest.

GROVE'S STORY DID not end with his death. It was to reappear as even more extraordinary than he had described it.

His family continued to live quietly. Leonard was not quite eighteen when his father died. He enrolled at Carleton University in Ottawa and when he graduated he became a patent attorney, an expert among other things, on the copyrights of publishers and authors. Catherine went on teaching — she had very little money, and her advancing age seemed to have no effect on her energy or high spirits.

In 1971, a collection of Grove's short stories, *Tales from the Mar-gin,* appeared edited by Desmond Pacey, his first biographer. Grove's voice from beyond the grave was full of bitter laughter, mocking at man and his futile attempts to outwit his fate.

It was inevitable that eventually Grove's puzzling and contradictory statements about himself should be challenged. There had been an upsurge of interest in him after 1957, when McClelland and Stewart republished *Over Prairie Trails* in paperback and followed it over the years with most of his other books. Before, they had been out of print and difficult to find. In 1967, Douglas Spettigue, a young professor of English from Queen's University had been particularly puzzled by Grove's autobiographical statement that he had been born in a manor house on the Russian border while his marriage certificate stated that it was Moscow. He inquired through the Soviet Embassy and Lenin Library and found there were no Russian birth records for Frederick Philip Grove. He thought it odd that Grove spoke no Swedish, although he said he had been brought up in Sweden, and of course most people who had known Grove in his early Canadian days had assumed that he was German. Grove's written English had contained some typically German usage and punctuation.

Dr. Spettigue went to Sweden to check Grove's birth record, his school attendance and his family. When he arrived, he found that Castle Thurow did not exist. He found that there were not and never had been any Groves in the neighbourhood of Lund, the city which Grove said was twenty-one miles from the Thurow estate. There is no record of his birth. No one with the name "Grove" had ever been registered at the schools Grove said he attended. In fact, Dr. Spettigue could find no trace of Grove in Europe at all. His book, *Frederick Philip Grove,* was published in 1969 and caused a stir. Really, it had raised more questions than it had answered; it had given some idea of what Grove was not, but it had given no clue as to what he was. Upon reading it, most people assumed that everything Grove had said about his European past was false. As it turned out, it was not all false.

In 1971, Douglas Spettigue was back in Europe on sabbatical leave from the university — not, he said, to pursue Grove. However, by this time Grove had become "his" man; the unanswered questions nagged. His wife, who was with him, could see that Grove **was** on his mind more than he admitted. She suggested that he go back to the British Museum where his research had led him previously and, once more, look up André Gide. Grove had mentioned Gide's name in *A Search for America,* and in the Prologue of *In Search of Myself* he had made a great point of a brilliant French writer who seemed to be Gide.

Spettigue did go back to the British Museum; he did look up André Gide — again. Studying some letters, he came across one from Gide to Paul Claudel, mentioning a quarrel between another friend and someone called Felix Paul Greve. Spettigue had seen the letter before, but at that moment the proverbial shivers ran up and down his spine. He had a feeling that these two might be the same man. For one thing, Grove had written a novel called "Felix Powell's Career"; the name was close to Felix Paul, and Mrs. Grove had burned the novel — why?

The next step was to look up Felix Paul Greve in the lexicons. Spettigue found that he had been born on February 14, 1879. Grove had always given his birth day as February 14, but he had been vague about the year — sometimes it was 1871, sometimes 1872, sometimes 1873. The records noted that Greve had died in 1910. Spettigue suspected that this had been a disappearance date, not a death.

He could not let go now. There was a new name, a German name, "Greve", to go on. Although he had found that Castle Thurow did not exist in Sweden, he knew that it is a common place name in East Germany. He went to East Germany. Sure enough, there he found not one village called Thurow, but five, running in a line through Pomerania and Mecklenburg. Finding Greve was another matter. Local authorities were not helpful, and furthermore, the area had been heavily bombed during the war, destroying records. He persevered to Bonn, the capital of West Germany, where Grove had said he had been at university. Here he struck gold. Felix Paul Greve had indeed attended university there. There were records, not only of his career in Bonn, but his complete school record from the time he started his education as a small boy in Hamburg.

Spettigue sought out every scrap of information he could find on Felix Paul Greve. There were letters to and from publishers. Greve had been a prolific writer and translator in Germany. There were newspaper accounts of the trial of a Felix Paul Greve and his imprisonment. Piecing the story together, he became convinced that Greve was Grove. There were a great many points at which Grove's account of himself and Greve's life intersected, although Grove shifted the time scheme in his later retelling, and had avoided or changed the most painful details about his early life. When Douglas Spettigue returned to Canada he wrote his second book on Grove. Published in late 1973, *F.P.G., The European Years* re-constructs the life of Felix Paul Greve and uses the information to argue fairly convincingly that Grove had been born Felix Paul Greve. It is a shadowy portrait still — there is much that is unknown. It does show an overwrought, gifted boy, at the mercy of erratic, distressing family and financial circumstances, a boy who would grow into a man with a need for fiction.

Felix Paul Greve's ancestors were not wealthy landowners. They were small farmers in Mecklenburg in the area surrounding the little city of Schwerin. The land is wild and often wooded, swept by fierce winds and bitterly cold in winter. When Grove recognized the Canadian prairie as his spiritual home, he was perhaps also recognizing his ancestral home. Felix Paul's father was Carl Eduard Greve; Grove had given his father's name as Charles Edward on his marriage certificate. His mother was Bertha Reichentrog; Grove had said his mother's name was Bertha Rutherford. She was the daughter of the steward of an estate and was comfortably well off.

On the whole, the picture of ancestral life which Spettigue provides shows generations of closely-knit, indeed intermarried, families living traditionally on the land. They combined farming with positions of minor officialdom — village mayors and the like. About the time that Felix's parents were married, however, young people were beginning to move off the land. It was becoming too crowded to support the farming population, and besides, a newly industrialized Germany was beckoning them to the cities where jobs could be found.

As soon as Carl Eduard and Bertha were married they moved away from the family neighbourhood, but not immediately to the city. Carl Eduard became manager of an estate near one of the Thurows. The first child, a daughter named Henny, was born there in 1887. Henny was Felix's only sibling; she must have cast a very large shadow indeed to be magnified into the nine or seven sisters whom Grove accounted for in his books. Spettigue was unable to find out much about Henny; she seems either to have died in early adolescence or run away, which would account for the vague role Grove's sisters play in the stories of his life. In *Our Daily Bread,* the difficult, sour daughter, Henrietta, is called Hennie from time to time.

The second child, Felix Paul Berthold Friedrich, was born at Rodomno in Germany, near the Russian-German border on February 14, 1879, and probably in a manor house (Carl Eduard had been relieved of his stewardship of the Thurow estate near the end of 1878). After the boy's birth they remained at Rodomno for five months, in Spettigue's opinion because they had no place else to go — a hint of anxieties to follow.

It seems that they then attempted to find their way back to familiar surroundings because they returned to the family neighbourhood of Schwerin. It was here that Carl Eduard began a career as a streetcar conductor. When Felix was two they went to Hamburg, no doubt in an attempt to better themselves. Carl Eduard again supported his family as a streetcar conductor, although when Felix was nine his father was given a small promotion, from conductor to collector. By the time the boy was seven the family had moved six times, from one pleasant middle-class apartment to another. Spettigue thinks that the apartments were more costly than Carl Eduard's small income could afford; perhaps the constant moving was the result of unpaid rent. In any case, a desire for luxury and resulting debt caused Felix Paul's later downfall.

He appears to have been the sickly child Grove described himself as being. Spettigue found a school record noting that the boy had weak lungs and that tuberculosis was a family disease. Grove was, of course, subject to pneumonia and it was the cause of his death.

When Felix was seven he was sent to St. Pauli School, a strictly-run institution controlled by the Evangelical Reformed Lutheran Church. (On his marriage certificate Grove had said that he was Lutheran.) The haphazard school career spent following his mother around Europe, which Grove describes in his autobiography, does not apply to Felix Paul. He spent eleven years at the St. Pauli School in Hamburg. It was a strict institution, but the nearby neighbourhood was disreputable, bordering on the docks. It is possible that the contrast between rigid school teachings and the licentious neighbourhood created Grove's later moralistic tone.

There was another child born to Bertha in 1885, but it was still-born. Felix was six at the time, old enough to understand. Nobody knows whether the baby died as a result of mistreatment by the father towards the mother, but the stillborn babies in Grove's novels are curious. Spettigue gives no hint of Carl Eduard's character. Was he as brutal as Grove describes in his autobiography? Was he like the tyrannical farmers? In 1892 the stresses in the family, from whatever cause, erupted, and Bertha left Carl Eduard, taking Felix and Henny with her. Later, Bertha and Carl Eduard were divorced. In Grove's farm novels, families break up when the children leave the old life on the soil and move to the city.

A strong link between the Grove autobiography and the Felix Paul Greve story emerges at this point. A man called Jacobsen attached himself to the separated mother and her children. He was a well-off ships' broker, as Grove had described his "Uncle Jacobsen" in *In Search of Myself*. The real one was born in Hamburg, not Denmark, although his name is Danish. Perhaps August Heinrich Jacobsen helped the family for, as far as Spettigue could make out, they were without resources.

Felix Paul was still attending the St. Pauli School. He graduated in 1895 when he was sixteen. His future was a pressing problem. His only resources were a penniless mother and her admirer. His father, with a salary of about two thousand dollars a year, could hardly provide much for future education and training. The "practical" course for Felix, as Grove's mother pointed out in the autobiography, would have been to go into commerce. In industrialized Germany, fortunes were being made by aggressive, talented business-men in the cities. But if Greve was Grove, he was well advised to shun business, for Grove's business ventures in Canada, be they publishing or farming, had a way of ending in disaster. Felix did shun business; he wanted to go to university, and he did so. Spettigue points out that the choice was unusual for a boy in Felix's position. Not only would he be unemployed for several years, he would need money to finance his studies and his living expenses, and from where was it to come? Only privileged boys attended university in those days, but Greve had good personal reasons, if not practical ones, for wanting to continue his studies. He was gifted, with a flair for mathematics and languages. University training would place him in a higher social sphere; he had a powerful longing to rise above his circumstances and become a man of account. He most certainly had intellectual interests.

But even to gain admission to a university he needed further schooling at an institution where Classics were taught. He entered a gymnasium in Hamburg as Grove said he had done in *In Search of Myself*. Spettigue thinks that he tutored to earn money, but debt was by now a way of life in his family. At the gymnasium, standards were stiff; Felix was introduced to the Classics for the first time and, though he did not win any prizes, his marks were good. Only twelve students in the graduating class had done well enough to enter university — Felix was one. In April, 1898, at the age of nineteen, he left home to enrol at Friedrich-Wilhelm University in Bonn. His course was philology, the study of languages. He had been at university only two weeks when his mother, the only support and guidance he had, died in Hamburg. By this time, his sister, Henny, had disappeared. He returned home for the funeral and seems to have taken on almost all the responsibility for the funeral arrangements himself, since it was he who filled out the death registration form. Carl Eduard remained in the background, but the mysterious Jacobsen appeared again and was present to help. Bertha died with only one hundred marks in her possession, or slightly over thirty dollars.

FELIX PAUL GREVE was a dandy. At the age of nineteen he was buying superb clothes and boots. He was also impressing his friends with his selection of fine wines and expensive books. He was a brilliant, erratic young man enjoying the life of a dilettante and aesthete.

Felix Paul was in search of an identity. It seems that he could not bear to be sneered at or looked down upon. His father's position as an employee of the streetcar company did not give him an acceptable background, and he may have suffered from this when he was a student at the gymnasium where the boys came from higher social and economic spheres. Later he was to tell stories about his father being a rich industrialist from Mecklenburg, or sometimes Hamburg, who had died ruined. In fact, Carl Eduard did not die until 1918, when Grove was settled and married in Canada.

Besides inventing a dead and rich father, what sort of persona should he create for himself? Dr. Spettigue's theory is that after intensive reading of modern literature, he assumed the lives of three writers as his own. They were Oscar Wilde, André Gide and Stefan George. Wilde was a fashionable, dissolute man, and Dr. Spettigue thinks that Felix discovered his young-man-of-fashion identity through him. Wilde was the "Son of a beautiful and talented mother whom he adored, of a very able father whom he jealously resented. . . ." We can see the germs of the Grove autobiography in this, and also, "Wilde grew up in an atmosphere of art and polite manners, of sensations and impracticalities."[122] This is the impression which Grove gave of his background, but it was hardly the reality of Greve's. As for Gide, he also was the child of wealthy parents; after his father's death he was brought up by his mother and her companion, Anna Shackleton. In Grove's autobiography, *he* is cared for by his mother's maid, Annette. Gide spent his early adolescence following his mother around France, rather in the manner Grove said he had trailed after his mother around Europe. Gide was introduced to literary circles in Paris and moved among writers such as Mallarmé, whom Grove also names in the stories of his life in Paris. By contrast there was the more austere Stefan George, who believed that art would lift mankind out of bestiality and materialism. There are strong echoes of this idea in Grove's essays *It Needs to be Said,* in which he pleads for the supremacy of man's godhead over his beasthood by way of the arts.

After only two years at university, spending money, which he did not have, like water, Felix threw up his studies, possibly because his creditors were after him. He began to write poetry and criticism and do translations (for which he was remarkably gifted) soon after he left Friedrich-Wilhelm University at Bonn in the fall of 1900. At the end of 1900 he suddenly went to Italy for at least ten months and there he wrote poetry. Back in Germany in the fall of 1901, he enrolled at university in Munich, not daring to go back to Bonn, Spettigue says, because he owed so much money there.

However, he had begun to make contacts with publishers; he had met well-known writers, and in 1901 he published two critical articles, one on Nietzsche. He had chosen his field and he gave up his formal education entirely, flinging himself into a chaotic existence of writing, intensive reading of modern authors, profligate extravagance and swamping debt.

In February, 1902, about the time of his twenty-third birthday, Felix Paul Greve published his first book. It was a collection of poems called *Wanderings,* reflecting the year he had spent travelling in Italy. No publisher was interested, so he published the slim volume himself in a beautifully produced, limited edition. The twenty-three poems, Dr. Spettigue says, "are dreamy, romantic, and they tend to show a youth prematurely beaten down, a loser in love, an aspirant to the heights who so often finds himself back down on the flats. . . ."[123] The perception of himself, generally, as a loser, is powerfully reminiscent of the Grove we know.

Ominously, the book was dedicated to a young friend of Felix's — one Herman Kilian. Spettigue thinks that Kilian, who was the son of a well-off doctor, paid for the publication of the poems, and it was Felix's later enormous debt to Kilian of thousands of marks which led him to utter disaster. To do Greve justice, he did not want to be in debt, and he was prepared to work tirelessly to pay what he owed and to earn his own living. Of course he was incredibly unrealistic about the difference between what he could earn and the expenses of his zestful life style.

In 1902 he published another volume of poetry privately, a verse drama, *Helena and Damon,* which Dr. Spettigue could not find but which was commented on by various sources. *Wanderings* was published again, this time by an established publisher.

Poetry was good for his reputation, but it didn't produce money. Felix was desperately in need of income. At this time German publishers were launching into a program of translations of foreign works into German; Oscar Wilde was a particularly fashionable writer and there was a lively market for his work. The situation was a godsend for Felix who was a gifted translator — and he knew Wilde's works well.

He began a career, not only as a poet, novelist, and critic, but as a translator of such a variety and number of works as to stagger the imagination. Spettigue's belief that Greve was Grove is strongly supported by Grove's speeches to the Canadian Clubs. In them, he demonstrated an intimate knowledge of Oscar Wilde, Edgar Allan Poe, Gustav Flaubert, George Meredith and others whose works were translated by Felix Paul Greve. He translated about forty works of significance; some of them are being republished in Germany today. He began by translating four plays by Oscar Wilde, which were produced by the Berlin Little Theatre. He followed these up with a volume of Wilde's sayings called *Intentions.*

At this point, Greve met a lady to whom he was to remain devoted for the rest of his European life. Dr. Spettigue was unable to find either her maiden name or her married one, so all we know about this influential person in Greve's life is her first name, Else, and the fact that she was married to an architect. Apparently Greve had met her at her house in Berlin and in November, 1902, he swept her off to live with him. In January, 1903, they went to Italy, but not before borrowing another six hundred marks from Herman Kilian. Kilian sent him another ten thousand marks later when Felix pleaded desperation.

Else and Felix travelled in Italy and Sicily, then settled down in a flat in Palermo. Felix plunged immediately into his work, translating some Browning and Walter Pater, and beginning a critical essay on Oscar Wilde. He also tutored to earn extra cash. For all his hard work and the strenuous attempts these two seemed to make to control their expenses (they lived in a "barren room", according to Felix's reports) Felix's debts finally caught up with him. He was earning the equivalent of only one thousand dollars a year; he owed thirteen thousand dollars.

Rather late, Kilian realized that Felix was not likely to pay him back. He wrote a crafty letter to his erstwhile friend, explaining that he was willing to give him more money if Felix would come to Bonn to collect it.

Felix went to Bonn without Else. As he stepped off the train two detectives arrested him for fraud. He had one pfennig in his pocket. He was convicted of fraud and sentenced to one year in prison.

No member of his family stepped forward to help him, not his father, nor his relatives in Mecklenburg. Felix was on his own, as he had been since his mother's death.

19 Wilhelm Street, Bonn-on-Rhine, became Felix's new office. "19 Wilhelm Street was, and is, the address of the Bonn prison,"[124]

Douglas Spettigue notes, and it was duly placed as the return address on Felix's business correspondence.

He began by writing to von Poellnitz of Insel Verlag, his publisher, begging him not to abandon him in his troubles, advising him that he was continuing with his translations of Browning and Pater and other works. He suggested that to avoid embarrassment, von Poellnitz might like to publish his work under a pseudonym, Friedrich Carl Gerden. Felix was to use several other pseudonyms during his German career, thus paving the way, we suppose, for the assumption of another name in Canada.

Von Poellnitz may have been startled by Felix's sanguinity under his new circumstances, but he agreed to the pseudonym and from the spring of 1903 until the spring of 1904, when Felix was in prison, his work poured forth. He began to translate George Meredith, Swinburne and more Browning; he asked for additional work and suggested that he translate H. G. Wells, Flaubert, DeQuincey and the Italian writer, Verga, besides works in classical languages. He started his first novel, *Fanny Essler*.

Not one penny that he earned went into his own pocket. By court order, Herman Kilian garnisheed all fees from his publisher, Insel Verlag, as payment on the debt. Felix attempted to find other publishers to avoid the disappearance of the money. Eventually he succeeded, but he also angered Insel Verlag to the extent that their association was severed for several years. Meanwhile, the steady stream of work from 19 Wilhelm Street was pouring just as steadily from the presses. This was partly due to the popularity of Oscar Wilde; Felix produced more work on Wilde — not only translations, but also criticism and biography — than any of his colleagues. Spettigue thinks it possible that within a year and a half he published twelve works on this English wit. He often spoke of doing a full biography but that never did materialize.

IN THE SPRING of 1904, Felix was released from prison. He immediately rejoined Else and looked about for ways to reestablish himself.

He went almost at once to Paris to meet André Gide in an attempt to make connections with the literary world. Douglas Spettigue's book climaxes with a piece by Gide called "Conversation with a

German," which Gide said he wrote down the day after his meeting with the German whom he identified as "F.P.G." It is an extremely cruel exposé of a man left frightened and vulnerable by a term in prison, bewildered by what he considered his friend Kilian's betrayal, and indeed, bewildered by all the events of his life. However, although the sketch is not admirable in any human sense, it is artistically so brilliant that one cannot help but wonder whether the artist in Gide tampered somewhat with details to give it shape, an impulse which attracted many a moral sneer to Grove himself.

Gide tells us that the German had a pale, smooth-shaven face "and the body so excessively tall that it made all the chairs too low. . . . F.P.G. was impeccably dressed, looking more English than German, so I was not at all surprised when he told me, a little later, that his mother was an Englishwoman."[125] F.P.G. offered Gide a cigarette from an exquisite silver box and a light from a matching silver matchbox. He was extremely nervous and confessed that he had just been released from prison, a fact which Gide knew, having been informed by the German who arranged the interview. He told Gide about the translating he had done in prison, although he exaggerated the quantity considerably; he spoke of his mother's death as a shocking and demoralizing blow which had left him rootless, and he told Gide that he had nine sisters, all of whom had died. (Spettigue is quick to point out the beginnings of the Grove legend here.) He said that his father was a rich industrialist from Mecklenburg who had died. The most disturbing element of the interview is that F.P.G. confessed to Gide that he was a compulsive liar, and that he had begun lying immediately after his mother's death. Pathetically, he seemed to think that only by telling lies could he hold his life together — at least he told Gide that it was his lies which kept his "wife" with him. ". . . it's when I'm with her that I tell lies most readily. That makes for some awful scenes between us. But in the end it's always the lying that wins out."[126] The interview ended inconclusively, and Gide did nothing to advance F.P.G.'s ambitions — all he did was to leave to posterity this distasteful portrait, with the supposedly guileless comment that it was presented solely for its "psychological" interest.

F.P.G. had referred to Else as his "wife" in his conversation with Gide, but at the same time he had told him that he expected to go to

Switzerland with her shortly so that they could be married. Spettigue is uncertain whether Felix and Else ever did marry. Married or not, they left soon after the Gide interview for Switzerland, Italy and northern France. He worked as hard as ever, and by using Else's name as translator on two volumes of Flaubert's letters he evidently tried to avoid having his fees deflected to Herman Kilian. He translated some De Quincey, George Meredith's *Diana of the Crossways*, and more H. G. Wells.

Gide had now replaced Oscar Wilde as the fashionable writer of the day and there was great demand for his works in translation. In 1905, two of Gide's most important works, *The Immoralist* and *Paludes* were translated by Felix and published in German. He also wrote and published an essay on Flaubert's critical methods. Along with this enormous amount of translation, Felix finished his first novel, the one begun in prison. *Fanny Essler* was published in 1905.

It tells the story of a young girl, Fanny, who had been a student at the Art Academy in Berlin until her mother died of cancer; then she had returned home to the country to live with her brutal father and younger sister. When her father catches her slipping home late one night after meeting a lover, he denounces her and she leaves home. She runs off to stay with an aunt, hoping for help and advice, but the aunt can offer no help and disapproves of Fanny. The girl realizes that there is no security at all now that her mother is dead; in both Greve's life and Grove's novels, the mother figure is the essential stabilizing force. Fanny goes to Berlin where she tries valiantly to make her own way. Her story is one of a rootless being who struggles against odds which are far beyond her strength. She decides that a rich husband is the only answer, and in order to attract one she studies drama and goes on the stage. She is talented, but actresses must provide their own expensive wardrobes and Fanny has no money, so she becomes a chorus girl. She passes from one lover to another; none of these men are any help to her since they are all either stingy or poor. However, some of her lovers are artists, and they encourage her natural artistic bent. She finally marries a writer, but the marriage is unhappy and Fanny falls in love with a rich archaeologist (who physically at least resembles Greve-Grove) and runs off with him. She now has money for the first time in her life, but the archaeologist sneers at her country manners and she is guilt-ridden when she finds that her former husband has committed suicide. Fanny, aged thirty, falls ill with malaria; she sinks into delirium, reliving her childhood in Pomerania, and dies. Like *The Yoke of Life, Fanny Essler* is a novel of unequal opportunities and it shows a remarkable sympathy for women.

During the period between 1904 and 1907, Felix wrote at least one other novel and perhaps two. *The Sentimentalist* seems to have disappeared and perhaps was never published, but in 1907, *Master-Mason Ihle's House* appeared. Suse Ihle is the daughter of the tyrannical master-mason Richard Ihle. His wife, Bertha, is a browbeaten, frightened woman, trying to protect her children from the father. The mother dies, but shortly before her death she runs away to a dance and tries to commit suicide. Dr. Spettigue recalls Martha Elliot in *Our Daily Bread* who runs off to make a spectacle of herself at a dance shortly before her death, and Grove's mother in *In Search of Myself* who abandons herself to a similar escapade. The bullying father remarries, but reaps the harvest of his cruelty for his second wife henpecks *him.* Greve, like Grove, was preoccupied with the struggle between overwhelming fathers and their children.

The flow of translation had slowed down while Felix was writing original work, but poverty pressed him back into it. He began to translate the *Arabian Nights,* Jonathan Swift's prose works, Balzac and Cervantes. But for all Felix's superhuman capacity for work, the pressure was beginning to tell. With creditors pushing him, he rushed through his translations and his work became slipshod; critics sneered and publishers complained. He wrote to Anton Kippenberg, a director of Insel Verlag, his publisher; ". . . and it happens that despite all my efforts my wife and I simply go hungry."[127] He begged for more work. His health was beginning to crack.

In spite of nervous strain and deteriorating health, 1907, the year of the publication of *Master-Mason Ihle's House,* was one of his most prolific. He produced a modernized version of some seventeenth-century German poems. The first five of the twelve volumes of his translation of the *One Thousand and One Nights* came out. It was one of his best-known translations and has been re-issued several times since. He translated three volumes of Balzac's twelve-volume *Comédie Humaine.*

But Felix Paul Greve was reaching the end of his rope. Any hopes of extricating himself from his mountainous debts were vanishing. He had worked like a Trojan and still he was bound hand and foot by those debts. A foreshadowing of flight occurred in 1908. Felix went to Sweden for the purpose of writing a travel article. He visited an area which was soon to be opened to pioneer farming. Who knows what thoughts were planted on that trip? Or at what moment the "Swedish" Grove was born?

ONE DAY IN 1909, Anton Kippenberg opened a letter from Else Greve. She told him that her husband had disappeared. He had left a note, telling her that he had boarded a steamer for Sweden "but would never get there."[128] Suicide was implied. Kippenberg suspected that the story was fabricated. His doubts were verified years later when he received a note from a New York clinic advising him that Felix Paul Greve had been admitted as a patient. So far as we know, that is the last that anyone in Germany heard of the brilliant, thwarted, struggling and finally desperate, Felix Paul Greve.

IN 1971, WHILE Douglas Spettigue was pursuing Felix Paul Greve across Europe, Catherine Grove in Simcoe, Ontario, had suddenly become ill. She was seventy-nine years old, but until November 25 she had enjoyed buoyant health, driving her own car to and from Toronto to visit Leonard and his family. She was stricken by a circulatory ailment and taken to hospital. On January 9, 1972, Catherine Grove died. Dr. Spettigue's findings about her husband's possible European existence were presented to her son, Leonard Grove. His response was cautious: "There are enough coincidences between Grove and Greve to go beyond coincidence."[129]

So far, Grove's years between leaving Europe and arriving in Winnipeg in 1912 are unexplored. With Dr. Spettigue's information that Greve left Europe in 1909, not 1892 as Grove said he had done, the unknown years have been reduced from twenty to two or three. The first indication of his appearance in North America is a poem, "At Sea," dated Nova Scotia, 1909. Perhaps he was on the ship which brought him here.

Grove's novels are peppered with references to changed or secret identities. In *A Search for America,* Phil Branden's waiter friend, Frank Carrol, says, "Carrol's as little my real name as yours is Branden."[130] In his autobiography, he comments on the remark of a critic who said that Abe Spalding "is a hero after Mr. Grove's heart." "I wondered who had told him that;" Grove said, "for I believe I have hidden myself fairly well."[131] In *The Master of the Mill,* a man named Ferguson is discussed at a dinner party at Clark House. This man had vanished, had been jailed for fraud and "had a string of aliases to his name."[132] Mr. Ferguson was also six foot three, Grove's height. Grove is reported to have said to his friend W. E. Collin, "I will confound my biographers.[133] He has indeed.

Grove's reputation as a writer has waxed and waned over the years; critics continue to comment irritably on his stilted dialogue and his tendency to use characters to illustrate philosophical points. He is, however, a hard man to dismiss. Perhaps more has been written about Grove than about any other Canadian writer. In May, 1973, a symposium was held on him at the University of Ottawa. It was attended by about two hundred scholars and students of his work from across the country. Few Canadian writers have commanded this sort of attention.

The late appearance of Douglas Spettigue at the Ottawa Symposium created a well-behaved academic stir. Although his book had not been published at that time, he had made the bare bones of his research known in two articles in *Queen's Quarterly,* so everybody was aware of his discovery of Felix Paul Greve and his belief that Greve was Grove. There were several skeptics in the audience. Tom Saunders of the *Winnipeg Free Press,* who has written a good deal about Grove, remarked that we should be as cautious about Spettigue's story as we are about Grove's. Dr. Spettigue managed a *coup,* however, when a paper on Grove's poetry was broken off to allow him to announce that one of Grove's poems, "The Flying Years," existing in both German and English among the Grove Papers at the University of Manitoba, is identical to a poem by Greve which Spettigue had found in Germany.

Leonard Grove attended the symposium on his father. His reaction was wistful: "If only he had been there. We could all have turned to him and asked, 'Now — tell us the true story'."[134]

Perhaps Grove would have told us the true story. Perhaps he

would have invented another, better one. It wasn't that Grove didn't know the difference between fact and fancy; no one knew better than he that every dream is destined to crack when it strikes reality. All but one of his novels are about smashed dreams. But without the dream, is life endurable? And without his dream of the Canadian west — a place where a man could begin anew — we would never have had the strange genius who was Frederick Philip Grove.

APPENDICES

NOTES AND REFERENCES

MARGARET LAURENCE

Brief quotations which are not acknowledged were provided to me by Margaret Laurence during a personal interview on August 31, 1972, and in written correspondence.

1. Letter from Mrs. C. Morden Carter, Margaret Laurence's aunt, to the author, December 8, 1972.
2. Letter from Mrs. C. Morden Carter to the author, December 8, 1972. Additional information from the Provincial Library, Winnipeg, Manitoba.
3. Donnalu Wigmore, "Margaret Laurence: The Woman Behind the Writing," *Chatelaine* (February, 1971).
4. Nadine Asante, "Margaret (Rachel, Rachel) Laurence," *Montrealer* (June, 1969).
5. Ontario Institute for Studies in Education, Toronto, "Canadian Writers on Tape: Margaret Laurence," Earle Topping, interviewer, 1971.
6. Wigmore.
7. *Annals of the Black and Gold* (Neepawa Collegiate Institute, Neepawa, Manitoba, June, 1943).
8. Margaret Laurence, "Jericho's Brick Battlements," *A Bird in the House* (Alfred A. Knopf Inc., New York, 1970), p. 199.
9. Wigmore.
10. Margaret Laurence, "Where the World Began," *Maclean's* (December, 1972).
11. Letter from Margaret Laurence to the author, August 23, 1973.
12. "Laurence of Manitoba," *Canadian Author and Bookman* (Winter, 1966).
13. Clara Thomas, *Margaret Laurence* (McClelland and Stewart Ltd., Toronto, 1969), p. 7.
14. *Ibid.*
15. *Vox* (United College student publication, Graduation Issue, 1947).
16. All information and quotations about Somaliland were taken from Margaret Laurence's travel book on that country: *The Prophet's Camel Bell* (McClelland and Stewart Ltd., Toronto, 1963).
17. Micene (Guthane) Mugo, untitled review of Margaret Laurence's *A Tree for Poverty,* in *Journal of Canadian Fiction* (Summer, 1971).
18. "Laurence of Manitoba."
19. *Ibid.*
20. *Ibid.*
21. Wigmore.

22. Margaret Laurence, "Ten Years' Sentences," *Canadian Literature* (Summer, 1969).
23. All information and quotations about the trials of rewriting *This Side Jordan* from Laurence's "Ten Years' Sentences."
24. *Ibid.*
25. Wigmore.
26. Margaret Laurence, *The Stone Angel* (McClelland and Stewart Ltd., Toronto, 1968), p. 129.
27. *Ibid.*, p. 292.
28. *Ibid.*, p. 304.
29. *Ibid.*, p. 3.
30. *Ibid.*
31. Asante.
32. Wigmore.
33. Thomas, p. 13.
34. Wigmore.
35. Margaret Laurence, *A Jest of God* (McClelland and Stewart Ltd., Toronto, 1966), pp. 123-124.
36. *Ibid.*, p. 201.
37. Asante.
38. Wigmore.
39. *Ibid.*
40. Asante.
41. *Ibid.*
42. *Ibid.*
43. Margaret Laurence, *Long Drums and Cannons* (Macmillan and Company Ltd., London, 1968), p. 9.
44. Laurence, "Ten Years' Sentences."
45. Margaret Laurence, *Jason's Quest* (McClelland and Stewart Ltd., Toronto, 1970), p. 60.
46. *Ibid.*, p. 204.
47. Asante.
48. Laurence, "Ten Years' Sentences."
49. Conversation with the author, August 31, 1972.
50. Margaret Laurence, *The Fire-Dwellers* (McClelland and Stewart Ltd., Toronto, 1969), p. 289.
51. Wigmore.
52. *Ibid.*
53. Letter from Margaret Laurence to the author, February 8, 1973.
54. *Ibid.*
55. Laurence, *The Prophet's Camel Bell*, p. 189.
56. Conversation with the author, August 31, 1972.
57. Wigmore.
58. Laurence, "Jericho's Brick Battlements," *A Bird in the House*, p. 205.

59. *Ibid.,* p. 207.
60. Laurence, "Ten Years' Sentences."
61. Wigmore.
62. *Ibid.*
63. *Ibid.*
64. Ontario Institute for Studies in Education, Toronto, "Canadian Writers on Tape: Margaret Laurence," 1971.
65. Conversation with the author, August 31, 1972.
66. Wigmore.
67. *Ibid.*
68. Letter from Margaret Laurence to the author, February 8, 1973.
69. Wigmore.
70. *Ibid.*
71. Laurence, "Where the World Began."
72. Letter from Margaret Laurence to the author, April 21, 1973.
73. Letter from Margaret Laurence to the author, February 19, 1973.
74. Margaret Laurence, *The Diviners* (McClelland and Stewart Ltd., Toronto, 1974), p. 319.
75. *Ibid.,* p. 370.

GABRIELLE ROY

1. Letter from Gabrielle Roy to the author, June 4, 1973.
2. *Ibid.*
3. Conversation with Gabrielle Roy, April 19, 1973.
4. Gabrielle Roy, "By Day and By Night," *Street of Riches* (McClelland and Stewart Ltd., Toronto, 1967), p. 145.
5. Conversation with Gabrielle Roy, April 19, 1973.
6. *Ibid.*
7. *Ibid.*
8. *Ibid.*
9. *Ibid.*
10. Tony Dickason, "Gabrielle Roy's Own Story Recalled by Sister Here," *Winnipeg Tribune* (March 1, 1947).
11. Gabrielle Roy, "Souvenirs du Manitoba," *Le Devoir* (November 15, 1955). Translated from the French by the author.
12. Conversation with Gabrielle Roy, August 27, 1973.
13. Conversation with Gabrielle Roy, April 19, 1973.
14. Alice Parizeau, "Gabrielle Roy, la grande romancière canadienne," *Châtelaine* (April, 1966). Translated from the French by the author.
15. Gabrielle Roy, "Souvenirs du Manitoba."
16. Gabrielle Roy, "To Earn My Living . . . ," *Street of Riches* (McClelland and Stewart Ltd., Toronto, 1967), p. 151.

17. Conversation with Gabrielle Roy, April 19, 1973.
18. Letter from Gabrielle Roy to the author, August 1, 1973.
19. Gabrielle Roy, "L'Enfant morte," *Cet été qui chantait* (Les Éditions Français Inc., Quebec, 1972).
20. Conversation with Gabrielle Roy, April 19, 1973.
21. Donald Cameron, "Gabrielle Roy: A Bird in the Prison Window," *Conversations with Canadian Novelists—2* (The Macmillan Company of Canada Ltd., Toronto, 1973), pp. 138-139.
22. Phyllis Grosskurth, *Gabrielle Roy* (Forum House Publishing Co., Toronto, 1972), p. 8.
23. Conversation with Gabrielle Roy, June 26, 1973.
24. Cameron, p. 130.
25. Letter from Gabrielle Roy to the author, June 4, 1973.
26. Cameron, pp. 129-130.
27. Marc Gagné, *Visages de Gabrielle Roy* (Librairie Beauchemin Limitée, Montreal, 1973), p. 23.
28. *Ibid.,* pp. 26-27.
29. *Ibid.,* pp. 27-28.
30. Gabrielle Roy, "Après trois cent ans," *le Bulletin des agriculteurs* (September, 1941). Translated from the French by the author.
31. Gagné, p. 39.
32. Cameron, p. 135.
33. Letter from Gabrielle Roy to the author, August 1, 1973.
34. Cameron, p. 134.
35. Gabrielle Roy, "The Road Past Altamont," *The Road Past Altamont* (McClelland and Stewart Ltd., Toronto, 1966), p. 146.
36. Conversation with Gabrielle Roy, April 19, 1973.
37. Dorothy Duncan, "Le Triomphe de Gabrielle," *Maclean's* (April 15, 1947).
38. Hugo McPherson, "Introduction," *The Tin Flute* (McClelland and Stewart Ltd., Toronto, 1969), p. v.
39. *The Canadian Forum,* unsigned article (July, 1947).
40. Duncan.
41. Conversation with Gabrielle Roy, April 19, 1973.
42. Duncan.
43. Newspaper clipping, source unknown, found in Central Reference Library, Toronto, file on Gabrielle Roy.
44. Letter from Gabrielle Roy to the author, August 1, 1973.
45. Gabrielle Roy, *The Tin Flute* (McClelland and Stewart Ltd., Toronto, 1969), p. 102.
46. Canadian Press, "Cleric Criticizes Miss Roy's Novel," *The Winnipeg Tribune* (June 6, 1947).
47. Conversation with Gabrielle Roy, April 19, 1973.
48. Letter from Gabrielle Roy to the author, June 4, 1973.

49. Gabrielle Roy, "Comment j'ai reçu le 'Fémina'," *Le Devoir* (Montreal, December 15, 1956). Speech given December 12, 1956 by Gabrielle Roy upon receiving the Prix Duvernay from the Saint-Jean-Baptiste Society. Translated from the French by the author.
50. Gagné, p. 226. Translated from the French by the author.
51. *Ibid.,* p. 228. Translated from the French by the author.
52. Gabrielle Roy, "Préface," *La Petite Poule d'Eau (Éditions du Burin et Martinsart,* Paris, 1967). Translated from the French by the author.
53. Cameron, pp. 131-132.
54. Gabrielle Roy, *Where Nests the Water Hen* (McClelland and Stewart Ltd., Toronto, 1970), p. 24.
55. *Ibid.,* p. 95.
56. *Ibid.,* p. 103.
57. *Ibid.,* p. 159.
58. *Ibid.,* p. 160.
59. F. Ambrière, "Gabrielle Roy, écrivain canadien," *La Revue de Paris* (December, 1947). Translated from the French by the author.
60. Cameron, p. 133.
61. Conversation with Gabrielle Roy, April 19, 1973.
62. Gabrielle Roy, *The Cashier* (McClelland and Stewart Ltd., Toronto, 1963), p. 102.
63. Conversation with Gabrielle Roy, April 19, 1973.
64. Roy, *The Cashier,* p. 180.
65. *Ibid.,* p. 188.
66. *Ibid.,* p. 205.
67. Gagné, p. 69. Translated from the French by the author.
68. Roy, "Petite Misère," *Street of Riches,* p. 15.
69. *Ibid.,* p. 19.
70. *Ibid.,* p. 20.
71. Roy, "My Pink Hat," *Street of Riches,* p. 23.
72. *Ibid.,* p. 24.
73. Roy, "The Voice of the Pools," *Street of Riches,* p. 132.
74. Roy, "To Earn My Living . . . ," *Street of Riches,* p. 158.
75. "St. Boniface Novelist Gets Canadian Award," *Winnipeg Tribune* (May 3, 1958).
76. Letter from Gabrielle Roy to the author, June 4, 1973.
77. Gabrielle Roy, *The Hidden Mountain* (McClelland and Stewart Ltd., Toronto, 1962), p. 62.
78. *Ibid.,* p. 82.
79. *Ibid.,* p. 83.
80. *Ibid.,* p. 98.
81. Gagné, p. 216. Translated from the French by the author.
82. Roy, *The Hidden Mountain,* p. 147.

83. *Ibid.,* p. 186.
84. Cameron, p. 144.
85. Conversation with Gabrielle Roy, April 19, 1973.
86. Gagné, p. 216. Translated from the French by the author.
87. Roy, *The Hidden Mountain,* p. 109.
88. Gagné, p. 261. Translated from the French by the author.
89. Conversation with Gabrielle Roy, April 19, 1973.
90. Gabrielle Roy, "Introduction," Man and His World. *Terre des Hommes* (Canadian Corporation for the 1967 Exhibition, Ottawa, 1967), p. 24.
91. Cameron, p. 142.
92. Gabrielle Roy, "My Almighty Grandmother," *The Road Past Altamont* (McClelland and Stewart Ltd., Toronto, 1966), pp. 6-7.
93. Roy, "The Old Man and the Child," *The Road Past Altamont,* pp. 52-53.
94. *Ibid.,* p. 75.
95. *Ibid.,* p. 80.
96. *Ibid.,* p. 81.
97. *Ibid.*
98. *Ibid.,* p. 86.
99. Roy, "The Move," *The Road Past Altamont,* p. 106.
100. *Ibid.*
101. Roy, "The Road Past Altamont," *The Road Past Altamont,* p. 139.
102. *Ibid.,* p. 146.
103. Brian Moore, "Gabrielle Roy," *Great Canadians: A Century of Progress,* Pierre Berton, ed. (The Centennial Book Publishing Company Ltd., Toronto, 1965), p. 96.
104. Conversation with Gabrielle Roy, April 19, 1973.
105. All quotations and information about Gabrielle Roy's trip to Fort Chimo are from a conversation with her, April 19, 1973.
106. Gabrielle Roy, "Les Satellites," *La Rivière sans repos* (Librairie Beauchemin Limitée, Montreal, 1970), p. 39. Translated from the French by the author.
107. *Ibid.,* pp. 49-50.
108. Roy, "Le Téléphone," *La Rivière sans repos,* p. 88.
109. Roy, "Le Fauteuil," *La Rivière sans repos,* p. 93.
110. *Ibid.,* p. 111.
111. Gabrielle Roy, *Windflower* (McClelland and Stewart Ltd., Toronto, 1970), p. 89.
112. *Ibid.,* p. 152.
113. Letter from Gabrielle Roy to the author, August 1, 1973.
114. Letter from Gabrielle Roy to the author, August 1, 1973.
115. Cameron, p. 136.
116. Letter from Gabrielle Roy to the author, August 1, 1973.
117. Gabrielle Roy, "La Gatte de monsieur Émile," *Cet été qui chantait*

(Les Éditions Françaises Inc., Quebec, 1972), p. 29. Translated from the French by the author.

118. *Ibid.,* p. 30.
119. *Ibid.*
120. *Ibid.,* p. 31.

FREDERICK PHILIP GROVE

1. Margaret R. Stobie, *Frederick Philip Grove* (Twayne Publishers Inc., New York, 1973), p. 25. Dr. Stobie interviewed Robert Fletcher and received the information from him about the telephone call. Grove's version is slightly different: he said in his autobiography that he had written to Fletcher, was too poor to afford a stamp, and had walked to his house with the letter.
2. Arthur L. Phelps, "Appraising a Passionate Enigma," *Globe Magazine* (November 29, 1969).
3. Stobie, *ibid.*
4. Stobie, pp. 28-29.
5. Frederick Philip Grove, *In Search of Myself* (McClelland and Stewart Ltd., Toronto, 1974), p. 266.
6. Stobie, p. 30. This anecdote is based on an account in Dr. Stobie's book.
7. Letter from Grove to John Warkentin, December 6, 1913.
8. Letter from Grove to John Warkentin, February 10, 1914.
9. "In Search of Frederick Philip Grove," radio documentary in two parts, produced by Allan Anderson for the Canadian Broadcasting Corporation, September 5 and 12, 1962.
10. Letter from Grove to Katrina Wiens, June 26, 1914.
11. Letter from Grove to Katrina Wiens, June 29, 1914.
12. Letters from Grove to Katrina Wiens, July 9 and 11, 1914.
13. Conversation with Mary Grove, November 30, 1973. The details of the courtship between Katrina and Grove were recounted much later by Mrs. Frederick Philip Grove to her daughter-in-law, Mary Grove, who told them to the author.
14. Grove, *In Search of Myself,* p. 275.
15. Conversation with Mary Grove, November 30, 1973.
16. Stobie, p. 33.
17. Stobie, pp. 34-35.
18. Frederick Philip Grove, *Over Prairie Trails* (McClelland and Stewart Ltd., Toronto, 1957), p. 117.
19. Stobie, p. 43.
20. "In Search of Frederick Philip Grove."
21. Grove, *In Search of Myself,* p. 296.

22. Stobie, pp. 47-50. Based on tape recorded interviews which Dr. Stobie made in 1970 with former pupils of Mrs. Grove.

23. Grove, *In Search of Myself*, p. 319.

24. Stobie, p. 47.

25. "In Search of Frederick Philip Grove."

26. Letter to Grove from McClelland and Stewart Ltd., January 29, 1920.

27. This anecdote is based on an account in Douglas O. Spettigue, *Frederick Philip Grove* (The Copp Clark Publishing Company, Toronto, 1969), p. 51.

28. "In Search of Frederick Philip Grove."

29. Stobie, p. 74.

30. Frederick Philip Grove, *The Turn of the Year* (McClelland and Stewart Ltd., Toronto, 1923), p. 179.

31. *Ibid.*, p. 26.

32. Arthur L. Phelps, "Introduction," *The Turn of the Year*, p. 9.

33. Stobie, p. 90.

34. "In Search of Frederick Philip Grove."

35. *Ibid.*

36. Grove, *In Search of Myself*, pp. 223-224.

37. Frederick Philip Grove, *Settlers of the Marsh* (McClelland and Stewart Ltd., Toronto, 1966), p. 154.

38. "In Search of Frederick Philip Grove."

39. Grove, *In Search of Myself*, p. 338.

40. *Ibid.*, p. 391.

41. "In Search of Frederick Philip Grove."

42. *Ibid.*

43. Grove adapted for May's tombstone the lines from *Adonaïs*, Shelley's lament on the death of Keats:
    He is a portion of the loveliness
    Which once he made more lovely: . . .

44. Frederick Philip Grove, *A Search for America* (McClelland and Stewart Ltd., Toronto, 1971), p. 322.

45. *Ibid.*, p. 392.

46. *Ibid.*, p. 382.

47. "In Search of Frederick Philip Grove."

48. Frederick Philip Grove, *It Needs to be Said* (The Macmillan Company of Canada Ltd., Toronto, 1929), p. 137.

49. Stobie, p. 121.

50. Letter from Grove to Catherine Grove, March, 1928.

51. Letter from Grove to Catherine Grove, March, 1928.

52. Letter from Grove to Catherine Grove, March 3, 1928.

53. Letter from Grove to Catherine Grove, March, 1928.

54. Letter from Grove to Catherine Grove, October, 1928.

55. Letter from Hugh Eayrs to Grove, July, 1929.

56. Letter from Grove to Watson Kirkconnell, June, 1929.

57. Grove, *In Search of Myself,* p. 399.
58. *Ibid.,* p. 424.
59. Letter from Hugh Eayrs to Grove, July 29, 1929.
60. Stobie, p. 133.
61. Grove, *In Search of Myself,* pp. 403-405.
62. *Ibid.,* p. 411.
63. Letter from Grove to Lorne Pierce, April 1, 1940.
64. "In Search of Frederick Philip Grove."
65. Conversation with Leonard Grove, November 30, 1973.
66. Frederick Philip Grove, *The Yoke of Life* (The Macmillan Company of Canada Ltd., Toronto 1930), p. 346.
67. *Ibid.,* p. 354.
68. William Arthur Deacon, a review, *The Ottawa Citizen* (October 11, 1930).
69. Grove, *In Search of Myself,* p. 419.
70. Stobie, p. 158.
71. Frederick Philip Grove, *Fruits of the Earth* (McClelland and Stewart Ltd., Toronto, 1965), pp. 118-119.
72. *Ibid.,* p. 118.
73. Stobie, p. 161.
74. Quoted in Douglas O. Spettigue, *Frederick Philip Grove* (The Copp Clark Publishing Company, Toronto, 1969), p. 55.
75. Grove, *In Search of Myself,* p. 445.
76. Conversation with Mary Grove, November 30, 1973.
77. Stobie, p. 161.
78. Conversation with Leonard Grove, November 30, 1973.
79. "In Search of Frederick Philip Grove."
80. *Ibid.*
81. Grove, *In Search of Myself,* p. 439.
82. Conversation with Mary Grove, January 6, 1974.
83. Stobie, pp. 178-179.
84. W. A. Deacon, a review, *The Globe and Mail* (August 5, 1939).
85. W. S. Milne, a review, *Saturday Night* (August 5, 1939).
86. Barker Fairley, untitled article, *The Canadian Forum* (October, 1939).
87. Stobie, p. 181.
88. "In Search of Frederick Philip Grove."
89. Conversation with Mary Grove, November 30, 1973.
90. "In Search of Frederick Philip Grove."
91. Stobie, p. 183.
92. "In Search of Frederick Philip Grove."
93. *Ibid.*
94. Frederick Philip Grove, *The Master of the Mill* (McClelland and Stewart Ltd., Toronto, 1961), p. 20 .
95. *Ibid.,* p. 105.
96. *Ibid.,* p. 217.

97. *Ibid.,* p. 332.
98. J. E. Middleton, "Of course any author has the right to his opinions, however distorted and unreal," *Saturday Night* (January 20, 1945).
99. Letter from Grove to Desmond Pacey, February 8, 1944. Published in *Canadian Literature* (Winter, 1962).
100. Stobie, p. 34.
101. "In Search of Frederick Philip Grove."
102. Letter from Grove to Desmond Pacey, February 8, 1944. Published in *Canadian Literature* (Winter, 1962).
103. Grove, *In Search of Myself,* p. 15.
104. Grove, *A Search for America,* p. 3.
105. Grove, *In Search of Myself,* p. 19.
106. *Ibid.,* p. 154.
107. *Ibid.,* p. 235.
108. *Ibid.,* p. 364.
109. *Ibid.,* p. 243.
110. "In Search of Frederick Philip Grove."
111. Stobie, p. 184.
112. Frederick Philip Grove, *Consider Her Ways* (The Macmillan Company of Canada Ltd., Toronto, 1947), p. 25.
113. *Ibid.,* p. 9.
114. *Ibid.,* p. 101.
115. *Ibid.,* p. 22.
116. *Ibid.,* p. 23.
117. *Ibid.,* p. 114.
118. *Ibid.,* p. 115.
119. Grove, *In Search of Myself,* p. 359.
120. Grove, *Consider Her Ways,* p. 253.
121. *Ibid.,* p. 201.
122. Douglas O. Spettigue, *F.P.G. The European Years* (Oberon Press Ltd., Ottawa, 1973), p. 52. Dr. Spettigue points out that this description of Wilde comes from two books on him by F. P. Greve.
123. *Ibid.,* p. 64.
124. *Ibid.,* p. 95.
125. *Ibid.,* pp. 119-120. This is presumably Dr. Spettigue's English translation of "Conversation avec un Allemand," by André Gide.
126. *Ibid.,* p. 123. See previous note.
127. Letter from Felix Paul Greve to Anton Kippenberg, April 15, 1907. Reprinted in Spettigue, *F.P.G. The European Years,* p. 151.
128. Spettigue, *F.P.G. The European Years,* p. 161.
129. Conversation with Leonard Grove, January 6, 1974.
130. Grove, *A Search for America,* p. 80.
131. Grove, *In Search of Myself,* p. 383.
132. Grove, *The Master of the Mill,* p. 141.
133. Conversation with Mary Grove, January 6, 1974.
134. Conversation with Leonard Grove, December 10, 1973.

BIBLIOGRAPHY

BOOKS BY MARGARET LAURENCE

A Tree for Poverty. (1954) McMaster University Press, Hamilton, 1970. Somali prose and poetry in translation.

This Side Jordan. (1960) McClelland and Stewart Ltd., Toronto, 1960. Novel.

The Prophet's Camel Bell. (1963) McClelland and Stewart Ltd., Toronto, 1963. Travel.

The Tomorrow Tamer. (1963) McClelland and Stewart Ltd., Toronto, 1970. Short stories.

The Stone Angel. (1964) McClelland and Stewart Ltd., Toronto, 1968. Novel.

A Jest of God. (1966) McClelland and Stewart Ltd., Toronto, 1966. Novel.

Long Drums and Cannons. (1968) Macmillan and Co. Ltd., London, 1968. Commentary on Nigerian writing.

The Fire-Dwellers. (1969) McClelland and Stewart Ltd., Toronto, 1973. Novel.

Jason's Quest. (1970) McClelland and Stewart Ltd., Toronto, 1970. Children's book.

A Bird in the House. (1970) McClelland and Stewart Ltd., Toronto, 1970. Short stories.

The Diviners. (1974) McClelland and Stewart Ltd., Toronto, 1974. Novel.

BOOKS BY GABRIELLE ROY

Bonheur d'occasion. (1945) Librairie Beauchemin Limitée, Montreal, 1948. Novel.

La Petite Poule d'Eau. (1950) Librairie Beauchemin Limitée, Montreal, 1965. Novel.

Alexandre Chenevert. (1954) Librairie Beauchemin Limitée, Montreal, 1964. Novel.

Rue Deschambault. (1955) Librairie Beauchemin Limitée, Montreal, 1967. Short stories.

La Montagne secrète. (1961) Librairie Beauchemin Limitée, Montreal, 1968. Novel.

La Route d'Altamont. (1966) Editions Hurtubise-H.M.H. Limitée, Montreal, 1966. Stories.

La Rivière sans repos. (1970) Librairie Beauchemin Limitée, Montreal, 1970. Novel and three stories.

Cet été qui chantait. (1972) Les Éditions Françaises Inc., Quebec, 1972. Stories.

IN ENGLISH TRANSLATION

The Tin Flute. (1947) McClelland and Stewart Ltd., Toronto, 1969. Novel.
Where Nests the Water Hen. (1951) McClelland and Stewart Ltd., Toronto, 1965. Novel.
The Cashier. (1955) McClelland and Stewart Ltd., Toronto, 1963. Novel.
Street of Riches. (1957) McClelland and Stewart Ltd., Toronto, 1967. Short stories.
The Hidden Mountain. (1962) McClelland and Stewart Ltd., Toronto, 1974. Novel.
The Road Past Altamont. (1966) McClelland and Stewart Ltd., Toronto, 1966. Stories.
Windflower. (1970) McClelland and Stewart Ltd., Toronto, 1970. Novel.

BOOKS BY FREDERICK PHILIP GROVE

Over Prairie Trails. (1922) McClelland and Stewart Ltd., Toronto, 1970. Essays.
The Turn of the Year. (1923) McClelland and Stewart Ltd., Toronto, 1923. Sketches.
Settlers of the Marsh. (1925) McClelland and Stewart Ltd., Toronto, 1965. Novel.
A Search for America: the odyssey of an immigrant. (1927) McClelland and Stewart Ltd., Toronto, 1971. Novel.
Our Daily Bread. (1928) Macmillan Company of Canada Ltd., Toronto, 1928. Novel.
It Needs to be Said. (1929) Macmillan Company of Canada Ltd., Toronto, 1929. Speeches and essays.
The Yoke of Life. (1930) Macmillan Company of Canada Ltd., Toronto, 1930. Novel.
Fruits of the Earth. (1933) McClelland and Stewart Ltd., Toronto, 1965. Novel.
Two Generations. (1939) The Ryerson Press Ltd., Toronto, 1939. Novel.
The Master of the Mill. (1944) McClelland and Stewart Ltd., Toronto, 1961. Novel.
In Search of Myself. (1946) McClelland and Stewart Ltd., Toronto, 1974. Autobiography.
Consider Her Ways. (1947) Macmillan Company of Canada Ltd., Toronto, 1947. Fantasy.
Tales from the Margin. (1971) Desmond Pacey, ed., McGraw-Hill Ryerson Ltd., Toronto, 1971. Short Stories.

ACKNOWLEDGMENTS

The author and publisher are grateful to the following copyright holders for permission to quote directly and indirectly from their works:

MARGARET LAURENCE

CANADIAN AUTHORS' ASSOCIATION "Laurence of Manitoba," by Gladys Taylor, *The Canadian Author and Bookman,* Winter, 1966.

THE JAMES PUBLISHING COMPANY "Margaret (Rachel, Rachel) Laurence," by Nadine Asante, in *The Montrealer,* June, 1969.

JOURNAL OF CANADIAN FICTION Review of Margaret Laurence's *A Tree for Poverty,* by Micene (Guthane) Mugo, Summer, 1971.

ALFRED A. KNOPF, INC. Acknowledgement is made to Alfred A. Knopf, Inc. for permission to quote from the following copyrighted works of Margaret Laurence: *A Bird in the House, The Tomorrow Tamer, The Stone Angel, A Jest of God, New Wind in a Dry Land, The Fire-Dwellers, Jason's Quest, The Diviners;* and for four lines from "The Gates of Damascus," by James Elroy Flecker.

MACLEAN-HUNTER LIMITED "Where the World Began," by Margaret Laurence, *Maclean's,* December, 1972.

MACMILLAN, LONDON AND BASINGSTOKE For permission to quote from the following novels by Margaret Laurence: *A Bird in the House, The Tomorrow Tamer, The Stone Angel, A Jest of God, Long Drums and Cannons, The Fire-Dwellers, Jason's Quest, The Prophet's Camel Bell.*

MARGARET LAURENCE "Ten Years' Sentences," first published in *Canadian Literature,* Summer, 1969, and "Where the World Began," published in *Maclean's,* December, 1972.

MCCLELLAND AND STEWART LIMITED and MARGARET LAURENCE from *A Bird in the House, The Tomorrow Tamer, The Stone Angel, A Jest of God, The Fire-Dwellers, Jason's Quest, Long Drums and Cannons, The Diviners,* by Margaret Laurence; and from *Margaret Laurence,* by Clara Thomas, reprinted by permission of The Canadian Publishers, McClelland and Stewart Limited, Toronto.

ONTARIO INSTITUTE FOR STUDIES IN EDUCATION "Canadian Writers on Tape: Margaret Laurence," interview with Earle Topping, 1971.

PRAEGER PUBLISHERS, INC. From *Long Drums and Cannons: Nigerian Dramatists and Novelists,* by Margaret Laurence, © 1968 in London, England, by Margaret Laurence. Excerpted and reprinted by permission of Praeger Publishers, Inc., New York.

THE UNIVERSITY OF WINNIPEG STUDENTS' ASSOCIATION, INC.   *Vox,* Graduation Issue, 1947.
DONNALU WIGMORE   "Margaret Laurence: The Woman Behind the Writing," published in *Chatelaine,* February, 1971.

GABRIELLE ROY

HARCOURT BRACE JOVANOVICH, INC.   *The Road Past Altamont,* by Gabrielle Roy, New York.
LE DEVOIR   "Souvenirs du Manitoba," November 15, 1955; "Comment j'ai reçu le 'Fémina'," December 15, 1956, by Gabrielle Roy.
LIBRAIRIE BEAUCHEMIN LIMITÉE and MARC GAGNÉ   For permission to quote from *Visages de Gabrielle Roy,* by Marc Gagné, Montreal, 1973.
LIBRAIRIE BEAUCHEMIN LIMITÉE and GABRIELLE ROY   For permission to quote from *La Rivière sans repos,* by Gabrielle Roy, Montreal, 1970.
MACLEAN-HUNTER LIMITED   "Le Triomphe de Gabrielle," by Dorothy Duncan, *Maclean's,* April 15, 1947.
THE MACMILLAN COMPANY OF CANADA LTD.   "Gabrielle Roy: A Bird in the Prison Window," from *Conversations with Canadian Novelists—2,* by Donald Cameron, 1973. Reprinted by permission of The Macmillan Company of Canada Ltd.
MCCLELLAND AND STEWART LTD. and GABRIELLE ROY   *The Tin Flute, The Road Past Altamont, Windflower, Where Nests the Water Hen, The Cashier, Street of Riches, The Hidden Mountain,* by Gabrielle Roy; material from *Great Canadians: A Century of Progress,* edited by Pierre Berton; reprinted by permission of The Canadian Publishers, McClelland and Stewart Limited, Toronto.
RÉALITÉS   "Gabrielle Roy, écrivain canadien," by F. Ambrière, in *La Revue de Paris,* December, 1947.
GABRIELLE ROY   For permission to quote from *Cet été qui chantait,* published by Les Éditions Françaises, Inc., Quebec, 1972; and the "Préface" to *La Petite Poule d'Eau,* Editions du Burin et Martinsart, Paris, 1967.
THE DEPARTMENT OF INDUSTRY, TRADE AND COMMERCE and GABRIELLE ROY   For permission to quote from Gabrielle Roy's Introduction to *Man and His World. Terre des Hommes,* The Canadian Corporation for the 1967 World Exhibition, Montreal, 1967.
THE WINNIPEG TRIBUNE   "Gabrielle Roy's Own Story Recalled by Sister Here," by Tony Dickason, March 1, 1947; "St. Boniface Novelist Gets Canadian Award," May 3, 1958.

FREDERICK PHILIP GROVE

ALLAN ANDERSON   "In Search of Frederick Philip Grove: A Symposium," CBC radio documentary, broadcast September 5 and 12, 1962.

THE COPP CLARK PUBLISHING COMPANY   For permission to use material from *Frederick Philip Grove,* by Douglas O. Spettigue, 1969.

JAMES EAYRS   Letters from Hugh Eayrs to Frederick Philip Grove, June 1929 and July 29, 1929.

GROVE COLLECTION, UNIVERSITY OF MANITOBA   Letter from J.F.B. Livesay to F.P. Grove, March 19, 1926. Copyright © Dorothy Livesay.

LEONARD GROVE   For permission to quote from F.P. Grove's personal correspondence, and from his books: *It Needs to be Said, The Yoke of Life, Consider Her Ways,* published by The Macmillan Company of Canada Limited; *In Search of Myself, Over Prairie Trails, The Turn of the Year, Settlers of the Marsh, A Search for America, Fruits of the Earth, The Master of the Mill,* reprinted by permission of The Canadian Publishers, McClelland and Stewart Limited, Toronto.

OBERON PRESS   The quotations on pages 200-202, 204, 206 are reproduced from *FPG: The European Years,* by Douglas O. Spettigue, 1973.

MRS. J.D. HAMILTON and MARGARET PHELPS   "Appraising a Passionate Enigma," by Arthur L. Phelps, *The Globe Magazine,* Toronto, November 29, 1969.

TWAYNE PUBLISHERS, INC.   *Frederick Philip Grove,* Margaret Stobie, New York, 1972.

Every effort has been made on the part of the publishers to locate all holders of copyrights and to make correct acknowledgments. For any oversights sincere regrets are offered.

INDEX

See also *In Search of Myself,*
185-6
Jeffers, Robinson, 14, 15
Je suis partout, 80, 81
Josephson, Hannah, 93-4
Joual, 115-16
Journalism, re: Margaret Laurence,
15-16; re: Gabrielle Roy, 80-3

Kennedy, Leo, 146
Kentucky, re: Grove, 137, 182,
183, 189
Kilian, Herman, 201, 202, 203,
204, 205
Kippenberg, Anton, 206, 207
Kirkconnell, Watson, 146, 154,
155, 156, 165, 169
Klein, A.M., 146
Knopf, Alfred, 34-5

Lakefield, re: Margaret Laurence,
55-6, 60
Landon, Munro, 178
Laurence, David, 26, 28, 29, 31,
40-1, 50-1, 53-4, 55
Laurence, Elsie Fry, 15
Laurence, Jack, 15, 16, 17, 18, 19,
21, 23-4, 25, 27, 28, 30-1, 36,
50, 51
Laurence, Jocelyn, 22, 24, 28, 29,
31, 40-1, 50-1, 53-4, 55
Laurence, Margaret
THEMES: ancestors, 25, 26, 27,
29-30, 48, 50, 54, in *A Bird in
the House,* 49, in *The Diviners,*
56-9, in *Jason's Quest,* 42-3, in
A Jest of God, 37-9, in *The
Stone Angel,* 32, 33; communication, 14, in *The Fire-Dwellers,*
44, 46, in *A Jest of God,* 38, in
The Stone Angel, 32, 33; divining power in *The Diviners,* 59;
the dispossessed in *The Diviners,*
57; freedom through self-knowledge, 46, in *The Fire-Dwellers,*
45,46, 48, in *Jason's Quest,* 43,

in *A Jest of God,* 39, 42, 46, 48,
in *The Prophet's Camel Bell,* 48,
in *The Stone Angel,* 33, 42, 46,
48; self-reliance, pride, independence, life force, 14, 20, 24, in
A Bird in the House, 48, in *The
Diviners,* 57, in *Jason's Quest,*
43, in *A Jest of God,* 37, in *The
Prophet's Camel Bell,* 48, in
The Stone Angel, 31, 32, 33,
34, 35; survival, 5, 21, 24, 48,
51, in *A Bird in the House,* 48,
in *The Fire-Dwellers,* 44, 46, in
The Stone Angel, 34
WORKS: *A Bird in the House,* 11,
46-9, 55, 56, 57; *The Diviners,*
7, 13, 53, 54, 55, 56-60; "The
Drummer of All the World,"
25-6, *see also The Tomorrow
Tamer; The Fire Dwellers,* 13,
37, 42, 43-6, 48, 52, 55, 56, 57;
"A Gourdful of Glory," 29, *see
also The Tomorrow Tamer;*
"Horses of the Night," 38, *see
also A Bird in the House; Jason's
Quest,* 42-3, 53, 55; *A Jest of
God (Rachel, Rachel),* 37-41, 42,
43, 44, 46, 48, 55, 57; *Long
Drums and Cannons,* 41; *New
Wind in a Dry Land* (Canadian
title: *The Prophet's Camel Bell*),
30, 31, 34-5, 48; *The Prophet's
Camel Bell* (U.S. title, *New
Wind in a Dry Land*), 30, 31,
34-5, 48; *This Side Jordan,* 13,
26-9, 31, 43; *The Stone Angel*
("Hagar"), 29-30, 31-5, 37, 39,
42, 43, 44, 46, 48, 55; "The Tomorrow Tamer," 13, 29, *see also
The Tomorrow Tamer,* 13, 28,
29, 30, 31, 34, 35; *A Tree for
Poverty* (translations of Somali
poetry and stories), 20-3, 36-7;
youthful writing, *see* 9, 10, 14
Laurier, Wilfrid, 66, 67-8